WHAT MOVES US
AN INTEGRATED LOOK AT HUMAN MOTIVATION

By: STEVEN SISLER

What Moves Us: an integrated look at human motivation
ISBN: 9781096808817
Copyright © 2019
Published by The Focus Media Group
Written by: Steven Sisler
All rights reserved.
Behavioralresourcegroup.com

This book is dedicated to our loving beagle, Couper. His life made all our lives better.
2006-2019

CONTENTS

1 DESIRE, MOTIVATION, AND FREE WILL 7
2 INTRODUCING MOTIVATION 21
3 GORDON ALLPORT AND THE PROPRIUM 50
4 ORIGINALITY AND AESTHETICS 66
5 EFFICIENCY AND ECONOMIC DRIVE 91
6 INDIVIDUALISM AND THE NEED TO BE OURSELVES 116
7 AUTHORITY AND POWER 139
8 PERSONAL SACRIFICE AND ALTRUISM 161
9 COMPLIANCE AND REGULATED THINKING 189
10 CURIOSITY AND THE NEED TO KNOW WHY...............213
11 DUEL MOTIVATIONAL AND BEHAVIORAL ORIENTATIONS CREATING FLOW...235
12 THE 37 MOTIVATIONAL STYLES 255
13 BEING THE BEST VERSION OF YOUR BEST SELF.......286
ABOUT STEVEN SISLER..300

1
DESIRE, MOTIVATION, AND FREE WILL

Are we free to do whatever we want? Can we easily change our behavior simply because we want to? I ate some blueberries this morning because I wanted to. Does this make me a free moral agent in the world—capable of doing whatever I desire? The idea that we humans are entirely free to do as we will is known in philosophical circles as *Libertarian Free Will*. This belief is based on the idea that metaphysically, we can act freely in the world.

The metaphysical component that allows for authoring prescribed behaviors is typically defined as a *soul*. Often labelled as a *ghost in the machine*, the soul is presumed to be separate from the brain. Furthermore, the soul according to this philosophy, affects the brain or *uses* the brain as an instrument or vehicle for carrying out its free will within the physical earth. This willingness is said to be autonomous (separate from the brain) and unrestricted.

The opposing philosophical position posits that every event has a cause that determines the event such that nothing other than what does occur could occur in the universe. This is known as *Determinism*. This idea that all things are governed by cause and effect consigns free will to an illusion. One cannot hold both philosophical views simultaneously. In an effort to better understand behavioral and attitudinal change, we must first understand the mechanisms at work in our brains that afford any opportunities for change if change is going to happen at all.

The Principle of Alternate Possibilities

This principle holds to the idea that an action is *free* only if the agent—that is, the person doing the thing—could have done otherwise. Free actions by default require options. Determinism, by its very nature, disallows options. If everything I do is because of a background cause known or unknown then according to determinism, I do not have free will. The fact is, we humans claim far greater autonomy than we actually possess. Libertarianism claims I did what I did simply because I decided to do it. I could have done otherwise, but out of the choices available, the thing that I chose to do was the thing that I did. We know that libertarianism runs counter to the way the physical world works so the proponents of this philosophy must find a way to account for their view of how free will works to avoid the conflict in reason.

The way libertarians do this is by coming up with two causations—*Event Causation* and *Agent causation*. Event causation says that no physical event can occur without having been caused by a previous physical event that affected it. They agree that the physical world is deterministic by its very nature. Agent causation says that an agent, a being provoked by a mind, can start a whole chain of causality that wasn't caused by anything other than the mind itself—I did thus and such because I decided to do it.

This begs the question; where do these free decisions to do whatever we choose to do and that launch a new causal chain of events come from? Why do we make one decision over another? The final philosophical view of free will is this: both determinists and libertarians are somewhat confused and free will is compatible with the underlying truths of determinism.[1]

According to neuroscientist Sam Harris, the only respectable way to endorse the premise of free will is to be a compatibilist because we know that determinism is true. Unconscious neural events determine our thoughts and actions. I may desire to lose 20 pounds, but I'm more often than not faced with competing commitments to not lose the weight. These competing commitments are unconscious to me. In fact, I've wanted to lose 20 pounds for an entire year. Why don't I just decide and do it? Some

---

1 Dr. Sam Harris, *Free Will*, copyright 2012; page 16.

might say that I really don't want to lose the weight but that would not be true—I do want to lose the weight. My reality is this; until my unconscious mind releases the *lose weight card* I'm pretty much out of luck in this arena.

You can desire to leave your job or to fix your marriage—fill in your own blanks here. What we desire is not what we end up doing; not by a long shot. We are *not* the conscious source of our thoughts and actions. Our thoughts do not begin in the area of our brain that is conscious witness to those thoughts. Decisions don't begin in consciousness; they only *appear* in consciousness only *after* the decisions have been made.

The Invisible Card Dealer

The physiologist Benjamin Libet is known for his remarkable findings after he proved using EEG that activity in the brain's motor cortex can be detected some 300 milliseconds before a person feels that he or she has decided to move a finger.[2] His work was further extended by others using functional magnetic resonance imaging (fMRI). These later experimenters found two regions within the brain that contained information about which button subjects would press a full 7 to 10 seconds before the decision was *consciously* made to press it.[3]

We do not deal our own cards. Cards (thoughts, decisions, and action steps) are dealt from the unconscious abyss of our minds and presented to our conscious self in the form of a seemingly random hand. For example; think about motivational guru Tony Robins. Why is there only one Tony Robins? Who else among the millions of available people who would love to help and motivate people and perhaps *believe* they could do what Tony does, actually do it?

---

[2] B. Libet, C. A. Gleason, E. W. Wright, & D. K. Pearl, 1983. Time of conscious intention to act in relation to onset of cerebral activity (readiness-potential): The unconscious initiation of a freely voluntary act, Brian 106 (Pt 3): 623-642; B. Libet, 1985.
[3] J. D. Haynes, 2011. Decoding and predicting intentions. *Ann. NY Acad. Sci.* 1224(1): 9-21.

Tony Robins has been dealt a few aces—I more likely have been dealt an eight of clubs. I can read, study, take speaking classes, receive professional coaching, you name it, but will I achieve the same result? I have spoken publicly over 3,000 times. Can I fill a stadium? Is anyone drooling to pay 60,000.00 for proximity space with me? Will this ever happen? Let's say it never happens. Would this be because I didn't know the formula? Is it because I didn't take your online coaching class? Is it because I don't *believe* in myself? Let's make this simple. How about none of the above.

You want to put away money each month for your retirement. How's that been working out for you? It's easy to do right? Just put aside a certain amount of money each month and when you turn 70, you'll be a millionaire. According to a recent article published on CNBC.com by Ester Bloom, if you're overwhelmed by the financial responsibilities of day-to-day life and more focused on making it to the end of the month than on the possibility of being able to save for the distant future, you're not alone. In fact, the vast majority of Americans have under $1,000 saved and half of all Americans have nothing at all put away for retirement.

"Nearly half of families have no retirement account savings at all," the Economic Policy Institute (EPI) reported, even in savings vehicles such as IRAs and 401(k)s. 69 percent of Americans have less than $1,000.00 in savings. The median for U.S. families is just $5,000, and the median for families with some savings is $60,000. And, according to a 2016 *GOBankingRates* survey, 35 percent of all adults in the U.S. have only several hundred dollars in their savings accounts and 34 percent have no savings at all—none.

Why is this? Does nobody care? Is everyone stupid? You might want to believe so, but you would be amiss if you did. You might think you can't afford to save a part of your income. Then just go get a better job, right? Hell, why don't you start your own business and be the next Jeff Bezos—he's worth 160 billion. He's the same age as me. Where did I go wrong? Or did I go right, and I've been comparing apples to oranges?

We cannot decide the life we are going to have. We can only play the life we've been dealt. Perhaps you have lost the weight you have been trying to lose for some time now. You can't account for why you were able to lose it this time but couldn't lose a pound every other time. You have no clue why you stuck with it this time and couldn't stick with it last time. Nobody knows why.

Post-Hoc Storytelling

Sure, you can produce a post-hoc story that tells your conscious self why you were so amazing and determined this time around, but it's just a made-up story to justify your current state of affairs, which could change tomorrow. We are incapable of verifying our failures in the past, so we justify our present no matter what it looks like.

You will justify your failed marriage or perhaps your failed business venture. You might think the economy wasn't in your favor or your mate wasn't as committed as you were. If you cheated on your mate and blew up your own marriage, the odds that you've already come up with a story to justify your actions is very high. The fact is, we don't know why we do the things we do, and we don't know why we can't do all the things we want to do like save our money or build a successful business.

This is nothing new. Humans have always struggled with free will. Even as far back as the first century, human beings were struggling with free will philosophy and coming up with post-hoc reasoning to justify their actions. Consider St. Paul in his letter to the Romans in the New Testament of the Bible:

> "I do not understand what I do. For what I want to do I do not do, but what I hate I do. And if I do what I do not want to do, I agree that the law is good. As it is, it is no longer I myself who do it, but it is sin living in me. For I know that good itself does not dwell in me, that is, in my sinful nature. For I have the desire to do what is good, but I cannot carry it out. For I do not do the good I want to do, but the evil I do not want to do—this I keep

on doing. Now if I do what I do not want to do, it is no longer I who do it, but it is sin living in me that does it."[4]

The author justifies his conscious self by claiming the entity of "sin" is wreaking havoc *within* him. He claims it is not actually *him* that is actually doing the wrong things, its sin residing in him that's doing it. According to his philosophy, sin has the ability to "take over the controls" and pilot his actions without his conscious permission—genius. He separates his sinful nature-self from his good natured-self creating a dual natured being. He can now go on living and blame his poor decisions on his sinful nature. But isn't this what we all do in one form or another?

We are all products of background causes out of our control. You did not choose your parents. You didn't choose you gnome, your brain type, your school, your peers, or your teachers. We are not responsible for the larger part of the life we have had up to this point. All we can do is build a story that suggests we are. "I knew that when I saw her, I was going to marry her." Oh, really? But you didn't know she was going to be your worst nightmare in 6 years.

The question persists; how are you playing your hand? Why am I not a sociopath? The real reason? I'm lucky. How did I get to this place in my life? I failed math in high school. I tried to go to community college, but it proved too difficult to continue. Even now, if it weren't for spell check this document would be laughable.

There are multiple thousands of problems, challenges, and opportunities we all face that are out of our conscious control. Sitting here right now thinking about the trajectory that my life has taken makes no sense at all. I could not have planned it this way if I had a degree in planning and a thousand years of planning time. I barely finished high school and then went on to enroll in the local community college. And as I pointed out, I didn't last one year in community college.

---

4 Romans 7:15-20 NIV.

I would get up in the middle of class and go to the mall and walk around aimlessly. Maybe I would go to the gym. The only class I enjoyed and pulled a decent grade in was art. I actually had a piece that was up for entrance into the Florida State Art Show in Tallahassee. I didn't make it through to the show, so I gave it away—what was I thinking?

In 1982 I went to work in a mobile home manufacturing plant. I was so terrible at my new job that they had to shut down the whole plant because of a massive number of mistakes that I made. The reason why I wasn't fired is because they wanted me to stay there alone for a few days to fix the problems I had created.

After that genius job I decided to go to an unaccredited seminary for two years. I decided? Really? What really happened was an uncle called me up and asked me about my schooling ambitions. If I was to choose a seminary, he would pay for it—that was easy. But he didn't pay for it; he left me in a terrible lurch in Broken Arrow, Oklahoma.

He justified his own post-hoc story by telling me that I needed to learn a hard lesson; "you had everything handed you growing up. You grew up with a silver spoon in your mouth," he said in a smug tone. There's no way I could have predicted this outcome and my subsequent so-called decisions were more or less survival instincts at full bore.

While schooling, I worked at Handy Dan's Home center cleaning floors. This was before Home depot existed. For extra money I would do odd jobs like pulling weeds for some unsuspecting victim. Unfortunately, I ended up pulling up all her annuals. As she stood there crying in her ruined backyard, I was abruptly told to leave the property. Nice going, Steve. Great brain you got going there.

I tried to be a minister upon graduation, but I couldn't remember to take up offerings. I quit after about three years of fumbling around in the dark while simultaneously working for a local painting company. My first day on that job I "geniusly" spilled five gallons of paint on the front lawn of the home we were painting. At this point it was as if I were dealt the card with the instructions on it and two jokers.

By sheer personality and a steady hand, I continued painting for eighteen years. I started to realize after about 15 years that people wanted to hear what I had to say about many things as they pertained to people, human nature, and life in general. Often, homeowners would request my presence in order to help them figure things out such as why they do certain things or why their children act the way they do. Simple conversations would morph into hours of talking and explaining my thoughts on matters of their interest.

Some people would slip me a $100.00 bill and say thanks so much for the conversation. Over time I was asked to speak to youth and church groups on a variety of subjects specifically related to religious ideas, human nature and life in general. I would often receive a standing ovation and rooms would be standing room only when the word was out that I would be speaking on some subject.

And then in 2003, my wife turned to me and said, "You need to get paid to talk to people." My response to this was, "nobody is going to pay me to talk to them." That was 16 years ago. Since that day I have spoken around the world. I have spoken in Athens Greece, Spain, New Zealand, throughout Australia, Canada, Newfoundland, and all over the United States. I've written 7 books (some I have taken out of circulation) and developed my own assessment tools with the help of some very smart people who were able to program them and create the analytics necessary for validation.

My life is a beautiful picture of randomness. I don't dare to imagine what will be going on in 5 years because the fact is, I have no idea what will happen. Does this mean I have no conscious part in my story? Absolutely not. It means I have consciously worked with the only cards that show up. This effort combined with circumstance and key relationships has afforded me the opportunity to go a greater distance than I would have imagined if left entirely to myself.

Desire, Discipline, and Destiny

What have I desired from a young age? Believe it or not, I have always desired to make a difference in the world. At 14 years of age I knew I wanted to help people. I was mesmerized by human beings and the way they acted. At age 22 I was visualizing myself on stages. As a teenager I could spot a liar a mile away. I could in fact read people's minds.

When you have this capacity and you're growing up in mainline Christianity you are considered a prophet; and that's what people called me. This became my post-hoc story to justify my ability to know people's thoughts. Currently I am no longer a Christian. I live as if there's a God, but I don't know exactly what that is.

But one thing is for sure; my capacity for reading people has never left me. It's my superpower. Do I think I'm psychic? No, not at all. I believe I have excellent body-language and people-reading skills—I have exceptional intuition. All my eggs have been in this basket for the last 15 years and it has enabled me to reach farther than anyone who knows me would have ever guessed possible. Businesses call and ask me to be their business psychic—I laugh at the notion. I have to inform them that I'm not psychic.

If I could simply guess at why I'm the way I am and what conscious efforts have contributed to where I am in the world right now, I would say this: *desire, discipline, and destiny*. I have always desired to have answers for the people I care about. I have sought very hard for those answers but have received more by accident than purpose.

I have spent literally thousands of hours in the study of ancient wisdom, story, and philosophy. Even now, I'm listening to 7 books concurrently. I listen to either books or lectures every single night often being awake for many hours thinking them through. My motor skills are terrible and I'm extremely uncoordinated, but my mind is on fire all the time.

My theoretical element is about a 98 and I still have trouble spelling simple words. What we desire is what we desire. What we do is what we do. King Solomon claimed that *"the discerning heart seeks knowledge."* He also claimed that *"knowledge comes easy to the discerning."*[5] I've often wondered what this means and after many years I have concluded on the matter.

I'm wired to wonder. There's no virtue in it for me—I can't seem to stop it. It's my only ace of spades. I cannot help but desire to know why and then seek out the answers like a bloodhound. Many things simply come to me. Much of what I use in my work just came from the top of my head. The discipline I have is not something I have had to muster up the strength to do—it comes easy but only in this one area. I cannot discipline myself to drink enough water, eat right or go to the gym regularly.

I struggle to remember birthdays or important appointments, but I obsessively clean the pool every day like an irrational person. Our desires are handed to us by our invisible card dealer. Our systematic behaviors are a product of our emotional consistencies, which are a product of our genome, DNA, and our environments with nearly equal affect.

We are what we are and it's mostly not our fault. It has little to do with any conscious efforts on our part according to current neuroscience. So, when I speak about the way we do things, I'm speaking about how our house is wired. Some people are low voltage

---

5 "The mocker seeks wisdom and finds none, but knowledge comes easily to the discerning." Proverbs 14:6, NIV.

and some people are high voltage. Some people are forgetful, and others have an enormous ability to remember details. Either way, you are what you are and there's not a lot you have to do with it.

Is Consciousness Magic?

In the words of Robert Wright speaking of Dan Dennett and others, "Of course the problem here is with the claim that consciousness is 'identical' to physical brain states. The more Dennett et al. try to explain to me what they mean by this, the more convinced I become that what they really mean is that consciousness doesn't really exist."[6] Dennett posits that "consciousness exists, it's just not what we think it is."[7] Jerry Fodor makes himself clear as he states, "One wants to be what tradition has it that Eve was when she bit the apple. Perfectly free to do otherwise. So perfectly free, in fact, that even God couldn't tell which way she'd jump."[8]

We are all looking for a more miraculous sense of self. We want to believe wholeheartedly that we are free to choose to bite or not bite the forbidden fruit. We long for the credit for walking in step with whatever map or plan seems most righteous for us to follow. Philosopher Galen Strawson, after reading Dennett's book *Freedom Evolves* reviewed in an article in the *New York Times* in 2003, "He doesn't establish the kind of absolute free will and moral responsibility that most people want to believe in and do believe in. That can't be done, and he knows it."

Eminent German neuroscientist Wolf Singer states concerning free will; "No one is responsible for their action since all is predetermined by the brain." The British neuroscientist Chris faith says, "Is it possible to predict peoples' actions on the basis of neural activity that precedes their conscious decisions? If so, then free will is an illusion. Distinguished Yale professor and editor and chief of

---
6 Wright, 2000, fn. 14, ch.21
7 Dan Dennett Ph.D., Lecture: Santa Fe Institute, May 14, 2014
8 Fodor, 2003

Behavioral Brain Sciences, Paul Bloom states in response to Harris' captivating book *Free Will*, "If you believe in free will, or know someone who does, here is the perfect antidote."

"In this elegant and provocative book, Sam Harris demonstrates—with great intellectual ferocity and panache—that free will is an inherently flawed and incoherent concept, even in subjective terms. If he is right, the book will radically change the way we view ourselves as human beings."[9]

"Many say that believing that there is no free will is impossible—or, if possible, will cause nihilism and despair. In this feisty and personal essay, Harris offers himself as an example of a heart made less self-absorbed, and more morally sensitive and creative, because this particular wicked witch is dead."[10] As you can see, there are pros and cons throughout the philosophical and neuroscientific world concerning the notion of free will. I don't see this issue as divisive or unconscionable. Like everything else, we must not get into any ditches on either side of the physiological road.

Although it has been proven that the unconscious brain is making many decisions without our conscious permission, the ability to choose is not completely lost. Not only have philosophers and neuroscientists thrown their hats into this physiological ring, physicist Stephen Hawking, and the late Albert Einstein have added their voices:

"Recent experiments in neuroscience support the view that it is our physical brain, following the known laws of science, that determines our actions, and not some agency that exists outside those laws... it is hard to imagine how free will can operate if our

---

9 V.S. Ramachandran, Director of the Center for Brain and Cognition, UCSD, and author of *The Tell-Tale Brain*.
10 Owen Flanagan, Professor of Philosophy, Duke University, and author of *The Really Hard Problem: Meaning in the Material World*.

behavior is determined by physical laws, so it seems that we are no more than biological machines and that free will is an illusion."[11]

"If the moon, in the act of completing its eternal way around the earth, were gifted with self-consciousness, it would feel thoroughly convinced that it was traveling its way of its own accord ... So would a being endowed with higher insight and more perfect intelligence, watching man and his doings, smile about man's *illusion* that he was acting according to his own free will."[12]

Although our emotions are fluid rather than static, we change and adjust as necessary with the world around us. I'm not addressing morality in this book because that's another subject altogether. I'm speaking of temperament and motivations and the idea of changing ourselves to fit whatever paradigm we deem necessary. Is behavioral change easy? You tell me.

How easy is it to change anything you don't like about yourself? Well, if you haven't noticed, it's as hard as hell. This is why I always say, if you're a tomato find a salad; if you're a hammer find a toolbox. Nobody likes a hammer in their salad. When you're a hammer everything around you becomes a nail and when you're a tomato, everything around you becomes a salad.

Can Change be Realized?

Yes. Change can happen albeit not easily. And it will more often than not be a change in your environment than it would be a change in your wiring. Changing the way we do things is possible, but not many are willing to do what needs to be done in an effort to secure it. It's far easier to use the tool for what it was designed for. Using a Philips-head screw driver on a flat-head screw will create more problems than it will solve.

---

11 Stephen Hawking, 2010, with Mlodinow.
12 Albert Einstein; in response to questions about belief in free will, responding with a comparison of the will of the moon. 1931.

But if you are dead set on doing it, you'll have to machine it first. Most people desire change because they are unhappy with who they are or because they live in an emotional system of comparison. In this context I'll tell you to be happy with who you are and determine the best environment for leveraging your authentic self.

How to change is another book I'm afraid. What about destiny—where does this fit in? I'm so glad you asked. You *are* your destiny. You can't chase it. You can't create it. You *are* it. You don't arrive at your destiny; you reveal it. So, you might as well embrace it for what it is. I want you to keep these concepts in mind as we explore the dynamics of human motivation and how motivation, emotions, and behavior work as a team. I agree that we are free to make choices; we decide to make choices every day. But we must remember; we do not decide to decide what to do. These decisions track backwards to greater depths of unconscious darkness.

What is revealed in our conscious minds are the cards we play, so play them well. That being said, in the next chapter I'll introduce human motivation—what great minds have discovered concerning it, and what we can ultimately do with it. I'll build a foundation for you and then we'll open up the fundamentals of personality, the 7 motivational elements, and then how behaviors play with our deepest desires in the game of our lives. A big thank you to you for taking this brave step towards a greater understanding of who you are and why you do what you do.

2
INTRODUCING MOTIVATION

The *Values Index* is a result of the combined research between Dr. Eduard Spranger[13] and Gordon Allport.[14] Its premise delves into what drives and motivates an individual. In this manuscript we will focus on seven specific dimensions of human value, or more importantly, what moves us.

The fascinating discoveries between these two researchers will not only help us to understand the sanities behind what drives us to utilize our talents in the unique ways we do, but these discoveries will also assist us in understanding how motivation works behind the scenes as a fundamental and synergistic counterpart to our emotions and values. It is this dynamic between emotions and values that insist on behavioral schemes designed to lessen brain tensions; allowing us to feel good about who we are and what we are doing in the world.

Although motivations[15] are a result of antecedent stimuli that have been paired with reinforcing consequences that activate certain centers within the brain, it is the consistent behavior in relation to the corresponding positive consequences that follow (postcedents) that cause us to desire particular scenarios and circumstances in life—why we value them. As is the values index, values scales are psychological inventories used to determine the

---

13 *Eduard Spranger* was a German philosopher and psychologist. A student of Wilhelm Dilthey, Spranger was born in Berlin and died in Tübingen. Spranger's contribution to personality theory, in his book Types of Men were his value attitudes.

14 *Gordon Willard Allport* was an American psychologist. Allport was one of the first psychologists to focus on the study of the personality, and is often referred to as one of the founding figures of personality psychology.

15 Yin, Henry H., Sean B. Ostlund, and Bernard W. Balleine. "Reward-guided learning beyond dopamine in the nucleus accumbens: the integrative functions of cortico-basal ganglia networks." European Journal of Neuroscience 28.8 (2008): 1437–1448.

values that people endorse in their personal lives. They facilitate the understanding of both the work and the universal values that individuals uphold. In addition, they assess the importance of each value in people's lives and how the individual strives toward fulfillment through work and other life roles, such as parenting.[16] Most scales have been normalized and can be used cross-culturally for vocational, marketing, counseling purposes, and many others largely yielding unbiased results.[17]

Moreover, many psychologists, political scientists, sociologists, economists, and others interested in defining values, use values scales to determine what people value and to evaluate the ultimate function or purpose of values. The values index I am about to explain, although derived from the original values index models, will help you understand your personal motivations and drivers and how you can maximize your own performance by achieving a more robust and advantageous alignment between what you inwardly desire (your learned motivators) and what you will ultimately do (behaviors spawned by emotions), by both understanding and integrating the *emotions* behind the things you do and the *drivers* behind why you do them.

Values scales were further developed by an international group of psychologists including Donald Super and Branimir Sverko. Their goal was to create a unique self-report instrument that measured intrinsic and extrinsic values for use both in the lab and in the clinic. The psychologists who gathered for this endeavor called their project the *Work Importance Study* (WIS).[18]

Donald Super was the international coordinator of the Work Importance Study. He was based in the Department of Psychology at the University of Florida and he was also professor emeritus of

---

[16] Super, Donald and Dorothy D. Nevill. "Brief Description of Purpose and Nature of Test." Consulting Psychologists Press'.' 1989: 3-10. Print.
[17] Beatty, Sharon E., et al. "Alternative Measurement Approaches to Consumer Values: The List of Values and the Rokeach Value Survey." Psychology and Marketing. 1985: 181-200. Web.
[18] Life Roles, Values, and careers: International Findings of the Work Importance Study: October 1995, Jossey-Bass, 397 Pages, ISBN: 978-0-787-90100-4

psychology and education at Teachers College, Columbia University. He was the author or coauthor of a number of human developmental books including; *Appraising Vocational Fitness, The Psychology of Careers, Computer-Assisted Counseling, Measuring Vocation Maturity*, and *Career Development* in Britain. He died in June 1994. Branimir Sverko is professor of psychology at the University of Zagreb, Croatia, where he teaches work and organizational psychology and is currently directing the chair for Industrial Psychology and Ergonomics.

The original values scale measured much more than we measure today. The following value descriptors used by researchers during the original values inventory boom were considered; I labeled those that are still in use:

- ability utilization
- achievement (still measured indirectly)
- advancement (still measured indirectly)
- aesthetics (still measured)
- altruism (still measured as *sacrificial*)
- authority (still measured)
- creativity (still measured)
- cultural identity
- economic rewards (still measured)
- economic security (still measured)
- lifestyle
- personal development
- physical activity
- physical prowess
- prestige (still measured indirectly)
- risk (still measured indirectly)
- social interaction
- social relations
- variety
- working conditions

Some of the above listed values were intended to be inter-related, but conceptually differentiable. Since the original Work Importance Study,[19] several scientists have supplemented the study by creating their own scale or by deriving and improving the original format. Theorists and psychologists often study values, values scales, and the field surrounding values, otherwise known as axiology.[20]

New studies have been published recently, updating the work in the field. Dr. Eda Gurel-Atay published an article in the *Journal of Advertising Research* in March 2010, providing a glimpse into how social values have changed between 1976 and 2007. The paper explained how "self-respect" has been on the upswing, while "a sense of belonging" has become less important to individuals.[21]

The Values Index measures the aspects of human motivation and impulses, which are those things we are naturally attracted[22] to and that are behind the "why" of our ultimate behaviors. As you make your way through this book you will begin to understand that in the end, and regardless of what you may actually want to do, your specific and largely predictable behaviors will always rule over your desires—our emotions trump our desires.

Gordon Allport was an early pioneer in the area of personality. He was often referred to as one of the founders of personality psychology. His main and most remembered contribution was his development of *Trait Theory*. This theory purported that every individual embodies formulations that include mixtures of the four

---

[19] Launched in 1979, the Work Importance Study (WIS) put the finishing touches to Super's lifework. WIS provides a richly cross-cultural exploration of peoples' life roles and values that people seek in their careers and life in general.

[20] Axiology is the philosophical study of value. It is either the collective term for ethics and aesthetics, philosophical fields that depend crucially on notions of worth, or the foundation for these fields, and thus similar to value theory and meta-ethics. The term was first used by Paul Lapie, in 1902, and then again by Eduard von Hartmann, in 1908.

[21] Gurel-Atay, Eda. "Changes in Social Values in the United States: 1976-2007, Self-Respect is on the Upswing as "A Sense of Belonging" Becomes Less Important." Journal of Advertising Research. 2010: 57-67. Print.

[22] The impulses within a person created by their worldview, ethical platforms, and emotional bents that will attract them to (create a desire within) specific wants such as control or a need to know a thing.

temperament types in differing consistencies, though one or two (and sometimes three) may be extra severe (consistent) than the rest. These are referred to as *Cardinal, Central,* and *Secondary* traits depending on how isolated they are within the context of the individual.

My partner Zeke Lopez and I have developed a new concept we are calling *Focal Consistency*.[23] This is the result of certain emotions consistently outplaying others in their quest for supremacy. Regardless of their usefulness in meeting practical needs, they remain the predominant go-to emotions when the chips are down.

In psychology, *trait theory* (also called *Dispositional Theory*) is an approach to the study of human personality—a method of observing it. Moreover, trait theorists are primarily interested in the measurement of traits,[24] which can be defined as characteristic prototypes of behavior; blueprints, if you will, including both thought and emotion with differing consistencies. A high consistency in the anger emotion will differentiate a person from one who has a lower consistency of this same emotion.

One person will be quick and decisive while the other slow and indecisive. We might say of a person of this less intense type, "Oh, don't call on him, he's as about as slow as frozen molasses!" In 1936, Allport found that one English-language dictionary alone contained more than 4,000 words describing different personality traits. He categorized these traits into three distinct concentrations. Let's take a deeper look into these three trait categories.

Cardinal Traits: Allport concluded that these are the traits that govern or control an individual's entire life, often to the point that the person becomes known unambiguously for these traits. These people can become so well known for these individualities that their

---

23 Focal Consistency: the most consistent primary emotions within our energy system.
24 There are roughly 638 different personality traits (ideonomy.mit.edu). Of these, 234 are positive, 112 are neutral, and 292 (almost half) are negative traits.

names become synonymous with them. Consider the origin and meaning of the following descriptive terms: Freudian, Narcissistic, Don Juan, Napoleon, Christ-like, etc. Allport suggested that cardinal traits are far more infrequent and tend to develop later in life. I'll elaborate on how Allport arrived at these traits in the following chapter.

Central Traits: According to Allport's findings, these specific traits are more foundational and will determine how one will act as a rule or most of the time. These are the general physiognomies that form the basic foundations of personality and behavior. These traits, while not as controlling or dominating as cardinal traits, are the foremost characteristics you might use to describe another person.

Terms such as *quiet, extroverted, anxious, complex,* or *shy* could be considered Central Traits. Saying, "He's hot-headed," or "Susan, she's the reluctant one," could be identifying statements that reflect the central traits among some of us because we become notorious for them. Unlike Cardinal Traits, these traits do not make up the whole of a person's personality.

Secondary Traits: These are traits that are only present under certain conditions. A good example of a secondary trait would be getting nervous before delivering a speech to an auditorium full of people. Although you might be fine with a small group of people you already know, a large group of strangers will generate feelings of insecurity thus creating both physical and behavioral responses that diminish your capacity to perform at your optimal level.

Similar to the four temperament types, the seven motivational elements we will soon discuss in detail are directly related to the four primary emotions; anger, optimism, patience, and fear. They also integrate or are *interconnected* with our personal trait system.

My goal is to break each of the seven motivational elements down into separate and unique "drivers" for better understanding, but when doing so, you cannot allow yourself to be fooled by these single overriding motivational elements in people. Everyone is a unique *combination* of all seven elements in differing consistencies, although several may have a greater impact among the rest. Keep this in mind as we move forward in unmasking the differences between them—it's the motivational *integration* of all seven dimensions that *really* matters.

In other words, you cannot decipher motivation with "singular" or specific separate elements contrary to what other analysts or assessment sellers may think. The seven elements are uniquely *coalesced* to formulate specific motivational types. Through our own extensive research we have identified 36 general types within the motivational framework. The seven elements when measured within their solitary specific modality encompass explicit levels of desire.

These levels of desire are categorized into three *basic* levels that include; high-desire, situational-desire, and indifferent desire. More specific overall measurements include; very-high, high, average, low, and very-low. These five *levels* of desire (sometimes referred to as *drive*), much like the four primary emotions[25] in our general behavior model, integrate with the seven motivational elements creating a specific type or *motivational matrix*.[26]

Both sets of behavior elements and motivation elements when integrated into a cohesive whole, produce an overall type of being. And not only that, but when behavior types (orientations) and motivational (preferences) types are integrated with each other, a collaborative event takes place that will either produce consistencies (known as flow) or inconsistencies (known as conflicts).

---

[25] The four primary emotions are: Anger, Optimism, Patience, and Fear.
[26] The Motivational Matrix is the sum of all seven elements creating a *type* of motivational matrix.

Understanding the Foundational Principles of Measurement

To fully understand how the seven motivational elements are measured to produce a type, we must take a look at two specific modes of measurement:

1. Bi-axial or bi-polar theory
2. Integrated measures

We will look deeper into the types much later in the book.

Bi-axial Theory

Bi-axial or bi-polar theory has been used and improved upon since the 1920's. In the domains of DISC, Work Motivations, and Axiology, we measure a person's reactions to stimulus words. Once this has been accomplished, we accumulate all measured responses to develop a measure of how consistently and inconsistently they responded to the stimulus words.

The cumulative effect of summing their answers provides us with a measure of consistency of responses. We then accumulate their responses into one score and place it on a bi-axial scale. Bi-axial signifies a person's response towards a stimulus word. These measurements will range somewhere between two end points:

1. One end point may be totally positive such as +100. It is more intuitive to think of 100 scales. Think of a score of a 100 as the maximum positive/consistency in a specific motivational element.
2. Another end point can be at the other end creating maximum negative/consistency such as -100. Again, it is more intuitive to think of 100 scales. Think of a score of zero as the maximum minimum negative/consistency in a specific motivational element.

Because 7 value elements are rank-ordered 10 times, the resulting top score can only measure as high as 70. In other words, if I rank order a power element as a first position out of seven available positions on each of the ten available questions, I will create a measured score of 70 for that specific motivational element. Likewise, if I rank order the sacrificial element in a last position (7th place) within all ten questions, I will create a score of 10.

Some tools use a 70-scale for this reason. We use a 100-scale in our IMO report. This means we must convert the 70-scale to a 100-scale using a specific algorithm. This allows an individual to score an 86, 98, or 8 on any given element. It's imperative that 70-scales are converted properly to 100-scales if 100 scales are being used—not all are. This ensures reliability and consistency among members of a measured group.

Think of consistencies such as hot and cold, bitter and sweet, East and West, or North and South poles. What is the halfway point between the north and south pole? The halfway point is known as the equator at zero degrees latitude. The equator lies between opposite ends or opposite poles. The name equator is derived from medieval Latin word *aequator*. In the phrase; "*circulus aequator diei et noctis,*" it means; "circle equalizing day and night," from the Latin word aequare, which means, to 'make equal'.[27]

It is for this reason that it is not the furthest distance from the *norm* that shows the greatest impact on any persons integrated motivator style, it is the furthest distance from the score of 50 or 0 (the midpoint between 0 and 100 or 100 and 100) that has the greatest impact on a person's overall integrated motivational style. In our IMO Report,[28] this is how we rank the seven motivational elements.

---

27 OxfordDictionaries.com. Retrieved 5 May, 2018.
28 The *IMO Report* is Behavioral Resource Group's motivational analysis. IMO represents; Integrated Motivational Orientation.

If we are accumulating responses and you have a score of 50 in the sacrificial element some call *Altruism*, a score of 50 means your response to the stimulus words associated with sacrificial values is situational or "neutral" and therefore will have minimal impact on your integrated orientation. This doesn't mean it won't have an overall impact because it will. Although it falls into a situational atmosphere, when taken into full consideration as it relates to the full matrix, the situational measurement will have an effect although not profound.

Because you selected a proportionately equal number of positive and negative responses for this specific motivational element, your score falls to the midpoint on the graph producing a balanced profile of that element. When you are neutral or "situational," it means you need more or less support or stimuli from your environment to access that attribute more fully. Greater or lesser consistencies create differing attributes.

For example, those who score within the very high and very low ranges within the curiosity element known as *Theoretical* would have greater consistency towards either a scholarly or disinterested value. Disinterested values cause individuals to rely more heavily on intuitive ideas and past experiences for learning and accessing necessary knowledge for moving forward in the world. Greater consistencies warrant a more in-depth factual knowledge of why something is what it claims to be.

Fig. 1

	Curiosity	Want Zone		Need Zone
100 90 80 70 60 50 40 30 20 10		10 20 30 40 50 60 70	80 90 100	
Dis-Interested		**Situational**		**Scholarly**

Another proof of this can be discovered in behavioral and emotional measurement. For example, if all scores were equal and fell on the energy line (50%) on a DISC scale, many DISC systems would kick the report out as invalid or "centered." This is known as *flatlining*. All scores of 50 would mean the person has a neutral response to *all* items—impossible. Centered scores are a product of transitional thinking or emotional confusion brought on by pressing circumstances.

There is no such thing as a person who scores "zero" in any motivational dimension. Consider the efficiency dimension known more popularly as the *Economic* dimension. There are people who consistently rank more consistently towards the southern pole within this dimension. We call this consistency level "satisfied" as opposed to "self-mastered," which is the northern position.

Fig. 2   The anger emotion on a bi-axial scale

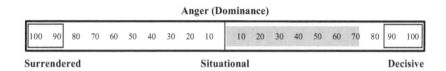

Integrated Measures

In an effort to force this idea home, I will repeat what I said above concerning integration. What matters most in the Motivator profile is the *integrated* motivator *style*, not any single score related to any single element. Even though we can measure 7 single elements of motivation, what matters most is their relationship to each other as a cohesive unit. What we care about most is how accurately we can explain in advance how a person will orient themselves in the more common situations in their role or work environment.

We share and show *individual* (separate) elements to create what is called "domains of influence or action." If you know a person's overall motivator style and you want to influence it or not we show you the individual domains that you can influence or not influence. Influencing where there's greater consistency will ensure a lessening of brain tension within the individual because their brain feels comfortable when leaning in that particular direction of value. This is known as value-consistency. It's when a person either consistently seeks power positions (high power) or positions that don't require shouldering more responsibilities than necessary (low power).

Motivation is more central to our lives when working. Having a systematic approach to motivating your behavior is what matters—yours and others. This is a skill that can be learned. The aim of this book as well as our IMO report, is to help you understand some of the hidden forces of your hidden motivators and to help you to increase the positive effects while reducing any of the potential harmful effects caused by your motivational orientation disagreeing with your environment.

Understanding the building blocks of your motivational system and the ways in which they can work better for you is essential for growth and happiness. The simpler you can create pathways to influence what energizes, orients, and directs you to behave in certain ways, the better you can arrange things in your environment to make your actions more useful. What matters most is to get started by understanding and having sufficient awareness and no more. Your goal is not to be an expert, but rather to sufficiently understand where you best fit in the universe.

A basic understanding of how your motivational system works will ensure a better and more tolerable relationship with yourself and your work-related activities. When using this resource and our reports, focus on *"what directly leads you to take action."* You won't make yourself more effective by copying other people's motives; you must first start with your own motivational nature and what serves you best and then make it automatic.

Your Environment and Motivation

The two main actors responsible for your success are your "Motivational Orientation" and your "environment." Your own unique *Integrated Motivational Orientation* (IMO) and how it fits into an existing environment is the central concept of importance to you. Your personal IMO describes and identifies:

- Your motivational direction: Specific goals to which your motivational energy will be directed.
- The types of work-related activities, events and structures that shape your IMO or agree with it.
- Your IMO factor potential from weak to strong.
- Your relative IMO motivational consistency level: The potential effort you can count on when the right motives are present. You will also discover the level of consistency most preferred by you.

Your IMO does not describe nor does it identify:

- What you do (behavior). Some of your behaviors (i.e., the characteristics you exhibit while you do things) are not aroused by motivation. For example; habits, reflexes, routines, and instincts are not aroused by motivation.
- Your IMO does not identify how well developed your preferences are or how well you use them.

At the heart of your IMO are specific preferences that are consistently important to you. Your specific preferences work together to form an overarching orientation that reflects the consistency of how you want to shape your behavior (intended behavior) and energize your efforts. What happens is this; your unique IMO acts as a set of requirements or demands you place upon yourself as part of your approach to fulfilling what is important to you. It also acts as a potential trigger point that can be activated by outside threats to what is important to you.

The 3 Sources of Motivational Preference

Your IMO identifies your sources of motivational preferences in *three specific domains* that all people feel are important. The fulfillment or thwarting of your motivational preference promotes in these three areas a sense of full engagement (flow); a feeling of being controlled and pressured; or a lack of intention (a-motivation). Your specific preferences within your IMO are measured using each pair of opposites below. I have included the graphs so you can visualize the motivational consistencies that reflect each of the three IMO's. There are opposite ends of these IMO's so watch for the distinctions when the consistencies change.

1
Freedom & Autonomy

Freedom and autonomy prioritizes our value preferences for shaping our behavior and being energized by experiencing and expressing our autonomy and freedom. This is a value for experiencing independence and uniqueness in the world. This framework is created by the engagement of two specific elements within the motivational system. The *individual* value element (Individuality) and the *regulated* value element (Compliance) work together to create a synergistic feeling of independence.

Fig. 3

Motivational Direction and Consistency Graph
Freedom-seeking

	0	10	20	30	40	50	60	70	80	90	100
ORIGINALITY	0	10	20	30	40	50	60	70	80	90	100
EFFICIENCY	0	10	20	30	40	50	60	70	80	90	100
INDIVIDUALITY	0	10	20	30	40	50	60	70	80	90	100
POWER	0	10	20	30	40	50	60	70	80	90	100
SACRIFICE	0	10	20	30	40	50	60	70	80	90	100
COMPLIANCE	0	10	20	30	40	50	60	70	80	90	100
CURIOSITY	0	10	20	30	40	50	60	70	80	90	100

When each value element seeks an opposite polar position, agreement is always achieved between the two values. When the individualistic value element achieves a northern position while the regulated value element achieves a southern position, the variation between the two creates a harmonious relationship less any perceived brain tensions—they agree with each other. This emotional agreement creates flow within the IMO. The opposite is also true.

Lesser consistent positions in individualism and greater consistency in regulation create the same harmonious relationship. This causes an individual to surrender to existing systems by integrating with what they believe or are told "should be." Lesser value within individualism creates a lesser need to be independent of and a greater need to be reliant on. The same goes for values of regulation. Less value towards regulated thinking creates a subversion towards existing structures.

2
Truth Seeking

Fig. 4   Motivational Direction and Consistency Graph
Truth-seeking

	0	10	20	30	40	50	60	70	80	90	100
ORIGINALITY	0	10	20	30	40	50	60	70	80	90	100
EFFICIENCY	0	10	20	30	40	50	60	70	80	90	100
INDIVIDUALITY	0	10	20	30	40	50	60	70	80	90	100
POWER	0	10	20	30	40	50	60	70	80	90	100
SACRIFICE	0	10	20	30	40	50	60	70	80	90	100
COMPLIANCE	0	10	20	30	40	50	60	70	80	90	100
CURIOSITY	0	10	20	30	40	50	60	70	80	90	100

Truth seeking prioritizes our value preferences for shaping our behavior and being energized by uncovering the objective truth to reduce any uncertainties. The need to uncover, discover, or recover the "why" concerning what is able to be known or expected of us takes precedent over the "how."

Those who have strong preferences towards truth seeking, which originates from a more consistent curiosity drive, believe the person who knows how will have a job, but the person who knows why should be the boss. Truth seeking by and large remains independent of all other values. No matter a group of individuals such as a group of law enforcement officers, values of curiosity by and large cannot be predicted. Although odds would be in favor of consistent regulated values within this group, consistent theoretical values would not be suspected. Their theoretical values could fall anywhere between say, 24 and 80. This is not always the case, but it is the case most of the time.

3
Self-Mastery

Self-Mastery encompasses the combination of originality (aesthetic values), efficiency (economic values), power (political and authoritative values), and sacrifice (altruistic values). Altruism cannot be confused with empathy. Altruism, as a value, embodies a sacrificial sense of equality. Sacrifice is about giving up our own sense of self, time, or property because we do not see the value of it. Empathy sees "into" others and has little to do with the "self" other than the diminishing of it.

Self-Mastery prioritizes our value preferences for shaping our behavior and being energized by our approach to self-enhancement and competency to assurances in reaching our desired outcomes. Self-Mastery involves a strong sense of personal efficiency and a heightened awareness of what we can lose if we are not paying enough attention. It's about thinking; "what am I getting out of this" before putting energy into something that has a potential outcome.

Fig. 5

Motivational Direction and Consistency Graph
Self-Mastery

	0	10	20	30	40	50	60	70	80	90	100
ORIGINALITY											
EFFICIENCY											
INDIVIDUALITY											
POWER											
SACRIFICE											
COMPLIANCE											
CURIOSITY											

Those who exhibit a Self-Mastered life have little willingness to sacrifice their own sense of self or their own property for those who cannot show a willingness to put forth the same amount of psychic energy when harnessing their goals. It is for this reason that the relationship between these four value elements are responsible for a self-mastered mindset.

The three IMO preference sets we discussed above (understanding that the curiosity element stands alone), because they are being measured using a Bi-axial scale, have opposite or opposing qualities as a united bi-axial dimension. Observe the opposite ends of these same spectrums as we describe them further below.

Rule Dependence

The opposite of freedom and autonomy is rule dependence. Rule dependence prioritizes our value preferences for shaping our behavior and being energized by the adherence to existing rules, standards, and structures. Similar to systemic or structured thinking, rule dependence ensures things are done according to *certain* specifications—it's all about no uncertain terms.

This IMO preference involves a lesser value towards unconventionality and a higher value towards adherence to certain standards or the suppression of creative and unconventional thought. Dependence involves a quality or state of being influenced or determined by or subject to another idea higher than our own.

Suppressing one's own desires in favor of what one believes is "supposed to be" creates a sense of captivity rather than freedom. Regulated thinkers are captive to ideas that originate outside of themselves. Out of all the preferences, this one may have the greatest impact on the self and others who fall into its gravitational field. We will discuss this in depth in later chapters.

Fig. 6

Motivational Direction and Consistency Graph
Rule Dependence

	0	10	20	30	40	50	60	70	80	90	100
ORIGINALITY	0	10	20	30	40	50	60	70	80	90	100
EFFICIENCY	0	10	20	30	40	50	60	70	80	90	100
INDIVIDUALITY	0	10	20	30	40	50	60	70	80	90	100
POWER	0	10	20	30	40	50	60	70	80	90	100
SACRIFICE	0	10	20	30	40	50	60	70	80	90	100
COMPLIANCE	0	10	20	30	40	50	60	70	80	90	100
CURIOSITY	0	10	20	30	40	50	60	70	80	90	100

Intuition

The opposite of truth seeking is intuition. Intuition prioritizes our value preferences for shaping our behavior and being energized by taking what we *currently* know and have already *experienced* as our primary approach to seeking and gathering information. When learning new things, those whose value preferences encompass intuition will rely more heavily on what they already have experienced for decision making.

Intuitive reasoning denies further investigation or study and accepts imagination and experience as its teacher. This is why some higher intuitive thinkers can imagine more than some others can acquire through reading and personal study. This type of intuitive reasoning works well with those who have strong practical thinking skills or an E1+ score in Formal Axiology—they hit the ground running even when unsure of what to do.

Fig. 7

Motivational Direction and Consistency Graph
Intuitive

	0	10	20	30	40	50	60	70	80	90	100
ORIGINALITY	0	10	20	30	40	50	60	70	80	90	100
EFFICIENCY	0	10	20	30	40	50	60	70	80	90	100
INDIVIDUALITY	0	10	20	30	40	50	60	70	80	90	100
POWER	0	10	20	30	40	50	60	70	80	90	100
SACRIFICE	0	10	20	30	40	50	60	70	80	90	100
COMPLIANCE	0	10	20	30	40	50	60	70	80	90	100
CURIOSITY	0	10	20	30	40	50	60	70	80	90	100

Accommodation

The opposite of Self-Mastery much like intuition and rule dependence is accommodation. Accommodation prioritizes our value preferences for shaping our behavior and being energized by our approach to supporting others even at personal cost or disadvantage. This value preference causes us to see the worth in others while missing our own worth within the world.

As we discussed in the Self-Mastery definition above, Sacrifice is about giving up your own sense of self, time, or property because you do not see the value of it and yielding to the better qualities you see in someone else. We will discuss this further in coming chapters when we explore the Altruistic value element in its singular form.

The IMO preference graph provides us a visual so we can see where our preferences are. In the IMO Preference Graph on the next page, you can see right away that freedom and autonomy are not preferential. This individual prefers truth seeking and self-mastery while at the same time they are likely rule dependent. Rule dependence is a perceived value. Pushing back or bending rules when necessary to achieve self-mastery will likely take place.

Fig. 8

Motivational Direction and Consistency Graph
Accommodating

	0	10	20	30	40	50	60	70	80	90	100
ORIGINALITY											
EFFICIENCY											
INDIVIDUALITY											
POWER											
SACRIFICE											
COMPLIANCE											
CURIOSITY											

When seeking answers, because of a higher curiosity element, this person may do "whatever it takes," especially if they have a diminished fear emotion (C in DISC and P in TARP) and even more so if we have limited patience (S in DISC and R in TARP). The IMO will not stand apart from an individual's consistent energies.[29] All

---

[29] Psychic or Consistent Energy refers to the 4 primary emotions and the energies they display. Whatever energies are in play will determine which are *relied upon* for forward movement.

these pieces work together to create our determined steps within the world.

IMO Preference and Consistency

Our IMO preferences are graphed (in our IMO report) and will indicate the sources within our motivational preferences that we use to organize, energize, and move ourselves towards any action.

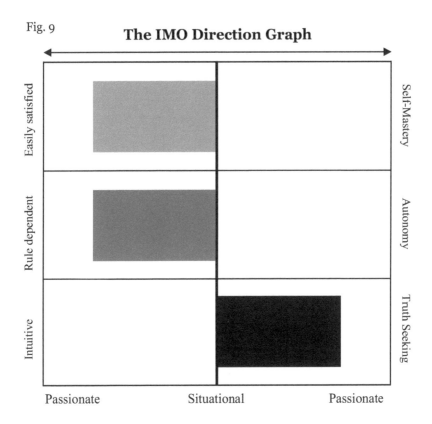

Fig. 9 **The IMO Direction Graph**

Much like our energy levels in behavior and emotions, our IMO consistency and direction graphs indicate the level of consistency (energy) and direction within our prioritized sources of motivation when engaging our motivational preferences. The IMO Preferences Graph identifies and describes our prioritized sources of motivational preference. This graph indicates how we organize and prioritize our approach to motivation. These different "approaches to organizing and prioritizing" the three areas of motivational importance (above) create our differences.

Our IMO Consistency Graph on the other hand, reflects our "direction" towards two "opposing sources" of motivation. The graph also reflects how consistently we prioritize a specific source of motivational preference over others. Figure 9 shows the IMO Preferences Graph and figure 10 shows the IMO Consistency Graph. Think of your motivational preferences as your right and left hands.

Fig. 10

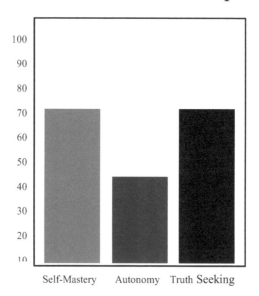

Most of us favor using one hand over the other to carry out specific tasks. In a similar way, we have favorite or specific preferences in how you shape and want to energize our behavior. Although our behavior always has the upper hand, our value preferences are always present to influence and shape our behavior as much as possible.

When what we desire and what we do find emotional alignment, behavioral synergy ensues and creates a clear path forward that includes minimal brain tensions and maximum results. We call this synergistic affect, *flow*.

The 7 Sources of Motivation Underlying Our IMO

Underlying your IMO are seven specific singular sources of motivation known as *separate motivational elements*. Each one of your 7 motivational elements will be measured using each pair of opposing sources of motivation according to Bi-axial theory. As we discussed above, our IMO organizes your seven specific motivational elements into three *cluster* groups (Self-Mastery, Freedom & Autonomy, and Truth Seeking) of integrated values containing higher and lower consistencies in unique and differing combinations.

Let's take a look at the seven separate motivational (value) elements with their opposing partners (higher and lower consistencies) for better clarity. In the chapters following this outline we will look deeper into each motivational element in an effort to help you gain the most clarity possible for deciphering any IMO preference.

The Aesthetic Element
with High and Low Consistencies

The Aesthetic Element (Originality) is a preference for shaping our behavior and being energized by achieving an equilibrium between life and work and emotional harmony between the world around us and ourselves. This element produces originality in those who are energized by it. Creative flow and creative expression are the result of higher consistencies within this element.

The Aesthetic Element when experiencing lower consistencies creates an opposing effect resulting in a *grounded* experience. *Grounding* is our preference for shaping our behavior and being energized by more pragmatic and tangible approaches to life and work that bring concrete and reliable results. When experiencing lower consistencies associated with this element individuals will desire to accomplish tasks using real-world approaches and may perceive those with higher consistencies as having their head in the clouds.

The Economic Element
with High and Low Consistencies

The Economic Element (Efficiency) is a preference for shaping our behavior and being energized by self-interest, real-world gains, and achieving functional returns on our efforts. This element is about *efficiency*. The idea of putting forth less energy while at the same time gaining more value. The word "economic" can be misleading to many simply because it promotes a monetary idea. While monetary gains can be associated with efficiency, functional returns on time and energy is the idea behind this specific value element.

The Economic Element when experiencing less consistency will result in a more *satisfied* state of mind. *Satisfaction* is a preference for shaping and being energized by less competitive approaches to life and work resulting in a more contented state of mind. Less energy is expelled and greater returns on efforts are not important when consistency levels fall below the equator within this element.

The Individualistic Element
with High and Low Consistencies

The Individualistic Element (Individualism) is a preference for shaping our behavior and being energized by expressing our autonomy and freedom from others' ideas and protocols. This element represents an *innovative* expression resulting in desiring our unique ideas to be heard and headed. Personal uniqueness must not only be realized in a personal sense, but also in a public sense— the desire to be in the spotlight and recognized by those around us.

The Individualistic Element when experiencing lower consistencies creates an opposing effect resulting in a *secure* world experience. *Security* is our preference for shaping our behavior and being energized by not seeking the limelight, keeping our ideas to ourselves, and a less likelihood of self-promotion. Those with lower consistencies within this element desire to be more cooperative and obliging and display a less self-seeking attitude.

The Power Element
with High and Low Consistencies

The Power Element (Authority and Control) is a preference for shaping our behavior and being energized by directing and controlling people, environments, and personal spaces. Formerly known as *Political*, this element seeks personal authority equal to or greater than personal responsibilities. In other words, individuals with high Power scores do not want to get into the car unless they're the ones driving it.

The Power Element when experiencing lower consistencies creates an opposing effect resulting in a more *submissive* experience. *Submission* is our preference for shaping our behavior and being energized by supporting other people's efforts and a less focused approach to owning our own personal space. Lower energy levels within this Power element will cause one to desire to yield personal positions to avoid controversial circumstances.

The Altruistic Element
with High and Low Consistencies

The Altruistic Element (Sacrifice) is a preference for shaping our behavior and being energized by assisting others through a *sacrificial* experience. The idea of "personal sacrifice" encompasses the *destruction* or *surrender* of something for the sake of something else. Seeing this element represents the individual comprehending it, the destruction of the self for the sake of someone or something of "greater value" is always the result. Do not think this is about helping others because benevolence is a thinly vailed cloth that covers a more sinister element—the diminishment of the self.

The Altruistic Element when experiencing lower consistencies creates an opposing effect resulting in a *self-focused* experience. Much like self-Mastery, lower consistencies in the sacrificial element create a preference for shaping our behavior and being energized by focusing on personal wants and needs and taking a more suspicious stance towards the motivations of others. This element when experiencing a lower consistency creates a guarded approach to others resulting in them having to *qualify* before they gain space within our world. In other words, only the worthy may enter.

The Regulation Element with High and Low Consistencies

The Regulation Element (Compliance) is a preference for shaping our behavior and being energized by establishing fixed routines and order, while setting boundaries for ourselves and others. Regulated thinkers live in a static world and will resist fluidity. They are narrower in their thinking and approach everything with a black and white mindset believing there's only one way to skin a cat.

The Regulation Element when experiencing lower consistencies creates an opposing effect resulting in a *defiant* experience. *defiance* is our preference for shaping our behavior and being energized by remaining independent and subversive towards the restrictive ideas of others. These individual's believe there's more than one way to skin a cat.

The Theoretical Element with High and Low Consistencies

The Theoretical Element (Curiosity) is a preference for shaping our behavior and being energized by activities towards knowing everything that can be known about what you believe to be important and truthful. Being theoretic is more about *curiosity* than conclusions. To conclude creates brain tensions that require a greater effort towards discovery.

It's very difficult to turn this brain type off. The Theoretical Element when experiencing lower consistencies creates an opposing effect resulting in a *dis-interested* experience. *Disinterest* is our preference for shaping our behavior and being energized by a more dismissive view of gathering more information and discovery while relying more on our natural instincts, intuition, and past experiences for answers.

The Combination Motivational Direction and Consistency Graph

The IMO elements listed above are structured into an *integrated* system of priorities by the dynamic relationships among them. This graph does not measure consistency, but rather it measures your motivational consistency (what you gravitate towards given the chance). You must remember, the ability to fully capture the IMO is through the *integrated* differences between each element. Interpreting single elements does not allow us to experience the full weight of what an IMO means.

The graph on the next page measures your unique motivational priorities identified by how you ranked the relative importance of the seven (7) IMO elements above. Your ranking is important because what affects your behavior is the trade-off (unique prioritizing) you make among *all* 7 elements, *not* the importance of any one element alone. These graphs are a snapshot of the whole of your motivational priorities including the greater and lesser elements as they produce a reliable blue print of how you will prioritize for greater success in the world of circumstance.

The graph on page 28 measures your unique motivational priorities identified by how you ranked the relative importance of the seven (7) IMO elements above. Your ranking is important because what affects your behavior is the trade-off (unique prioritizing) you make among *all* seven elements, *not* the importance of any one element alone.

Fig. 11

Motivational Direction and Consistency Graph

ORIGINALITY	33	7	0	10	20	30	40	50	60	70	80	90	100
EFFICIENCY	86	1	0	10	20	30	40	50	60	70	80	90	100
INDIVIDUALITY	75	3	0	10	20	30	40	50	60	70	80	90	100
POWER	61	5	0	10	20	30	40	50	60	70	80	90	100
SACRIFICE	24	6	0	10	20	30	40	50	60	70	80	90	100
COMPLIANCE	28	4	0	10	20	30	40	50	60	70	80	90	100
CURIOSITY	78	2	0	10	20	30	40	50	60	70	80	90	100

These elements have been ranked highest to lowest (ranging from 1-7). Your consistency in selecting individual preferences is expressed by the length of a bar. A shorter or longer bar indicates a consistency of preference for one motivational element over another. The shorter the bar the more inconsistent your preference, the more moderate your bar the more situationally oriented you are in that specific element. The longer the bar the more you consistently prefer a specific element and the more you will favor environments that favor that element.

The Motivational Word Matrix

The graphic below denotes a matrix of specific descriptor sets using the traditional elemental names: aesthetic, economic, individualistic, power, altruism, regulatory, and theoretical. The motivator element word matrix translates numeric scores into a one-word descriptor and places each word in a relative position to the other descriptors. By labeling your numeric score with one word you can better understand, describe, and locate both your motivator orientation and its direction.

Fig. 12

Eccentric	Self-mastered	Unrestricted	Domineering	Pushover	Black & White	Scholarly
Impractical	Maximized	Independent	Forceful	Sacrificial	Fixed	Fact-Finder
Unconventional	Competitive	Self-Reliant	Authoritative	Accommodating	Systemic	Studious
Divergent	Incentivized	Creative	Controlling	Obliging	Orderly	Investigative
Imaginative	Practical	Balanced	Directive	Supportive	Disciplined	Inquisitive
Sensible	Judicious	Cooperative	Influential	Helpful	Open-Minded	Reflective
Realistic	Relaxed	Accommodating	Supportive	Self-Protective	Flexible	Street-Smart
Practical	Aloof	Supportive	Yielding	Suspicious	Independent	Intuitive
Real World	Apathetic	Apprehensive	Passive	Distrusting	Spontaneous	Superficial
Grounded	satisfied	Secure	Submissive	Self-Focused	Defiant	Dis-Interested
ORI	EFF	IND	POW	SAC	COM	CUR

This graph is found in our IMO Report and is useful for quick analysis. In the next chapter we will begin breaking down the 7 motivational elements to ensure a greater understanding of how each element contributes to the whole of our integrated motivational orientations.

3
GORDON ALLPORT AND THE PROPRIUM

A significant story often mentioned by Allport in his biographies displays the potential depth of psychological analysis. When Allport was 22, he traveled to Vienna. This trip was important as he was scheduled to meet with Sigmund Freud. When he arrived in Freud's office, Freud simply sat in silence and waited for Gordon to begin. After a short period of uncomfortable silence, Gordon blurted out an observation he had made on his way to meet him. He mentioned that he had seen a little boy on the bus who was very upset at having to sit where a dirty old man had sat previously.[30]

Gordon rationalized this was likely something he had learned from his mother, a very well ordered and apparently rather overbearing type. Freud, instead of taking it as a simple observation, took it to be an expression of some deeper, unconscious process in Gordon's mind, and said, "And was that little boy you?" it was this particular experience that made him realize that depth psychology sometimes digs too deeply, in the same way that he had earlier realized that behaviorism often doesn't dig deeply enough.

Allport received his Ph.D. in Psychology in 1922 from Harvard, following in the footsteps of his brother Floyd, who became an important social psychologist. His career was spent developing his theory, examining such social issues as prejudice, and developing personality tests.

---

[30] Cornelis George Boeree (born January 15, 1952) is an American psychologist and professor emeritus at Shippensburg University, specializing in personality theory and the history of psychology.

One of the greatest human motivators is to satisfy natural biological survival needs. Allport referred to this essential human need as Opportunistic Functioning. He surmised that this opportunistic process could be characterized as a biologically reactive and past-oriented functioning. He assessed that when it came to most human behaviors, Opportunistic Functioning was not responsible. His belief was that the majority of human motivations were not biological, but rather individualized expressions of the self. He surmised that our actions and motivations at root level were simply we being who we are. He called this *Propriate Functioning*.

The word "propriate" comes from the word proprium, which was the term Allport came up with for his self-concept. After reviewing hundreds of definitions for his self-concept he felt that, in order to sound more scientific, it would be essential to dispense with the common word "self" and substitute something else in its place. His word "proprium" never gained traction. To better understand Propriate Functioning, think of what you do as a means of self-expression.

I don't mean expressing yourself in any evolutionary or biological sense, but rather expressing your "creative side" or perhaps your logic-based cognitive ability or your personal need for structure and life-organization. Some people, before putting a puzzle together, will organize all the pieces into perfect piles representing their specific color schemes. These type behaviors are not representative of all people across the boards, but rather they are behavior traits we display as individuals; they become personal extensions of ourselves. We human beings *act* in keeping with who we *are*.

Allport's Proprium

Allport's definition of the self-concept (or ego) was bi-directional. First, Gordon Allport believed the self-concept was *experiential*. Our experiences over time develop into a self-concept built upon what we have learned throughout our lifetime. Later on in the book we'll visit the neuroscientific idea that purports the *self* as an illusion. As we move through space-time, our experiences become opportunities to discover what moves us. Allport's proprium addresses our deeper desire to behave (function) in ways that ultimately express our true self. This leads to the second direction, which is *functional*. Our experiences assist in our ultimate functioning (behaviors).

Let's not confuse motivation and drive with the primary emotions that energize our behaviors or ways in which we "act out" desires. Motivation is associated with the "why" of behavior not the "how." For a better understanding of human behavior, see my book; *The Four People Types and What Drives Them* available on Amazon and Audible.

To further make sense of this two-pronged idea of experience and function, I will give you an example of something that happened to me while in high school. When I was a freshman, a young girl brought some drawings to art class that her late grandfather had secretly drawn. After her grandfather's passing, her grandmother discovered a secret room in the basement where her husband would retreat for solace. He would create pencil drawings late into the night.

When he died, her grandmother showed them to the family. These drawings were unlike anything I had ever seen up to that time. One stands out to this day. It was a pencil drawing of a child standing up in a child's pool in the backyard of a home. Perhaps it was one of his grandchildren. The image portrayed the child's wet face with water pouring down through his hair.

In the detailed water droplets on the face you could make out distinct images; reflections of the woods and trees including branches. I was so inspired by them that I went home that afternoon and drew a picture in an effort to capture the realism her grandfather had done. My first drawing was that of a bat out of a

National Geographic magazine. It looked just like the magazine image. I was astonished.

My second drawing was a famous picture of Rita Hayworth. I showed the drawings to my mother and her mouth fell open. "You drew these?" she asked shockingly. For whatever reason, I became an artist that very afternoon. Since then I have taken first prize in shows and have dazzled friends and family for years. In my junior year, teachers in the school would line up to purchase my artwork. My former "experience" with those secret drawings ultimately became a "functional" part of who I am today.[31] Now, to Allport's point; did I become an artist or was I already an artist?

Here's what happened. I was already an artist. The girl who brought the drawings into class was a trigger to an already present capacity—I just didn't know it. The "experience" my brain went through when handling the original drawings connected me to them. My innate desire to try it at home was the proof that she had awakened a sleeping giant already resent within me.

Fig. 1

My mother's duck painting (watercolor) she made as a teenager

---

[31] Unfortunately, I have not drawn with pencil or watercolor in years.

The DNA was already there. Later I found out that my mother's brother was an artist, my mother's sister was a poet, and my mother had painted when she was young. My art *is* my way of self-expression. I'm expressing *who I am*. This is "phenomenological expression."

Fig. 2

My horse drawing: 1984, graphite.

Before moving ahead, I want to make a general distinction that goes largely unnoticed by many analysts. There's a difference between an artist and a talented person. Artists are not as much talented as they are *gifted*. I am not a gifted artist. The gentleman who drew those pictures I witnessed as a teenager was gifted. I'm talented. Unless discovered or moved by some other outside force such as a planetary alignment or cosmic ray bombardment, artists more often than not do not make a good living with their work.

They are usually starving in some parking lot with their amazing work displayed in a makeshift booth they purchased for a day at the town art fair. Talented people are better at monetizing their talent than artists are. The singer Jewel lived in a van with her mother singing in honky-tonks until discovered years later by someone else.

Phenomenological Expression

Phenomenological expression is the self as *experienced*. It's us experiencing ourselves in varying degrees. Allport deduced that the self was composed of several levels of experience. He claimed that we experience ourselves essentially, warmly, and centrally. This is where he comes up with his *trait* theory I mentioned in chapter one. These are a generalization of his levels of self-experience:

Essential: Experiencing our self as an *essential* part of who we are; not accidentally or incidentally. This self-experience is cardinal. It's primary. My art is an essential, self-expressive part of who I am and it can be conveyed in many ways. It began as a pencil drawing and now 40 years later it has morphed into writing, speaking, all my self-branding including working with Photoshop, graphic design, web development, assessment development, and many other creative expressions. According to the Hartman Values profile, I'm unconventional.

Warm: This denotes "precious" as opposed to a state of emotional coolness. Precious is a word that symbolizes closeness, as one would deem a favorite stuffed animal—it's not with you all the time. It's not a cardinal trait but rather a warmer friend that is visited upon on occasion. Not essential, these areas of self-expression are not deeply rooted in who we are, but rather the parts of ourselves we associate with as on occasion. These are branches on our tree as opposed to our trunk and roots.

Central: This signifies a focal sense of self and not a peripheral sense of self. It represents our middle selves albeit not cardinal. These traits are apparent but not dominant. Central traits are part of who we are but they don't necessarily drive us—passengers as opposed to the driver. They are on the bus but do not determine its course.

Propriate Striving

In this concept as postulated by Gordon W. Allport, Propriate Striving emerges in adolescence with the search for identity. The concept goes on to state that experimentation is common among early adolescents before endeavoring to make long-range commitments. Adolescence is considered significant because it's a time of conscious intention and planning for the future. This is a time of defining our objectives, which will later become the standard operating procedures within our personality.[32] Propriate Striving therefore, consists of formulating goals and strategies for the future.

Consider deciding to go to junior college to get an Associates of Arts degree. This is *Propriate Striving*. It's imagining your future self based on what you know about yourself in that moment and developing a path towards it that makes sense to you. Often encouraged by parents, teachers, and peers, our adolescent self makes poor or inappropriate career decisions.

Unfortunately, the brain is not fully developed until around age 26, so although your striving may lead you to take a degree in engineering, you may not end up an engineer in the end. Only 1 out of 4 graduates ultimately end up using their college degree and the average graduate changes careers three times before they ultimately settle into their best niche.

Functional Autonomy

Allport was one of the first researchers to draw a distinction between motive and drive. He suggested that a drive forms as a reaction to a motive, which may outgrow the motive as the reason for a behavior. The drive then becomes autonomous and distinct from the original motive, whether the motive was human instinct or something else. The idea that drives can become independent of the

---

[32] Nugent, Pam M.S., "Propriate Striving," in *PsychologyDictionary.org*, April 28,

original motives for a given behavior is known as functional autonomy. Functional autonomy is thought to underlie adult obsessions and compulsions.

Although our adult motives develop from infantile drives, they eventually become independent of them through further learning and experience. Allport's approach favored an emphasis on the problems of the *adult* personality rather than on those of infantile emotions and experiences. In other words, the experiences of adulthood override the early drives.

An example of this would be experiencing economic gains through your work that over time become driving forces in and of themselves. Although you may have been more passive and easily satisfied in your younger years, experiencing the functional worth of receiving such returns on your energy compel you to earn more returns.

Allport gives the example of a man who seeks to make accurate his task or craft. His original motive may be a sense of inadequacy engrained in his childhood, but his new diligence in his adult work and the motive it acquires is a need to excel in his chosen profession, which becomes the man's contemporary drive replacing the original compulsion fueled by inferiority.

Allport says that the theory avoids the absurdity of regarding the energy of life now, in the present, as somehow consisting of early archaic forms (instincts, genetic reflexes, or some never-changing Id). Learning brings new systems of interests into existence just as it does new abilities and skills. "At each stage of development these interests are always contemporary; whatever drives, drives now."

McClelland offers a critical evaluation of Allport's theory that certain acts can provide their own motivation after the original incentive has disappeared, as against the traditional theory that secondary drives are learned elaborations of primary drives. According to behaviorists, there are 3 parts to any behavioral sequence: instigation, instrumental acts, and goal response. According to McClelland, the problem is, can instrumental acts persist when the instigations, which started them in the first place no longer exist? According to Allport, yes, under three conditions: (1) removal of the instigation, (2) replacement by a more successful instrumental act (3) elimination of the goal response or reward resulting.

McClelland hypothesizes that it's "difficult to prove that each of these conditions actually exists, due to inadequate criteria of their presence, or of the presence of conditioned substitutes. Removal of reward is technically 'extinction,' and this may be delayed by many factors. Hence, until all such possibilities are removed, Allport's main argument for functional autonomy loses force. It must be considered a gratuitous concept until an experimental instance can be found where an act continues even with all delaying factors ruled out."[33]

Observations made by J. P. Seward on the structure of functional autonomy are also at odds with Allport's theory. "An organism approaches and withdraws, explores and manipulates, as a function of specific differences between the present situation and the expectancies built into his schema of the world. I believe this view deserves consideration as a substitute for Allport's. In a literal sense exogenous motives (forces outside the self) are functionally autonomous; since they began that way, a theory of functional autonomy becomes superfluous."[34]

Although I understand these arguments, Allport's functional autonomy theory still makes sense. If we think in terms of our own lives we can reflect on the emergence of specific drivers we did not possess in our past and the resulting motivations that occasioned. I

---

[33] McClelland, D. C. (1942). Functional autonomy of motives as an extinction phenomenon. Psychological Review, 49 (3), 272-283 (PsycINFO Database Record (c) 2016 APA, all rights reserved).
[34] Seward, J. P. (1963). The Structure of Functional Autonomy. American Psychologist, 18 (11), 703-710 (PsycINFO Database Record (c) 2016 APA, all rights reserved).

am a good example of this. I left high school at age 18 wanting to be an artist, later attended seminary at age 22 and became a minister at age 25. I started a painting company at around age 29. I later returned to seminary at age 38. After experiencing a behavioral analysis in one of my seminary classes called *Leadership and Spiritual Formation*, I became a behavioral analyst and started *The Behavioral Resource Group* around age 40. I left the faith at age 48 and started developing my own IP and analytical tools by age 51.

Not only have I developed personal attitudes and drives much different than I had in my early years, I appear nothing like the person I used to be in the 1970's. I have fully outgrown previous motives that acted as drives resulting in new motivations. Motives are learned and much like our emotional make-up, they change over time to fit everything we have come to know through our experiences.

The Big Five

Allport's understanding of our hidden desires to self-express was elaborated into a developmental theory. In this theory, he developed seven operational functions that emerge at certain stages of human development. Self-imaging for example can emerge between the ages of four and six. According to his theory, as our proprium develops, personal dispositions emerge. Cardinal and central traits (some temperament based) are more or less the building blocks of our personalities as a whole and become largely responsible definitions of who we are.

A modern personality assessment tool known as the Big Five was later developed based on Allport's original heuristic work in the 1950's and was defined by the letters OCEAN. In modern contemporary psychology, the *Big Five traits of personality* are five broad domains that define human personality and account for the five basic individual differences. Several independent sets of researchers discovered and defined the five broad traits based on empirical, data-driven research. Ernest Tupes and Raymond

Christal advanced the preliminary model, based on work done at the U.S. Air Force Personnel Laboratory in the late 1950's.[35] J. M. Digman propositioned his five-factor model of personality[36] in 1990, and Goldberg[37] extended it to the highest level of organizations in 1993. In a personality test, the Five Factor Model or FFM[38] and the Global Factors of personality may also be used to reference the Big Five traits.[39]

The Big Five (OCEAN) personality traits are:

Openness
Conscientiousness
Extraversion
Agreeableness
Neuroticism

Openness: People who like to learn new things and enjoy new experiences usually score high in openness. Openness includes traits like being insightful and imaginative and having a wide variety of interests much like those who exhibit high *optimistic* and low *fear* emotions.

Conscientiousness: Those who have a high degree of conscientiousness tend to be reliable and prompt. Traits include being organized, methodic, and thorough much like those who exhibit high *patience* and *fear* emotions.

---

[35] Tupes, E.C., Christal, R.E.; "Recurrent Personality Factors Based on Trait Ratings," Technical Report ASD-TR-61-97, Lackland Air Force Base, TX: Personnel Laboratory, Air Force Systems Command, 1961.
[36] Digman, J.M., "Personality structure: Emergence of the five-factor model," Annual Review of Psychology, 41, 417-440, 1990.
[37] Goldberg, L.R., "The structure of phenotypic personality traits," American Psychologist, 48, 26-34, 1993.
[38] Costa, P.T., Jr., McCrae, R.R.; Revised NEO Personality Inventory (NEO-PI-R) and NEO Five-Factor Inventory (NEO-FFI) manual. Odessa, FL: Psychological Assessment Resources, 1992.
[39] Russell, M.T., Karol, D.; 16PF Fifth Edition administrator's manual." Champaign, IL: Institute for Personality & Ability Testing, 1994.

Extraversion: Extraverts receive emotional energy from interacting with others (having a less excited amygdala), while introverts (more excited amygdala) get their energy from within themselves. Extraversion includes the traits of energetic, talkative, and assertive types (high optimism, and low patience).

Agreeableness: These individuals are friendly, cooperative, and compassionate. Those with low agreeableness are more distant. Traits include kindness, affectionate, and sympathetic. These are indicative of high or *exaggerated* patience with low dominance.

Neuroticism: Neuroticism is also sometimes called Emotional Stability. This dimension relates to one's emotional stability and degree of negative emotions. People that score high on neuroticism often experience emotional instability and negative emotions. Traits include being moody (low optimism) and tense (high dominance with a negative view of the world).

Allport's 7 Functions of the Self

You cannot display all Big Five traits at once. You will exhibit one or two of these traits mainly because some of these five traits have competing energies such as dominance and patience and optimism and fear. According to Allport, having a well-developed and rich and adaptable set of dispositions, you are considered psychologically mature. These traits are defined using seven characteristics.

- Involvement with the world understood as extensions of the self (self-esteem).
- Dependable and technically adept in relationship to others.
- Self-accepting whilst begetting emotional security and decorum (self-esteem).
- Having a realistic sense of self without emotional defensiveness (self-esteem).
- Problem-centeredness resulting in effective problem-solving skills.

- Self-insight with the ability to laugh at one's self (self-esteem).
- Having a unified philosophy of life and a personalized conscience.

Four of the seven traits are strictly self-esteem related. This proves that self-esteem is essential not optional for mental health. Our motivation can be stalled or energized by low or high self-esteem levels. Having a high sense of self-worth to many feels like egocentrism. This fallacy has been one of the largest roadblocks to emotional health and sustainability.

Allport's 8 Stages of Self

What is the self? According to William James, the "me" involves objective materials and social and spiritual characteristics. This is the social and material self as a functioning entity in the world. The "I" involves more subjective matters including your life history and life experiences on a time continuum—pure ego. Winncott identifies a true and false self that could use some definition. Winncott's "true self" is all about being.

It's our natural existence including spontaneity and non-verbal gesturing. The "false self" is made up of other people's expectations (us in shared existence) overriding the true self. In my book, *The Four people Types and What Drives Them* I call this lifestyle the Eros Prison. The Eros prison is a false life created by behaviors and relationships that lack the spontaneity that comes from separate existence. The false self is performance driven.

The self in cognitive developmental theory focuses on the quality, rate, and general thinking processes of human beings. Self-awareness and self-concepts are studied through either *stage* or *layer* theories. *Stage Theories* assume development occurs in a linear progression and that ultimately divide child development into distinct, linear stages characterized by qualitative differences in behavior. Each stage must be complete before advancing to the next stage. There are a number of different views about the way in which psychological and physical development proceed throughout the life span.

Layer Theory is "Distinct layers of awareness about objects, people, and the self, mature from an implicit biologically given core at birth. Each added layer of subjective experience would correspond to major qualitative shifts; the emergence of a contemplative stance by 2 months, self-consciousness from around 21 months and the manifestation of an ethical stance by 3–5 years.

"This new 'onion' way of looking at psychological experience is meant to capture the fact that a new emerging layer of awareness does not block, re-construct, or fundamentally re-structure "à la Piaget" the expression of those ontogenetically anterior via bounding up equilibration and other reflective abstraction 'bootstrapping' mechanisms."[40] In other words, each layer is an expansion of the first core, building on pre-existing layers cumulatively. Each layer adds on to what already exists without restructuring or changing pre-existing layers.[41]

Researchers have developed a test known as the "rouge test" in which toddlers and infants are presented with a mirror for self-reflection. Children under 18-months fail to recognize the connection between the mirror image and themselves. After 18-months, the connection is made resulting in an awareness of the self in the world as an objective reality. These connections are staged by age and are presented below using Gordon Allport's 8 stages.

Sense of Body (infancy): Is a sense of one's own physical body, including bodily sensations and feelings. It attests to one's existence in the world and therefore remains a lifelong anchor for being alive

---

[40] Philippe Rochat, "Layers of awareness in development," dans Developmental Review, Elsevier, vol. 38, December 2015, pp. 122-145.
[41] Tanya Maria Geritsidou (Tantz Aerine), Director at MindPower Publishing; Psychopedagogue at Private Practice.

and self-aware. Imagine spitting in a cup, waiting a few minutes and then drinking it. The realization that a bodily fluid has left the "body envelope" initiates a psychological disgust meter in an effort to protect the body from toxins.

Self-identity (first 18 months): The second aspect of the proprium is self-identity and emerges in the first 2 years. This is most evident when the child, through acquiring language, recognizes his or herself as having a name and that they are a distinct and constant point of reference apart from everyone else. Self-awareness takes place when we as individuals can examine ourselves from a point of view other than our own.

Knowing what you might think about what I'm about to say means I am self-aware. Self-consciousness can only occur after becoming self-aware. This level of awareness involves understanding the self through two sets of eyes; our own and someone else's. this is the basis for identity development.

Self-Esteem (2-3 years): This is an individual's evaluation of his or herself and the urge to want to do everything for oneself and take all of the credit for gains made. Self-esteem starts off with an "A" and over time, we diminish our grade often to a state of utter failure.

Self-Extension (4-6 years): This occurs during the third year of life, which states that even though some things are not inside my physical body they are still very much a part of one's life.

Self-Image (4-6 years): How others view "me" is an aspect of selfhood that emerges during childhood. This is the "looking-glass self." It includes social imaging, role-awareness, and social status. This can be lost or exaggerated.

Self as a Rational-Coping Agent (6-12 years): The child begins to realize fully that he or she has the rational capacity to find solutions to life's problems, so that they can cope effectively with reality demands.

Propriate Striving (13 years): Allport believed this to be the core problem for the adolescent. It is the selection of occupations or other life goals; the adolescent knows that their future must follow a plan. This includes a sense of direction and purpose and in this sense makes them *lose* their childhood.

Self as a Knower (Adulthood): The last part of proprium that unifies and transcends the other 7 stages. The thinker is different from his or her thought-feelings. This is contrary to William James, who maintains, "The thoughts themselves are the thinker."

Understanding where we sit in relationship to ourselves and the world around us will ensure a greater connection with what moves us through the world, we live in. when we integrate our primary emotions with what moves us, a picture of who we are emerges with greater clarity. In the following chapters we will look into the 7 specific motivational elements that make up our Integrated Motivational Orientation.

Eduard Spranger contributed to personality theory in a more important way when he wrote his book, 'Types of Men' in 1928. His six value attitudes (Aesthetic, Utilitarian, Individualistic, Religious, Theoretical, and Altruistic) were paramount in unearthing what moves us. These six passions (now seven since the Individualistic attitude was divided to also include a Power attitude), combined with the four behavioral temperament dynamics originating with Hippocrates, have become the general framework for fully drilling down into the how and why of personality today.

4
ORIGINALITY AND AESTHETICS

Aesthetics is the first of the seven elements we will discuss. I want to reiterate something about all these motivational elements. None of them stand alone and none are meaningful without integration—none. They are all part of a highly complex fabric of being; a tapestry of the four emotions, the seven attitudes, and the six value foundations put forth by Dr. Robert S. Hartman (I call this the Holy Trinity). Each are varied in their individual consistency or weakened intention, and all are resting upon different character dimensions. We will not be discussing Hartman's six value dimensions in this work although I may allude to them from time to time.

These styles vary between individuals and will either create dissonance or cultivate resonance when acting in concert in families, relationships, partnerships, and the work world. This in no way is a full explanation of all that these individual and collective styles encompass, but rather it is a brief overview of each. These are just a few examples of what a motivational graph can look like.

"If there is nothing but the fanciful enjoyment of a single situation, we have only a poetic mood, or an aesthetic whim. But if the whole soul acts as a forming power in every bit of life, giving color, mood, and rhythm, then we have the aesthetic type."[42] Perhaps the most ardent proponent of the theory that men are best known through their evaluative attitudes is Eduard Spranger in his book, Types of Men. The types fall into six categories: theoretical, economic, aesthetic, social, political, and religious.[43] These he describes as "the ideally basic types of individuality."[44]

---

42 Eduard Spranger, Types of Men, (Halle, 1928) p. 111-112.
43 Annie Willie Young, Thesis, Department of Education, Atlanta, GA, June,1942.
44 Eduard. Spranger, Types of Men, Authorized Version of 5th German Edition by Paul J. W. Pigors (Halle, 1928) p. 108.

The aesthetic person sees and understands the highest value in appearance and synchronization. Each experience is judged from the standpoint of refinement, proportion, or suitability. He regards life as a procession of events; each event experienced for its own sake. She need not be an uncommon artist, nor need she be decadent; she is aesthetic if she but finds her chief interest in the splendor of life.

According to Mencken, "the aesthetic person either chooses to consider truth as equivalent to beauty or agrees that, 'to make a thing charming is a million times more important than to make it true'."[45] In the economic sphere the aesthetic person sees the process of manufacturing, advertising, and trade as a wholesale destruction of the values most important to her.

Be it known that the aesthetic attitude is opposed or "conflicted with" the theoretical attitudes. Whereas the aesthetic mind is concerned with diversity, the theoretical mind is concerned with identities of experiences. He is also opposed to the economic attitude. The economic mind is concerned with efficient means while the aesthetic mind is concerned with *unconventional* means. It is for this reason that the aesthetic mind becomes hopeless and helpless when faced with practical demands that require an objective and efficient stance.

Seeing this aesthetic sense of being is rooted in individuality, it holds hands with the individualistic attitude. When both attitudes are in play, a sense of satisfaction with a life that "now is" emerges free from excessive needs to act responsibly or rationally. Excessiveness within this dimension can lead to eccentricity and self-absorption (not in an ego sense). Aesthetics, for this reason can become lost into themselves and devoid of useful reason.

---

[45] Henry Louis Mencken, (September 12, 1880 – January 29, 1956).

The main motivation when an aesthetic impulse is in full swing is the strong desire and need to achieve equilibrium between the world around them and the world within them. Creating a sustainable work/life balance between the two dimensions becomes necessary. Creative, imaginative, arty, mystical, and expressive, those with higher aesthetic impulses may redefine and resist everyday approaches to current problems, challenges, and opportunities.

People with a higher consistency in this dimension will think in unconventional ways likely leading to inefficient processes to real-world problems. If this is you then the tendency to think outside the box and preferring to be your own person will be commonplace. You may have a high interest in protecting wildlife, the environment, and the distinctive. Minority groups of animals and people matter. You may feel as though you were born out of time or you may feel misunderstood by others. Like all life, they become objects themselves of aesthetic enjoyment and differentiating empathy.

Fig. 1 (This is a very rare profile 11/1250)

Motivational Direction and Consistency Graph
Intuitive

	0	10	20	30	40	50	60	70	80	90	100
ORIGINALITY											
EFFICIENCY											
INDIVIDUALITY											
POWER											
SACRIFICE											
COMPLIANCE											
CURIOSITY											

Resisting inner strength, aesthetic types prefer outer influences such as the natural order of things to motivate their person. These outer influences act as mediums to paint an artistic portrait of the self that harmonizes with the natural world and its surroundings. The aesthetic language of influence thus affects others through a creative sense of responsibility and a creed that is a religion of exquisiteness.

Aesthetic styles display a strong appreciation for uncommon and original approaches to life and work. They have a "hyper-awareness" of their surroundings and they will need to feel right before engaging with circumstances or other people. High aesthetically driven styles will show a very strong desire for expressing their talents and fulfilling their dreams. Aesthetic types will struggle with deciding what to do with their life. Higher education may seem daunting to original thinkers. Aesthetics or original types often care less about monetary values and creature comforts and more about gravitating towards feeling happy and fulfilled in life.

When original thinkers sport low dominant behavior, they become "floaters." This means they allow circumstances to frame their world, but they will lack the fortitude and personal incentive to create the world they want—they end up settling for whatever world they can get. Rather than paddling against the current in an effort to reach a desired destination, they float down the river and "set up camp" wherever the raft leads. Destinations become secondary to journeys.

Some of the key strengths to this style involve not being moved by monetary or tangible rewards or being bullied into the status quo. Instead, they are looking for personal fulfillment and peace of mind. They see things differently than most because their insights are highly intuitive rather than rational and mechanical. They are big on helping others to find creative alternatives to everyday problems.

They believe people should do work that is an expression of who they are as opposed to a job that simply must get done. Because they are a contributor and not a consumer, they believe more in giving and less in taking. When accompanied by higher theoretical mindsets this style may experiment with alternative or unorthodox sexual practices outside the national norm. They're sensitive and empathetic to the plights of others and will resonate with their inner longings. They may demonstrate a very high personal and professional regard for the feelings and emotions of those outside the "machine." They uncover, discover, and recover creative ideas and solutions to all the challenges they face.

If you are like this, you should remember that it is okay that some people won't "get" you or understand your unconventional ideas. You may end up feeling somewhat out of place in this world and inadvertently sideline yourself for not knowing what to do or why you are here, but know you are here for a reason. At times, you may try to be too much of a non-conformist and may rebel against established systems and systemic processes. You might tend to have your work back up because you're using impractical means to accomplish work tasks. You likely get lost in creative intuition if not kept somewhat reined in and on target by peers, partners or managers.

You would likely benefit from having your feet on the ground as opposed to your head always in the clouds. Because you may place too great an emphasis on unconventional alternatives in the workplace, leading to impractical outcomes or not meeting deadlines, you may experience excessive turnover within your work or love life.

Low Aesthetic Consistency

On the lower end of the aesthetic consistency, the opposite attractors will be experienced. You'll believe something's usefulness is more important than its appearance. You'll likely believe artistic people to be time vampires and focused on non-essentials. You'll be a strong advocate of process and productivity and won't want to waste resources on things that don't affect productivity.

Those with low aesthetic drive are not likely to connect with unreasonable ideas, either emotionally or professionally like those on the higher end of this scale. You may view "feeling good inside" as secondary and not primary when working with other people. You will prefer your time not to be wasted by others who dilly-dally or take the unconventional approach to solving problems. You could also have a strong practical and innovative logic-sense accompanied by good horse sense.

Fig. 2 (Entrepreneurial drive)

Motivational Direction and Consistency Graph

Category	Score	Rank	0	10	20	30	40	50	60	70	80	90	100
ORIGINALITY	33	7											
EFFICIENCY	86	1											
INDIVIDUALITY	75	3											
POWER	61	5											
SACRIFICE	24	6											
COMPLIANCE	28	4											
CURIOSITY	78	2											

If you're more economically driven you won't share emotions or your true feelings with others and you may approach business as just that; simply business, nothing personal. Because of your economic drive and bottom-line approach to business transactions, you may put people off. Those who have a very less consistency in the aesthetic sphere with higher economic or power drives are likely surviving difficulty rather than thriving in difficulty and may fight as opposed to negotiate to win battles.

Low aesthetic styles have a practical approach to life and business and won't like wasting people's time with things that won't increase their bottom line, salary, or standing. They may be more talented than artistic when developing ideas and others. Odds increase they will cut to the chase more than they will beat around the bush. They might also have the gift of faultfinding. They could have a heightened awareness of wasted time and energy and will stick to what works most of the time.

If this is your style, don't assume that aesthetic workplace changes or remodeling would be welcomed or overly appreciated by you—it likely won't matter because you will be tempted to connect improvements in function to success. To you, rational goals are what matter the most. Those with high aesthetic drive will not move you since yours it's very low. So in order to maintain your highest level of motivation, avoid getting involved with emotional issues.

Because you teach/learn in a very practical way, you may not appreciate things that you don't understand. Make sure to connect training benefits to business opportunities when working. Because you are not aesthetically driven, you will likely stick to practical motivations only. You'll probably avoid lots of team interaction just for the sake of interaction so be certain there is a practical reason for opting out.

Some might consider your uncaring attitude about what people are feeling to be too critical. You should try to appreciate the value others have for the environment and nature as a whole, as well as the impractical ideas they may settle upon. You will have to remember to respect the creativity and quirky ways of others.

Aesthetic as an Attitude

To go even deeper into the aesthetic mind, "If we wished to summarize the essence of aestheticism we should say, 'It is formed expression of an impression.'"[46] Spranger imagines three stages contained in the aesthetic attitude which he calls; *impression*, *expression*, and *form*. Spranger's "impression" denotes a "sensuous

---

46 Eduard Spranger, Types of Men, (1928), p. 147.

concrete objective" picture either introduced in reality or created by one's imaginative faculties that can be physically experienced through an emotional conduit.

The expressive stage is also a sensuous concrete presentation of the same psychological content. He claims it to be *enlarged* by our imagination in either a physical or imagined material.[47] And the final stage is said to be a product of both the infused impressive and expressive stages and their *subjective* and *objective* faculties if a condition of *equilibrium* and *synchronization* is established.

> "Aesthetic attitude theories are marked by their general insistence on the fundamental importance of the aesthetic attitude. Some of these theories hold that the nature of art is explained by the aesthetic attitude. This is generally accepted as an insufficient way of setting the boundaries of art, for reasons we have already seen, since nature, too, is a perfectly fine thing to take the aesthetic attitude toward.
>
> Most aesthetic attitude theories thus offer subtler and more complex accounts of the interaction among the aesthetic attitude, art, and beauty. Indeed, many of these philosophers have been keen on distinguishing a variety of different aesthetic qualities. In addition to beauty, they are interested in sublimity, novelty, charm, and so on."[48]

The problems related to aesthetic attitudes is found in the fine line between an object and the creative and emotional attributes we assign to it. Defining an object strictly through theoretical concepts isolates the object. This is known as the *naïve aesthetic enjoyer*.[49] The objects attributes 'live,' according to Spranger, inside the aesthetic object and can be experienced simultaneously between both the object and the self who beholds it.

---

47 Ibid.
48 Alexandra King, Brown University, *The Aesthetic Attit*ude, The Internet Encyclopedia of Philosophy.
49 Joseph Strzygowski elevates this unsafe positivistic procedure to a fundamental methodological principle whenever he wants strictly to differentiate between Sachforschung and
Beschauerforschung in aesthetics, (Die Krisis der Gesteswissenschaften, Wien 1923).

This process is clearly seen in those who's world revolves around art appreciation, environmental caregiving, music, creative writing, healthy and alternative food sources, etc. The aesthetic mind is not only *called out* by a great work of art, it is enabled to create the work itself.

Unicorns and Gypsy Spirits

Aesthetics' is about an 'inner rhythm' that is somehow translated into an inner vision that gives birth to great forms and harmonies. This is why aesthetic driven people types in affect, see the world through a prism. Non-aesthetic types see only through plate glass and wonder what the aesthetic type is talking about when they attempt to describe the rainbow they so clearly see. This is why I refer to higher aesthetic types as *unicorns* and *gypsy sprits*.

Higher theoretic types who experience the higher aesthetic elements are mostly rare. If you measure above a 65 on the aesthetic scale and above a 65 on the theoretical scale you are likely one of 10 out of about 1200 random people. Greater consistencies than 80 may put you in a category all your own. This is more attuned to an anomaly. Consistencies on levels like this is where we find banjo players, harpists, and those who film wild elephants in Asia and live in a tent. These are often complex or quirky people—experimental in thought and deed. More about this in chapter 9.

Someone once said, *Raphael would have been a great painter even if he had been born without hands.* What they mean is that he could not help but view the world through the eyes of a painter. How many aesthetic types are out in the world today with great ability and don't really know it? More often than not I have had debriefings with high aesthetic types and suggested creative writing, blogging or some other creative outlet only to be told they were thinking the same thing.

It's often our low self-esteem that gets in the way of our creative flow and creates a roadblock to exceptional personal discoveries.

Spranger speaks of aesthetic types "letting themselves go" in the manifold nature of actual or imagined objects.[50] Absolute connection with the world is always 'passionate' and abounds with the struggle for both material and spiritual existence.

Aesthetic types shroud themselves with a "veil of imagination" through which they recreate the pain and suffering of the past through a process of transmuted emotional alchemy into a bearable essence of contemplative assurance. This imaginative process enlarges their view of the world and allows a maintenance of prolonged mediation between pain and suffering and joy.

It, therefore, becomes increasingly difficult for higher aesthetic theoretical types to live in the *real* world. A haunting need to escape the trappings of real-world objects such as houses and cars and real jobs claws at their minds with a relentless aggression. They can often feel nomadic and will identify with the famous quote, "Not all who wander are lost."[51] Experience becomes the mother of all creativity.

Aesthetics' place an almost religious level of importance on experiencing the world and its objects. The ability to *feel into* their surroundings and experience a deeper sense of harmony between themselves and objects is no less than astounding. Never satisfied with a single situation of poetic mood or fanciful appreciation for a single object in time, the whole of a person with all forms of impressions filling their soul as a flooded plain giving forth a whole spectrum of color, mood and rhythm is an aesthetic soul.

Aestheticism and Individualism

The aesthetic soul is an aesthetic phenomenon. The combination of aestheticism and individualism devoid of economic or efficient

---

50 Ibid. p. 148.
51 "Not all those who wander are lost," a line from the poem, "All that is gold does not glitter," written by J. R. R. Tolkien for The Lord of the Rings.

drives is a marriage made in heaven. The unification of these two elements brings the aesthetic type to a higher level of aesthetic awareness. The relatedness between individualism and aesthetics is an emotional glue binding the highest qualities of both interests that always results in the *forcing out* of philosophies of efficiency and functional worth.

Functional worth becomes an albatross around the neck of the aesthetic soul burdening it with unnecessary and banal mandates devoid of mood and meaning. The greater the individualistic and aesthetic flow, the lesser the functional and material worth. Nearly all who display these traits fail to exhibit a materialistic view of the world. Objectivity gives way to subjectivity. These types live so intensely as to color every part of their inner and outer being with an aesthetically biased hue.

Fig. 3 (The starving artist)

Motivational Direction and Consistency Graph

ORIGINALITY	81	3	0	10	20	30	40	50	60	70	80	90	100
EFFICIENCY	18	1	0	10	20	30	40	50	60	70	80	90	100
INDIVIDUALITY	89	2	0	10	20	30	40	50	60	70	80	90	100
POWER	37	5	0	10	20	30	40	50	60	70	80	90	100
SACRIFICE	24	4	0	10	20	30	40	50	60	70	80	90	100
COMPLIANCE	28	6	0	10	20	30	40	50	60	70	80	90	100
CURIOSITY	60	7	0	10	20	30	40	50	60	70	80	90	100

Spranger incites the aesthetic soul believing they lack any possibility of an objective relinquishment to the concrete and visible objectives of life. Power *over* circumstances becomes weakened while a truce with what one can stand emerges. This is what I mean when I say, settling for what they can get rather than fighting for what they want. To want is at odds with their soulish needs. Wanting becomes an anathema to them. To want is to align oneself with greed and materialism. To desire to become one with the universe is characteristic of the aesthetic nature in its basic form. They are themselves part of a larger tapestry of form and universal harmony.

Spranger notes a difference between an externally creative artist and an internally purposed soul—the advantage of being able to project her experience into any external form including colors, tones, and poetic pictures.[52] Still, the individualistic aesthetically driven soul must disassociate herself from the objective realities of life.

An Aesthetic Nature

The aesthetic man's conception of the essence of nature is opposed to the theoretic man. The theoretical man binds himself to a reasonability akin to logic and reason as understood in the thinking brain whereas the aesthetic feeler disassociates with objective reality and takes on a mythological method of thought. Mythological characters make sense whereas real people do not. An organically developed *sense* (interpretation) of life is transposed onto whatever is real.

Aesthetic souls are in continued conflict with mechanical conceptions of nature. All that is living represents a much deeper sense of empathetic force. This is why higher aesthetic types are drawn to yoga, meditation, and Buddhism. Ignoring the diaphragm in its mechanical sense, the aesthetic gives way to the imaginative form as seen by the inner eye as it embraces and imagines the body being pulled up through the heard by an invisible string with each breath. All is one. Nature and soul are bound in unity and partnership. All that destroys and affects its course must be condemned.

---

52 Eduard Spranger, Types of men (1928), p. 151.

Plastics, tires, and all that litters its oceans become enemies of her fury. Environmental activism is fueled by high aesthetic types whose mission is to rescue mother earth from the soiled hands of the unnatural mechanical man and his machine.

Aesthetics and Originality

I like the word *original*. From a Spranger perspective, I may not receive the tipping of his hat on this one. But I have noticed something profound after nearly 15 years of debriefing and tens of thousands of motivational orientations; high aesthetic types are originalists. Creative, unorthodox, and unconventional, yes, but originality is at its root. What is an *original* but a product of one's imagination? Unusual? Novel? Innovative? Yes—all of the above.

An aesthetic drive finds its fuel in a deep and fanciful imagination; an imagination that is axiomatic of the full capacity of a feeling type. Yes, unconventionality is very original as it is disassociated with pragmatic thought. "What's in it for me" gives way to "What can I imagine." Experimentation is often the aesthetic type's highest form of *experience*. Novel ideas, new paths, new scenery, and new and exciting relationships built on the foundation of harmony and form are consistently pouring out of the aesthetical existence.

Unfortunately, the down side to novel ideas and an anti-pragmatic viewpoint is hardship. Originalist's in this particular sense do not value monetary returns as much as they value how they feel and how they fit within a natural dynamic. They work only to live but will never live to work. Working is more about contributing to the natural world and less about building wealth.

Often we here about communal living and socialistic programs where all are part of the producing of goods and services and the benefits that are imagined to follow. Yes; this is an aesthetically driven utopian image of the world. Sure, it works in small groups of likeminded people as long as they are devoid of efficiency and power drives.

Only IMO's whose altruistic drives are increased and whose economic and power drives are diminished will this model have a snowball's chance to work.[53] Yielding one's position to avoid controversial encounters and contributing more than one consumes is a convergence within the motivational framework that will keep one from *taking* over. This idea is found thousands of years in the past, about the sixth century BCE to be exact.

> "The wolf also shall dwell with the lamb, and the leopard shall lie down with the kid; and the calf and the young lion and the fatling together; and a little child shall lead them.
>
> "And the cow and the bear shall feed; their young ones shall lie down together: and the lion shall eat straw like the ox. And the sucking child shall play on the hole of the asp, and the weaned child shall put his hand on the cockatrice' den."
>
> Isaiah 11:6-8

Oh, how wonderful this image of life is. Humankind has longed for a world that demonstrates the highest of virtues in all that participate in it. This is an aesthetic type's dream. A utopian world where we are moved to contribute and consume in equal parts. Like the native American's who spared nothing after the kill.

"Native Americans highly respected animals. As they were a part of their livelihood. If the animal was hunted, not one part of the animal was wasted.

"They used bones from the animal to make tools and weapons, the hides for clothing and tipi's, blankets, and protection from the elements. Horses were the highest form of currency and played a crucial role in Native American survival. Especially for tribes like

---

[53] This has never worked long-term on a communal scale and it's never worked on a societal scale.

the Comanche who were possibly the best horseman to ever live. They domesticated dogs, and even children got their own pony by the age of 4 or 5 to start caring for it and learning to ride.

"Every animal had a purpose either physically or spiritually and every animal was treated with respect (not other humans so much but usually that was in defense of people 'trespassing' on their hunting grounds or in retaliation from ongoing wars). I haven't read any books on Native Americans that implied anything other than respect for animals."[54]

Compared to today's world, these ideas are novel. They are out-of-the-box and sidelined as silly or impossible. Only the aesthetic knows the deeper natural meaning underneath the veneer of commonality. Natural, novel, and unique; yes, the aesthetic mind sees the world through this natural prism where rainbows reign and rubbish retreats. Where unity and harmony are the fundamental forms of relationship, work, and spiritual investment. Where communal and harmonious living occurs between man and beast, earth and sky, and heart and mind.

Duel Aesthetic Convergences

Duel convergences are a combination of two separate value elements. How each element contributes to the total factor set will differ as each value element contributes an essential component that offsets the other component to create a synergistic outcome that will contribute to the whole of each IMO. In the first set represented below, for example, a higher consistency in the economic value element (ECO/H)[55] when associated with a lower consistency in the aesthetic value element (AES/L) synergizes into a competitive desire free from creative intrusions.

---

54 Kevin Maher, Quora.com, Oct 11, 2014.
55 H=high and L=Low.

Self-mastery, which is a derivative of the higher consistency of economy, joins with a real-world attitude found in the lower consistencies associated with creativity, harmony, and form (aesthetic). Alone, this will build a competitive desire, but when combined further to include the other five value elements this factor set can take on further characteristics. Later on in the book we will several styles that cover all convergences (all seven value elements) giving you a taste of what the total factor set can mean for you.

I have discovered (after 13 years of research) a series of particular patterns that we have translated into 27 styles. We will cover those as well. But for now, let's take a look at a few duel factor sets that include the Aesthetic value element.

AES/H-IND/L (Accommodation): This value factor associates *creativity* with *accommodation*. Individuals who score higher on the aesthetic element and lower on the individualistic element will feel the need to deliver creative ideas and results for those who are willing to cooperate.

AES/H-IND/H (Creative-Independence): This value factor associates *creativity* with freedom and *independence*. Individuals who score higher on the aesthetic element and lower on the individualistic element will feel the need to deliver creative ideas and results for the common good.

AES/H-ECO/L (Unconventionality): This value factor associates a *creative* need disassociated from *pragmatism*. Because aesthetic value is disassociated with personal returns, individuals who score higher on aesthetic elements while scoring lower on economic elements will feel the need to experiment for the sake of *experiencing* the results as opposed to benefitting from them.

AES/H–ECO/H (Crafty): This value set associates *self-mastery* with *unconventionality*. These two competing forces are disassociated when together. When the economic value is high, and the aesthetic value is high you will have inner conflict. This will create a strong need to diverge while desiring to make personal gains. The process to this end can be emotionally compromised when the need to *experience* those gains competes with practical rationale; if all goes well, one attains cleverness.

AES/H-POL/L (Apprehensive): This value factor associates *creativity* and alternative thinking with *submissive* and supportive thinking. Low power values are disassociated with owning the rights to its benefits. Individuals who score higher on aesthetic elements and lower of power elements will feel the need approach experiences within established groups and social structures of likeminded people with caution.

AES/H-POL/H (Creative-Leadership): This value factor associates *creativity* and alternative thinking with *ownership* and *authority*. Higher power values are seeking authority and control over circumstances. Individuals who score higher on aesthetic elements and higher on power elements will desire to use their creativity thinking to direct and control their immediate space and those who are in it.

AES/H-ALT/L (Precautionary): This value factor associates *creativity* and *alternative* thinking with *distrust* and *suspicion*. Individuals who score higher on the aesthetic element and lower on the sacrificial element will feel the need to explore and *experience* the world around them while being detached from others who might ruin it.

AES/H-ALT/H (Experiential): This value factor associates *creativity* and alternative thinking with *self-sacrifice*. Individuals who score higher on the aesthetic element and higher on the sacrificial element will feel the need to *experience* other people and seek creative outlets where they can share like experiences. These types may appreciate communal living.

AES/H-REG/L (Unrestricted): This value factor associates *creative* experiences and *alternative* thinking with *subversion* and *independence*. Individuals who score higher on aesthetic elements and lower on regulated elements will feel the need to explore and experience the world around them while being independent from authorities, powers, and unnecessary restrictions.

AES/H-REG/H (Circumscribed): This value factor associates *creative* experiences and *alternative* thinking with *discipline* and *order*. Individuals who score higher on aesthetic elements and higher on regulated elements will feel conflicted. The need to explore and experience the world around them while adhering to what is reliable and socially expected can cause tension. They may seek to build creative systems where none are present without crossing lines.

AES/H-THE/L (Imaginative): This value factor associates *creative* experiences and alternative thinking with *intuition*. Individuals who score higher on aesthetic elements and lower on theoretical elements will feel the need to explore and *experience* the world around them while being detached from the need to know everything about it.

AES/H-THE/H (Alternative Complexity): This value factor associates *creative* experiences and *alternative* thinking with *curiosity*. Individuals who score higher on aesthetic elements and higher on theoretical elements are very rare. They will feel the need to experiment with the senses and experience alternative impressions. This type may seek alternative sexual experiences, mushrooms, and diverse fields outside the scope of social normalcy.

AES/L-IND/H (Unobstructed): This value factor associates *freedom* with *real-world* attitudes built on self-reliance. Individuals scoring higher on individualistic elements and lower on aesthetic elements will feel the need to use *conventional* and *reliable* means to gain personal freedom and autonomy.

AES/L-IND/L (Reasonable): This value factor associates *sensibility* with *supportive* attitudes. Individuals scoring lower on aesthetic elements and lower on individualistic elements will feel the need to use *conventional* and *reliable* means to gain personal security and self-sustenance without frills or nonsense.

AES/L-ECO/H (Discrete): This value factor associates *freedom and uniqueness* within a practical, *real-world* environment. Individuals scoring higher on individualistic elements and lower on aesthetic elements will feel the need to be their own person by sharing their own unique ideas while not being an extremist or unorthodox in the process.

AES/L-ECO/L (Gratified): This value factor associates *satisfaction* with a practical, *real-world* environment. Individuals scoring lower on aesthetic elements and lower on economic elements will feel the need to hang back while resisting competitive forums. These types are usually grounded and content with what they already have.

AES/L-POW/H (Coordinated): This value factor associates *ownership and control* over one's own space within a pragmatic environment absent from nonsense. Individuals scoring higher on the power element and lower on the aesthetic element will feel the need to control their own destiny and influence their surroundings while maintaining common sense strategies and real-world approaches to problems, challenges, and opportunities.

AES/L-POW/L (Relinquished): This value factor associates *surrender* with *sensibility*. Individuals scoring lower on the power element and lower on the aesthetic element will feel the need to yield to those who know better while resisting excessive responsibilities.

AES/L-ALT/H (Practically Supportive): This value factor associates *assisting* others at personal expense through real-world solutions and everyday means. Individuals scoring higher on this end will feel the need to assist others through practical processes that benefit others at a degree of personal expense stemming from an inability to perceive their own value.

AES/L-ALT/L (Self-Protective): This value factor associates *suspicion* with *sensibility*. Individuals scoring lower on aesthetics and lower on the altruistic element will post a guard at their emotional gate. Those who seek closeness will have to qualify to enter their private space.

AES/L-REG/H (Restrictive): This value factor associates the need to follow *established systems* and consistent rules through practical, common sense processing. Individuals scoring higher on regulated elements and lower on aesthetic elements will feel the need to live within a narrowly structured system devoid of creative or alternative influences.

AES/L-REG/L (Candid): This value factor associates the need to follow *their own path* without unnecessary frills. Individuals scoring lower on regulated elements and lower on aesthetic elements will feel the need to live and let live. Usually spontaneous, these types may try anything once.

AES/L-THE/H (Analytical): This value factor associates the need to uncover, discover, and recover the facts in a *useful* way. Individuals scoring higher on theoretical elements and lower on aesthetic elements will feel the need to establish the facts through analytical reasoning and rational thought.

AES/L-THE/L (Common): This value factor associates the need to rely on existing pathways forward in a *useful* way. Individuals scoring lower on theoretical elements and lower on aesthetic elements will not feel the need to establish the facts through analytical reasoning and rational thought, but rather to utilize existing ideas.

Aesthetic Ranges and Results

Seeing that the main motivation in this element is the strong desire and need to achieve equilibrium between the world around us and ourselves (within) while creating a sustainable work/life balance between the two, consistency levels will produce differing motivational desires as they move from the mid-point to both higher and lower regions. Below we will look into the diversity of desires within this element covering assets, advantages, insights and intuitions, learning paths, and growth opportunities.

Situational Aesthetic Consistency

Remember, these are values not behaviors. Values speak of our *desires* and what moves us in a directional effort. Keep also in mind that this list is associated with a single element and not the *integrated motivational orientation*. What we desire can often conflict with what we actually do.

Individuals with *general* or situational (situational/midpoint) consistency and direction within the *single* motivational element of aesthetic will likely desire to (keep in mind that this list is in no way exhaustive):

1. Keep impractical, creative, and mystical types grounded.
2. Appreciate others' needs to express their creativity.
3. Work equally well with the imaginative and pragmatic types.
4. Possess a healthy balance between style, purpose, and function.
5. Possess the average level of aesthetic appreciation, near the national mean.
6. Work well with others to create and transform.
7. Live on an even keel and not likely become to obsessed with things.

8. Desire a sense of balance between work and life but are not crippled without it.
9. Appreciate nature and its beauty and will likely protect it when possible.
10. Recognize conservation but may or may not participate in them.
11. Be willing to help others especially if you appreciate their uniqueness.
12. Enjoy certain creative expressions, but you are not head over heels over it.
13. Appreciate the world around you including natural wonders, good art, and solitude.
14. Believe that creativity is available to everyone, but it depends on how one defines it.
15. Equalize team efforts between doing it right and enjoying being innovative.
16. Possess a level of artistic interest or appreciation that is right at the national mean.
17. Believe offsetting work and play is important for emotional health.
18. Participate in a variety of training and professional development efforts.
19. Work well with either groups, or individuals.
20. Appreciate developing soft skills and will care about emotional health.

Very High Aesthetic Consistency

Remember, these are values not behaviors. Values speak of our *desires* and what moves us in a directional effort. Keep also in mind that this list is associated with a single element and not the *integrated motivational orientation*. What we desire can often conflict with what we actually do.

keep in mind that this list is in no way exhaustive. Individuals with *very high* (situational/midpoint) consistency and direction within the *single* motivational element of aesthetic will likely desire to:

1. Think in unconventional ways likely leading to inefficient processes to real world problems.
2. Think outside the box and prefer to be your own person without apologizing for it.
3. Have a high interest in protecting wildlife, the environment, and the distinctive.
4. Feel as though you were born out of time and feel misunderstood by most.
5. Display a very strong appreciation for uncommon approaches to life and work.
6. Have a hyper awareness of your surroundings and will need to "feel" right.
7. Show a very strong desire for expressing your talents and fulfilling your dreams.
8. Struggle with deciding what to do with your life. Higher education may feel daunting.
9. Gravitate towards being happy and fulfilled.
10. Not be moved by monetary rewards, but rather look for personal fulfillment and peace of mind.
11. See things differently than most because your insights are intuitive not mechanical.
12. Be helpful in helping others find creative alternatives.
13. Believe people should do work that is an expression of who they are as opposed to a job that simply must get done.
14. Be a contributor not a consumer.
15. Believe in giving and not taking.
16. Be sensitive to the plights of others and will resonate with their inner longings.
17. Demonstrate a very high personal and professional regard for the feelings and emotions of those outside the machine.
18. Uncover, discover, and recover creative ideas and solutions.

19. Have the ability to act as a go-between and integrate people's imaginations with certain tasks.
20. Increase the meaning of people's by acting as a facilitator between people's gifts and talents and meaningful jobs that might require them.

Very Low Aesthetic Consistency

Like the descriptors above, keep in mind that this list is in no way exhaustive. Individuals with *very low* consistency and direction within the *single* motivational element of aesthetic will likely desire to:

1. Believe something's usefulness is more important than its appearance.
2. Believe people to be time vampires focused on non-essentials.
3. Be a strong advocate of process and productivity, and don't want to waste resources on things that don't affect functional outcomes.
4. Not connect with unreasonable ideas emotionally or professionally.
5. View "feeling good inside" as secondary rather than primary when working.
6. Not like their time to be wasted by others who dilly-dally.
7. Have practical innovative logic and some horse sense.
8. Not share emotions or their true feelings with others.
9. Believe its simply business and not personal.
10. Take a stronger stance.
11. Put people off with their bottom-line approach.
12. Survive difficulty rather than thrive difficulty.
13. Battle as opposed to negotiate to win.
14. Have a real-world approach to life and business.
15. Not like wasting their time with things that do not produce results.
16. Be more *talented* rather than *artistic* when developing ideas.

17. Cut to the chase.
18. Have the gift of faultfinding.
19. Have a heightened awareness of wasted energy.
20. Connect improvements in function to success.

The aesthetic element, as you can now see, is the unconventional part in an engine containing many parts. Alone, this part has nothing to offer. It will remain motionless like setting a carburetor on the surface of a table. Together with the rest of the engine parts, this piece offers an unconventional *addition* to how this engine runs. Much like putting a turbo charger on an existing engine, the engine will perform differently now that this part has been added.

In the coming chapters we will look at the remaining parts associated with the motivational engine. Keep in mind that as we go through each additional component, we will observe its quality and function and, in the end, we will examine how these differing parts organize themselves to create a particular type of performance as each engine whirs to life.

5
EFFICIENCY AND ECONOMIC DRIVE

One of the strongest natural drives in humans is self-preservation. As we increase in age, our needs both natural and unnatural begin to increase with changes in degrees of responsibility. Although basic needs may be satisfied, to continue to advance will require greater motivational reach. The capacity of natural products to satisfy needs by maintaining and developing physical life is called their *utility*.[56]

What is useful will always be a physical means to satisfy needs. Maintenance of life by means of appropriate adjustments to given conditions is the sum of the process of basic achievement. Our individual aims in the direction that is our best interest will encompass feelings of pleasantness or pain. Pleasantness being feelings associated with a satisfactory process of attaining desired results and pain being feelings associated with an inability to achieve one's goals effectively or in a timely manner.

These levels of satisfaction can be measured. And not only that, but the levels of the "desire to be satisfied" can be measured. Goods in the form physical products and forces including intellectual and emotional achievements, must be attained in order to be experienced. While aesthetic aims can be fulfilled by simply experiencing form and beauty around and in us, economic aims cannot be fulfilled without physical achievements.

For example; many physical processes are assembled together in order to achieve a great painting. One must purchase a canvas, brushes, oil paints, graphite, an easel, wood, a frame, etc. Without the commission of a specified amount of human and psychic energy,

---

56 Eduard Spranger, Types of men (1928) p. 130.

the creation of a great painting will never be realized. If I desire to obtain a great painting, those mental and physical utilities employed to create it will be transferred to me and I will have to pay a price for the consumption of energy and goods used to create it.

Such utilities are not unlimited. The expulsion of human energy used to bring goods from different places and to transform them by the application of known natural laws is called work. Work is the expenditure of energy. *Economic* energy is energy that *gains* more than what you started with by achieving *greater* returns than the energy used to capture them.

This is achievement. To achieve is to gain through the expulsion of energy. To achieve *economically* is to achieve more by using less energy. The greater our returns in proportion to the lesser energies needed determines the amount of utility. A very characteristic quotation is the following: "This book," the author says, "tells you how to be twice the man or woman you ever were before—happy, well, brimming with energy, confident, capable, and free of care. You are required to follow on laborious mental of physical program; it is much simpler than that. As laid down here the route to that promised profit may appear strange, for a few of us can imagine *getting without striving* . . . Yet that is so, as you will see."[57]

The Productive Orientation

In his work, Social Character in a Mexican Village, Erich Fromm outlines The Productive Orientation (PO) of personality. According to Fromm, it refers to an axiomatic attitude, a mode of affiliation in all realms of human experience. It covers the physical, mental, emotional, and sensory responses to others, to oneself, and to things. Productiveness is man's ability to use his powers and to not only realize the potentialities inherent in him, but to expel his energies to fulfill these potentials. Saying one uses their powers implies that they must be free and not dependent on someone who

---

[57] Hal Falvey, *Ten seconds That Will Change your Life* (Chicago: Wilcox & Follett, 1946)

controls their powers. The key to the economic drive is potential or *product* fulfillment.

It implies, furthermore, a practical understanding that they are *guided* by reason (in a functional sense), since they can make use of their powers only if they understand what they are, how to use them, and what to use them for. Productiveness means that one experiences themselves as the incarnation of his or her powers and as the *player*; that one feels himself or herself as the subject of their powers, that they are not alienated from their powers, i.e., that these powers are not masked from him or her and transferred to an idolized object, person, or institution. Productiveness is to say that the productive person animates that which he or she touches.[58]

The full unfolding of biophilia[59] is to be found in the Productive Orientation. The person who fully loves life is attracted by the process of life and growth in all spheres. They prefer to *construct* rather than to retain. This means holding the fort is worse than taking the hill. One is capable of wondering, and prefers to see something new to the security of finding confirmation of what one already knows. They love the adventure of living more than they love inevitability.

Their approach to life is *functional* rather than mechanical. They see the whole rather than only the parts, and the structures rather than summations. "They desire to mold and to influence by reason, by example; not by force, by cutting things apart, by the bureaucratic manner of administering people as if they were things, but by a more civilized means. They enjoy life and all its potentials rather than mere excitement."[60]

---

58 Fromm-online.org: *Social Character in a Mexican Village*. 1970b [with Michael Maccoby]: *A Sociopsychoanalytic Study*, Englewood Cliffs (Prentice Hall) 1970, pp. 71f.
59 Edward O. Wilson introduced and popularized the hypothesis in his book, Biophilia (1984). He defines biophilia as "the urge to affiliate with other forms of life."
60 *The Heart of Man. Its Genius for Good and Evil*, New York (Harper and Row) 1964, pp. 46f.

Productiveness is an attitude that every human being is capable of, unless he or she is mentally or emotionally compromised. That being said, not all people *choose* to live a highly productive life. Do not confuse production with actions. Productivity is an active response to stimuli, but *activity* as it stands is not productive by nature. In other words, being active does not equate with being productive. Behavior and emotion play large roles in production as do desires and motivations. But one can also desire a more productive life yet not easily achieve it.

Activity is behavior that brings about a change in an existing situation be an *expenditure* of energy. In contrast, "a person is described as passive if they are unable to change or overtly influence an existing situation and thus are influenced or moved by forces outside themselves."[61] The level of change as it relates to the level of expenditure of energy determines its economic value. This description of Productive Orientation is thus representative of the economic value element.

Fromm uniquely analyzes the characteristics of productivity as they relate to certain people types in a behavioral sense. But the economic drive under discussion in this book is a value orientation and is separate from a person's behavioral orientation.

Productiveness as a Value Orientation

As a value orientation, productiveness becomes sidelined to a dimension that desires rather than dictates. In other words, to *desire* productiveness does not make one physically or emotionally productive. That being said, one can highly value or dislike productiveness and achievements. Valuing achievements and economic returns means you understand productivity and you value what it brings; i.e., you value less of an expenditure of energy and a greater return on that lesser expenditure of energy.

---

61 Erich Seligmann Fromm, Man for Himself: an inquiry into the psychology of Ethics, Fitzhenry & Whiteside LTD. 1947.

You may have heard it said that the lazy man is the efficient man. I would not go as far to agree with this statement on its face, but I understand what is meant by it. A lazy man will seek the most advantageous means and the road of least resistance in an effort to expel the least amount of energy. But this is separate from making gains. A lazy man will not benefit much from his laziness if he is passive and not active in nature. If he is not economically driven or if he does not desire to achieve greater outcomes proportionate to his efforts and energy then he will lose with passive behavior orientations.

Greater needs to gain can be either offset or aligned by differing consistencies associated with altruism and self-sacrificial needs. My productive needs can align with assisting others in attaining their needs by sacrificing my position power. There are those who gain by *losing* to another—this is the loss-winner. My productive needs can also be attained by assuming a *me first* position in relationship to others. Both positions will meet the need to be productive but the outcomes will be different.

The Loss-Winner

What will I do if I see old Mrs. Jones walking home from the grocery store (as is her routine) with her small cart of groceries and I know it is about to rain heavily. Let's say she's not close enough to her house and she will get soaked to the bone if it starts raining in the next few minutes. To add to this scenario, I'm already late for an important meeting with my manager. To add further, I was late already this week. What would you do? For some, the answer comes quickly but for others, more energy is required to think it through.

Depending on where your economic and altruistic orientations are located on the values index will determine how easily this question can be answered. Higher economic consistencies coupled with lower altruistic consistencies may cause one to think Mrs. Jones isn't very smart for deciding to walk to the store when rain was in the forecast for several days—serves her right if she gets wet. But if your economic consistencies are highly diminished and your altruistic consistencies are more accelerated, you may stop and insist she gets in your car before the rain starts (see the below graph).

Fig. 1 (Low Economic drive)

Motivational Direction and Consistency Graph

ORIGINALITY	80	2	0	10	20	30	40	50	60	70	80	90	100
EFFICIENCY	18	1	0	10	20	30	40	50	60	70	80	90	100
INDIVIDUALITY	65	5	0	10	20	30	40	50	60	70	80	90	100
POWER	37	6	0	10	20	30	40	50	60	70	80	90	100
SACRIFICE	84	3	0	10	20	30	40	50	60	70	80	90	100
COMPLIANCE	55	4	0	10	20	30	40	50	60	70	80	90	100
CURIOSITY	60	7	0	10	20	30	40	50	60	70	80	90	100

Not only would this individual (above) take Mrs. Jones home before the rain starts, they might also help her bring the bags in and refuse the ten dollars she offers for their act of benevolence. Being rewarded for what they believed was *doing what is right* would feel terribly wrong. Let's take a look at a few losses incurred for this behavior. We'll call this person Susan.

1. Susan is late to work again.
2. Susan has to explain why she is late again.
3. Susan lost out on a $10.00 tip.

Does Susan believe she lost anything? Absolutely not. Let's take a look at the gains Susan made. Susan believes . . .

1. Mrs. Jones is not soaking wet and therefore may have avoided a cold.
2. Mrs. Jones did not harm herself hurrying home in the rain.
3. Mrs. Jones was able to keep $10.00 that she may have lost to someone else.

We gain when our brain feels good; we lose when it doesn't. The gains we make are therefore subject to the motivational orientations we consistently experience. In the above scenario, Susan may have felt like she won the lottery by helping Mrs. Jones. But someone with a greater consistency towards the economic orientation and a much-diminished altruistic orientation would not feel that way at all. Sure, they may assist Mrs. Jones simply because they're not a cruel bastard, but they probably won't feel as good as Susan felt about it.

Brain Tension

The reason is clear—brain tension. Those who are more efficient-minded or economically driven will feel brain tension when they do not make critical gains. Much of what we desire is about eliminating brain tension and *not* about fulfilling a specific desire. Our brains and our emotions do not like tensions that build. The fulfillment of the economic desire is therefore, the brains way of eliminating unwanted anxieties associated with the negative feelings produced when the failure to realize productive outcomes happens.

This is purely a physiological experience. This is true for each value interest. Whether it's the economic interest or the individualistic interest, built up tensions occur when we fail to realize what we (our brains) inherently value.

Higher Economic Consistency

The higher economic impulse is largely opposed to the higher aesthetic impulse as well (by default). When the economic impulse is more intense while the aesthetic impulse is less intense you will resolve the conflict between the two dimensions. High economically driven styles are real-world thinkers (feet on the ground) while high aesthetic thinkers are more abstract and intuitive (head in the clouds).

When it comes to getting what they need, those with a high economic impulse may believe the ends justify the means especially if they are low regulatory thinkers and low fear oriented (-C in DISC or -P in TARP). People who are motivated this way tend to like rewards based on the results they achieve rather than on the method used to obtain those results. They not only compete with others, they compete with themselves. They are typically interested in what makes logical sense and what gives the greatest return for their efforts.

Because they don't typically do nonsense, they will struggle with work-life balance and could become over worked because of their high degree of self-interest. They always think in terms of, "me first–you second." Other people may imagine this style as selfish. If this is you, you'll likely have strong horse sense and you'll probably work hard to become debt free in relationship to people and money. You never lose in the end because you do not appreciate being on the end that owes.

You'll work long and hard to meet personal needs and you'll desire to save your money when you can if your behavior warrants it. Your decisions are made with yourself and bottom-line thinking in mind and you'll be highly driven by competition, challenges, and economic incentives. This attitude makes one able to multi-task in a variety of areas and keep important projects that will bring both reward and challenge while rejecting those that don't. I want to reiterate the fact that your behavior has a big impact on whether or not your desires are realized.

People with this strong attitude *desire* to be highly industrious— to maximize efforts and returns. They want returns that are "equal to" or "greater than" whatever energies they put into something.

They have high motivation to achieve and win in a variety of areas. If this is you, you'll ask yourself, "What am I getting out of this" before engaging in opportunities and challenges involving shared interests. Also, those with a higher economic attitude, a higher level of curiosity, and lower sacrificial sense within this framework likely won't have time for stupid and others may see it.

Economic types may be more focused on their future and less on their present situation. When coupled with a highly charged optimistic brain type, the future is all they think about. If your power orientation is above average, you'll have an entrepreneurial spirit and you might seek status symbols. You won't like or put up with excessive credit card debt and if a door closes in front of you, you are hoping to find a window.

Because the economic type provides substantial room for financial rewards and excellent performance, they have no problem rewarding others for high performance in tangible and monetary ways. They realize that it's not just money that motivates, but also autonomy and personal fulfillment in the job. They understand that people should provide recognition and rewards (e.g., bonuses) as soon as possible, not just at the end of the quarter or year.

Remember that people like this have a heightened awareness of wasted time and materials. They will not like their time being wasted by nonsense and therefore will not likely waste someone else's time. They will appear selfish to those of lower economic consistency. They may even find it difficult to balance work and life or *doing* and *being*. They will not like moochers, time vampires, or people who take credit for the accomplishments of others.

If this is you, if possible, you should not think of everything as a competition. You should link learning outcomes to the ability to become more effective in increasing earnings for both yourself and the organization you are a part of. If you run a business, you should think about providing some rewards or incentives for participation in additional training and professional development. You may need to focus more attention on others and less on yourself.

You may need to slow down and enjoy being with others not just competing and comparing yourself to them. People may see you as intense and more focused on your own personal needs and not the needs of others. You may judge the efforts of others by the amount of work, energy, and time they put in. If your economic attitude is over-extended you may need to work on balancing other dimensions of the values scale and appreciating the creative people who are less practical in their approach to things. You may also need to know that not having excessive means is not a sign of laziness or social or ethical weakness.

Low Economic Consistency

The lower economic impulse can sometimes indicate that you have already begun to reach your own level of financial security, to the extent that things other than monetary increase may now become motivating drives. While not driven by a need to "get yours," you may be sensitive to perceived injustices and discriminations among your peers and may be compelled to fight for them. A lower economic drive can indicate that you are not solely motivated by competitive financial incentives, but are easily satisfied with what you already have. Those who constantly talk about their great accomplishments and financial gains may turn you off.

For these people, life isn't about what you get out of it, but rather what you contribute to it. Using monetary or material gains as a yardstick to measure one's worth or impress others is considered distasteful. This lower consistency will work well with a high altruistic value sense because of the strong absence of self-interest at its root. Lower economic consistencies are far more focused on others and less focused on the self. They rarely (if ever) look at a project with a "what's in it for me?" perspective.

They are likely more sensitive and responsive to the lives of others than they are their own. You see a much wider spectrum of the picture, not just your own view when you think this way. You consider the world in terms of "we" and less in terms of "me." You are less concerned with personal gain and more with personal contributions. Also, when people are lower in consistency in this realm, they may need more creative options for taking on tough challenges. They should avoid measuring their performance by "feeling good about it" only.

Fig. 2 (High Economic drive)

Motivational Direction and Consistency Graph

ORIGINALITY	26	2	0	10	20	30	40	50	60	70	80	90	100
EFFICIENCY	79	4	0	10	20	30	40	50	60	70	80	90	100
INDIVIDUALITY	65	5	0	10	20	30	40	50	60	70	80	90	100
POWER	37	3	0	10	20	30	40	50	60	70	80	90	100
SACRIFICE	84	1	0	10	20	30	40	50	60	70	80	90	100
COMPLIANCE	55	4	0	10	20	30	40	50	60	70	80	90	100
CURIOSITY	60	7	0	10	20	30	40	50	60	70	80	90	100

Because these people prefer when job "enrichment" strategies are structured into the reward system, they may end up with the short end of the stick monetarily speaking. Preferring praise for continued contributions to the job, as opposed to monetary rewards for high productivity, they won't be incentivized by rewards like some people.

Lower economic styles should remember that *helping hands* behind the scenes might not get them where they need to be. Because they consider the strengths of the total person to be important, they may miss some significant singularities. They should be aware that some people can see them coming a mile away and may take advantage of their willingness to help.

These lower economically driven styles enjoy *being* more than they enjoy *doing*. They are more cooperative and less competitive. They may prefer group-oriented activities to work, having fun, and sharing ideas with others. They will not come to a training or development function without a 'What's in it for me?' attitude. If your attitude is low here, you may need to learn that saying "no" does not make you're a bad person. In fact, by embracing "no" occasionally, you will avoid some potential conflicts.

Time Awareness

Lower consistencies (0-34) within the economic driver means one will not be time-sensitive and therefore may end up taking longer to complete something than people expect. You will mistake saying "I can't" for saying "I won't." You may tend to over-commit for fear of letting people down. You likely pay more attention to the needs of others and as a result might miss meeting important personal needs.

Time is the one thing we cannot get back. This is why strong efficient types are so aware of it. And its why higher aesthetic and lower economic types are unaware of it. If your economic drive consistency is below 30 on the values index you may be living outside of time. You may not even notice the time staring you in the face when looking directly at your phone screen. If these values are coupled with high optimism and low fear then you won't know what time is. Time will be an albatross imposed on you by annoying timekeepers who's only role is to cramp your style.

If your altruistic consistency is high and your economic consistency is low, you may be ten times the person you think you are. If this describes you then you should find personal time during each week to simply waste on yourself. If you need to say "no" you should tell people you'll get back to them with your answer at a later time.

Saying "no" is much easier when you're in another space away from the person. This can also be done through a text or email, which is also less confrontational. I call this the one-way glass method. Texting or email is akin to pointing out a perpetrator in a line up behind one-way glass—it's much easier than doing it in front of a clear glass window. More on this when we delve into the altruistic attitude.

Economy and Cognition

Economic types are purposeful not whimsical. While theoretical types desire answers for no other reason than to *know* them, economic types will only view knowledge for its utility. *Because I know this I can now put this information to good use!* Whatever is not useful is taxing to the brain and will raise tensions. Application of knowledge is all that knowledge is for. Wisdom becomes more essential as wisdom applies knowledge for personal advancement.

The economic attitude is therefore, the mother of pragmatism. All knowledge is measured by its ability to increase one's self-preservation and the degree in which it can enhance one's position in the world. The limits of cognition will define the limits of economics.[62] Those who gender lower consistencies in the theoretical attitude will rely on their intuitive sense and their past exploits for learning their way forward. With no time to waste, they will be apt to *jump* to conclusions based on what they already have stored in their databanks.

This causes the brain to scan rather than study—images are preferred over words. Quick scanning becomes the mode of operation when lower consistencies abound within a theoretical context. Innovation is a time sensitive orientation because it

---

62 Eduard Spranger, Types of Men (1928), p. 134.

combines higher economic drives (and usually higher individualism) with lower or moderate theoretical drives. *I don't have time to waste, therefore I am forced to innovate.* Creativity abounds when lower consistencies are found in the theoretical dimension.

The reasons for this should become clear. Much like the competing emotions of optimism and fear, there's a semi-contradiction between individualism and curiosity. While optimism is a creative, non-thinking emotion, so also is lower theoretical interest. The less I rely on rational thought, which takes a certain amount of concentration energy, the more I depend on the automatic *flow* of information *already* obtained. Relying on what we already know takes far less energy than coming up with something new.

When we connect economic consistency and creative individualism with lower theoretical interests, the process of learning is short-cutting. This is known as thinking on your feet. Desiring to utilize my need to think on my feet will determine the level of tension experienced when forced to "study to know" in an effort to make quick gains. This is why many with this motivational dynamic merely "study to pass." More about this chapter nine.

Economy and Beauty

Spranger speak openly about the exclusivity between the aesthetic and economic components. The aesthetic component is characterized by the fact that it has an *experiential* rather than a *utilitarian* value. The useful therefore becomes an anathema to the beautiful. What brings more destruction to the pristine landscapes, lovely oceans, and stunning forests of the earth than economic motive? Would the earth agree that there is room for both values?

When the aesthetically important is viewed from an economic vantagepoint it is considered a *luxury*. For those who have higher aesthetic and economic consistencies, luxury items may be desired.

But when one value overrides another with considerable distance on the values scale, a disposition occurs that sets one against the other.

The general rules between economic interest and aesthetic interest when positioned against one another could not be more contrasted. One will sacrifice the luxuries of life for natural harmony of all things while the other sacrifices a few trees for fine furniture. In the end, an oxymoron emerges between these two components; those with the greatest economic standing become patrons of art. Expensive art initiates social elevation and becomes the authentic sign of one's utilitarian nature.

Economy and Self-Preservation

An excessively driven economic type endeavors to preserve the self above anything else. Often viewed as ego-driven or even selfish, the high economic type places little importance on the needs of others. Their rationale insists on every human being taking personal responsibility for their own welfare. If one chooses to sacrifice their own welfare for another then that is their prerogative.

They may miserably fail to understand why this may happen but will nonetheless cater to themselves more vigorously than to others. Higher economic types believe we have choices—we choose to live the way we want to. That being said, there's a disconnection with the reality of differing mindsets. Although a highly aesthetic style realizes they have little to no utility, they may still long for a more secure and stable life.

The starving artist never decided one day that they would live a life of starvation. Neither did they set out to struggle with objective day-to-day decisions that make their brain hurt. Our lives encompass many variables that ultimately shape our direction of motivational consistency. Unfortunately, the economic person often fails to *feel* into the soul of the aesthetic type and much misunderstanding ensues. The higher economic system has no real place for charity.[63] Their economic interests are strictly limited to a utilitarian perspective. By nature, the focus is strictly on the self and the preservation of its earnings. It is for this reason that others are judged by their ability to produce. Wealth is often used as a yardstick to measure one's worth to society. Efficient, reliable, and thrifty, the economic type caters to self-sufficiency first while thereafter determining the worthiness of the extension of resources to another.

Duel Economic Convergences

Duel convergences are a combination of two separate value elements. I talked about these in the last chapter so I will not further elaborate on how these factors work. You may reference the former if you need to brush up on convergences.

ECO/H–AES/L (Competitive): This value factor associates *self-mastery* with *pragmatism*. These two forces are disassociated (in conflict) when both are in play. When the economic value is high, and the aesthetic value is low you will have no inner conflict. This will create a strong real-world and conservative approach to solving problems, finding opportunities, and making personal gains.

ECO/H–AES/H (Cleverness): This value factor associates *self-mastery* with *unconventionality*. These two forces are disassociated when competing. When the economic value is high, and the aesthetic value is high you will have inner conflict. This will create a strong need to diverge while desiring to make personal gains. The process to this end can be emotionally compromised when the need to *experience* those gains competes with practical rationale; if not, one attains cleverness.

ECO/H–IND/L (Compromising): This value factor associates *self-mastery* with *security*. These two forces are neutralized when both are in play. When the economic value is high, and the

---

63 Eduard Spranger, Types of Men (1928), p. 136.

individualistic value is low you will have no inner conflict. This individual will feel free to cooperate without the need of a spotlight to highlight personal accomplishments.

ECO/H–IND/H (Instruction): This value factor associates *self-mastery* with *self-reliance*. These two forces are neutralized when both are in play. When the economic value is high, and the individualistic value is high you will have no inner conflict. This individual will desire to have their opinions and ideas heard in an effort to secure what they believe to be coming to them. They will need to be autonomous and free from the constraints that may diminish their ability to leverage resources.

ECO/H–POW/L (Yielding): This value factor associates *self-mastery* with *submission*. These two forces are maximized when both are in play. When the economic value is high, and the power value is low you will have some inner conflict. This individual will desire to maximize personal gains but may lack the fortitude to make it happen.

ECO/H–POW/H (Dominating): This value factor associates *self-mastery* with *power*. These two forces are maximized when both are in play. When the economic value is high, and the power value is high you will experience maximum leverage. This individual will desire to maximize personal gains while controlling input and outcomes. They will desire to win or will resist playing if winning doesn't appear evident.

ECO/H–ALT/L (Self-centered): This value factor associates *self-mastery* with *suspicion*. These two forces are disassociated (conflictive) when both are in play. When the economic value is high, and the altruistic value is low you will have no inner conflict. This individual will prioritize personal wants and opportunities in line with their personal agenda while largely distrusting others and leaving them to fend for themselves.

ECO/H–ALT/H (Torn): This value factor associates *self-mastery* with *sacrifice*. These two forces are disassociated when both are in play. When the economic value is high, and the altruistic value is high you will have inner conflict. This individual will prioritize personal wants and opportunities in line with their personal agenda while struggling with a need to please others. This creates a me-me conflict response; should I sell it or give it away?

ECO/H–REG/L (Flexible): This value factor associates *self-mastery* with *independence*. These two forces are neutralized when both are in play. When the economic value is high, and the regulated value is low you will have no inner conflict. This individual will insist on multithreaded and subversive approaches to solving problems and meeting personal needs.

ECO/H–REG/H (Forceful): This value factor associates *self-mastery* with *systemic thinking*. These two forces are neutralized when both are in play. When the economic value is high, and the regulated value is high you will have no inner conflict. This individual will insist on specific ways of attaining what they desire and will hold others to the same standard of operation by force.

ECO/H–THE/L (Street-smart): This value factor associates *self-mastery* with *intuition*. These two forces are neutralized when both are in play. When the economic value is high, and the theoretical value is low you will have no inner conflict. This individual will rely on intuition and past experiences for learning what to do next. They will study to pass rather than learn to know.

ECO/H–THE/H (Shrewd): This value factor associates *self-mastery* with *investigation*. These two forces are neutralized when both are in play. When the economic value is high, and the theoretical value is high you will have no inner conflict. This individual will rely on proof, facts, and excessive amounts of knowledge for leveraging how to maximize their current position in the world. These types can be very clever.

ECO/L–AES/H (Unconventional Surrender): This value factor associates *satisfaction* with *unconventionality*. These two forces are disassociated (in conflict) when both are in play. When the economic value is low and the aesthetic high you will have no inner conflict. This will create unconventionally imaginative and original approaches to life that many will not relate with. You may settle for what you can get rather than fight for what you want.

ECO/L–AES/L (Settling): This value factor associates *satisfaction* with *realism*. These two forces are disassociated (in conflict) when both are in play. When the economic value is low, and the aesthetic value is low you will have inner conflict. This will create a practical yet apathetic need center. This style is rare but if it occurs, you can expect a level of apathy.

ECO/L–IND/H (Creative Independence): This value factor associates *satisfaction* with *independence*. These two forces are neutralized when both are in play. When the economic value is low, and the individualistic value is high you will have no inner conflict. This individual seeks creativity, the spotlight, and non-competitive environments where they can shine.

ECO/L–IND/L (Collaborative): This value factor associates *satisfaction* with *apprehension*. These two forces are neutralized when both are in play. When the economic value is low, and the individualistic value is low you will have no inner conflict. This individual seeks group activity, team orientation, and extended collaboration. This outlying style typically desires to help at personal loss.

ECO/L–POW/H (Controlling): This value factor associates *satisfaction* with *authority*. These two forces are maximized when both are in play. When the economic value is low, and the power value is high you will have some inner conflict. This individual desires control over their surroundings but may struggle to gain it.

ECO/L–POW/L (Self-deprecating): This value factor associates *satisfaction* with *submission*. These two forces are maximized when both are in play. When the economic value is low, and the power value is low you will have no inner conflict. This individual resists responsibility and will yield their position to avoid controversy. Passive by nature, they may seek to diminish their personal worth.

ECO/L–ALT/H (forfeiture): This value factor associates *satisfaction* with *sacrifice*. These two forces are in conflict when both are in play. When the economic value is low, and the altruistic value is high you will have no inner conflict. This individual is the "lose-winner" and will suffer personal loss while creating value for others. They will likely see others as more important than themselves.

ECO/L–ALT/L (Measuring): This value factor associates *satisfaction* with *distrust*. This style match is rare. These two forces are in conflict when both are in play. When the economic value is low, and the altruistic value is low you will have minor conflict. This will create an aloof distant style who resists assisting others who do not qualify. They could potentially have hidden agendas.

ECO/L–REG/H (Compliant): This value factor associates *satisfaction* with *black and white thinking*. These two forces are in minor conflict when both are in play. When the economic value is low, and the regulated value is high you will have no inner conflict. This individual is rigid and may be punitive in nature. They may use other people's mistakes against them in order to gain personal strength.

ECO/L–REG/L (Passive-Resistant): This value factor associates *satisfaction* with *subversion*. These two forces are in minor conflict when both are in play. When the economic value is low, and the regulated value is low you will have no inner conflict. This individual may be passive-resistive. In other words, they may covertly seek to do things their own unique way.

ECO/L–THE/H (Fact-Finder): This value factor associates *satisfaction* with *curiosity*. These two forces are neutralized when both are in play. When the economic value is low, and the theoretical value is high you will have no inner conflict. This individual has little time awareness and may seek inordinate amounts of information beyond the allotted time necessary.

ECO/L–THE/L (Floater): This value factor associates *satisfaction* with *dis-interest*. These two forces are neutralized when both are in play. When the economic value is low, and the theoretical value is low you will have no inner conflict. This style is intuitive and resists over-working their cognitive mind. They may be subject to errors in judgment.

Situational Economic Consistency

To reiterate, these are values *not* behaviors. Values speak of our *desires* and what moves us in a directional effort. Keep also in mind that this list is associated with a single value element and not the *integrated motivational orientation*, which includes all seven value elements. I'm going to say this again because it bears repeating; what we desire can often conflict with what we will actually do.

Individuals with *general* or situational (situational/midpoint) consistency and direction within the *single* motivational element of economic will likely desire to (keep in mind that this list is in no way exhaustive):

1. Make modest gains in return for their efforts.
2. Not need to win when engaging with others.
3. Keep a balance between being satisfied with what they have and a need for more.
4. Be more or less realistic and down-to-earth in regards to getting what they believe they deserve.
5. Identify with and understand individuals who have both high and low satisfaction rates.

6. Be fine with helping others with projects and initiatives without experiencing an overextended need to "get yours."
7. Not be an extremist and therefore a stabilizing force when winning is required.
8. Be able to balance both needs and perspectives of those with substantially different attitudes towards financial gain.
9. Play well with others especially because they do not try to compete to the extent of creating dissension within the group, team or office.
10. Not come to a training session asking, "How much more will I earn as a result of this course?"
11. Be somewhat flexible between being cooperative and competitive.
12. Engage in training and development activities in a balanced and supportive method.
13. Not think too much about where they'll be in five years and whether or not their current path will get them there.
14. Work to live as opposed to living to work, you could be missing out on greater opportunities.
15. Be moderately satisfied thus needing to get into a different gear in order to get what they want.
16. Need to think about their financial future with stronger urgency, less it come upon them unawares.

Very High Economic Consistency

Remember, these are values not behaviors. Values speak of our *desires* and what moves us in a directional effort. Keep also in mind that this list is associated with a single value element and not the *integrated motivational orientation*. What we desire can often conflict with what we will actually do. Keep in mind that this list is in no way exhaustive.

Individuals with *very high* (situational/midpoint) consistency and direction within the *single* motivational element of economic will likely desire to:

1. Believe the ends justify the means.
2. Be motivated by winning and overcoming difficult assignments.
3. Appreciate sales, technical, or management training programs that demonstrate a bottom-line gain as a result of their participation.
4. Want to surpass others in material and monetary rewards.
5. Like rewards based on the results they achieve rather than on the method used to obtain the results.
6. Not only compete with others but compete with themselves as well.
7. Think in terms of "real world."
8. Be interested in what makes logical sense and gives a greater return for their efforts.
9. Not do nonsense.
10. Struggle with work-life balance.
11. Be a workaholic.
12. Have a high degree of self-interest.
13. Think, "me first – others second."
14. Have strong horse-sense.
15. Work hard to achieve a secure future.
16. Never lose in the end.
17. Work long and hard to meet personal needs.
18. Save their money when they can.
19. Judge the efforts of others based on the amount of energy they put into it.
20. Compare themselves with those who have more than they do.

Very Low Economic Consistency

Like the descriptors above, keep in mind that this list is in no way exhaustive. Individuals with *very low* consistency and direction within the *single* motivational element of economic will likely desire to:

1. Have already begun to reach their own level of financial security, to the extent that things other than money may now become motivating drives.
2. Be sensitive to perceived injustices and discriminations among their peers and may be compelled to fight for them.
3. Not be solely motivated by competitive financial incentives, but are easily satisfied with what they have.
4. Be turned off by those who constantly talk about their great accomplishments and financial gains.
5. Believe life isn't about what you get out of it, but rather what you contribute to it.
6. Think that using monetary or material gains as a yardstick to measure one's worth or impress others is distasteful.
7. Not have a centered interest in getting an equal or greater return on their time, talent, and personal efforts.
8. Rarely (if ever) look at a project with a "what's in it for me?" perspective.
9. Be more sensitive and responsive to the lives of others than they are their own.
10. See a much wider spectrum of the picture, not just their own view.
11. Think in terms of "we" and less in terms of "me."
12. Need more creative options for taking on tough challenges.
13. Avoid measuring their performance by "feeling good about it" only.
14. Prefer when job "enrichment" strategies are structured into the reward system and thus end up with the short end of the stick monetarily speaking.
15. Prefer praise for continued contributions to the job, as opposed to monetary rewards.
16. Need to understand that 'helping hands' behind the scenes may not get them where they need to be.
17. Consider the strengths of the "total person" to be important and so miss some important singularities.
18. Need to be aware that some people may see them coming from a mile away and therefore may take advantage of them.
19. Enjoy "being" more than just doing.

20. Prefer to work with non-competitive teams as opposed to going it alone or competing fiercely.

The economic element, as you can now see, is the pragmatic part in an engine containing many parts. Alone, this part has nothing to offer. It will remain motionless like setting a carburetor on the surface of a table. Together with the rest of the engine parts, this piece offers a conventional and practical *addition* to how this engine runs. Much like putting a turbo charger on an existing engine, the engine will perform differently now that this part has been added.

Next we will examine individualism. This component will have a whole set of new desires and interesting attributes. As we consider this value element, keep in mind its propensity towards insecurity.

6
INDIVIDUALISM AND THE NEED TO BE OURSELVES

I want to establish a framework surrounding the idea of being human, human need, human wants, and what it means to *be* ourselves.[64] The ability to be yourself is an art. And because of the social orders we've created and live within, being ourselves doesn't seem to come easily anymore.

Our goal throughout this treatise is to uncover, discover, and hopefully recover many of the nuances associated with human behavior and to better understand them. But first we have to define what it is to be a human being within your own social circle and in-group (which could include your family, work, a local bar, a church, school, or peer group). To begin with, there are three important aspects about being human:

1. We are not alone and we are wired for meaningful connection.
2. We travel in packs (families, friendships, social groups, and sub-groups).
3. Our behavioral decisions always include the fact that we live in community and will always directly or indirectly reflect this shared existence with other people—like it or not.

Oscar Fingal O'Flahertie Wills Wilde was an Irish playwright, author, and poet. Known for his satirical wit and a variety of adages, he became one of the most successful playwrights of the late Victorian era in London, and one of the greatest celebrities of his day.

---

[64] Much of this first chapter is derived from my last book; The Freedom of Being. The concepts of being human, self-worth, and real are expounded upon in greater detail in that book.

Wilde once said, "Be yourself, because everyone else is already taken."[65] This phrase probably speaks to all of us on some level. If you take a moment to think about it, you'll come away wishing it were that easy, but we all know it isn't. It is our *differences* that not only define us, they drive us within this community model of shared existence.

If you were the only human being on earth, your behavior would not be what it is today—you would not likely hang paraphernalia from your rearview mirror, place bumper stickers on your car, buy big tires or place stuffed animals in your back window. Every decision you make, and every behavioral action you perform, will instinctively take into consideration the other humans around you. This begins with immediate family members, it extends beyond that circle into the community at large, and then, ultimately, to the greater culture.

If you're an individualist, you think for yourself and desire to do things your own way—you have individualistic values that spell independence and creativity. Not many realize how much creative influence is in the individualistic value element. But what is an individual? An individual is a person or any specific object in a collection of many objects. It is singled out *from* among them and *distinct* between them.

In the 15th century and earlier, individual means "indivisible," usually describing any numerically singular thing, but in this case meaning "a person." From the 17th century, the word individual has indicated separateness, as in individualism. Individuality therefore, is the state or *quality* of being an individuated being; a person separated from everything (in this case, *everyone*) with unique characteristics by possessing his or her own needs, goals, and desires in comparison to everyone else.[66]

---

65 Although often attributed to Wilde, most authorities do not believe he was the author of this.
66 Gerald N. Izenberg (3 June 1992). Impossible Individuality: Romanticism, Revolution, and the Origins of Modern Selfhood, 1787-1802. Princeton University Press. pp. 18+. ISBN 1-4008-2066-9.

Gordon Allport's Trait Theory is also known as the "psychology of individuals." It is our individual traits that set us apart as different from each other—uniquely different. Remember, Allport differed from other psychologists and behaviorists of his day in that he adopted a radical view regarding the dynamics within each individual person. His belief that motivation occurred independent of one's past experiences and was catalyzed by current or newly *learned* personal interests, attitudes, and values.

Allport's 8 Criteria of Dispositions

1. Have more than nominal existence.
2. Are more generalized than a habit.
3. Are dynamic, or at least determinative.
4. May be established empirically or statistically.
5. Are only relatively independent of each other.
6. Are not the same as our moral quality.
7. Acts and habits inconsistent with a disposition are not proof of the non-existence of the disposition.
8. Are present within the personality that contains it or within a population at large.

But, individualism as a single motivational element is not the same as a trait or disposition. Although we experience personal traits that make up our personalities as a whole, individualism is selective of the individual components among our common traits. Consistencies along the bi-axial scale are representative of how much a person will emphasize *individual* components within the trait or disposition dynamic. The individualistic motivational element is just one of many. It denotes a personal sovereignty and is energized by one's ability to experience their own personal uniqueness.

Personal Sovereignty

What is meant by personal sovereignty? This is the heart of the individualistic value. A longing to be seen as unique and special among the species. Those who experience higher consistencies within this value element have a greater focus on themselves as an individual and a lesser focus as one within a collective.

Fig. 1 (High Individual drive)

Motivational Direction and Consistency Graph

			0	10	20	30	40	50	60	70	80	90	100
ORIGINALITY	26	3	0	10	20	30	40	50	60	70	80	90	100
EFFICIENCY	40	4	0	10	20	30	40	50	60	70	80	90	100
INDIVIDUALITY	80	2	0	10	20	30	40	50	60	70	80	90	100
POWER	37	6	0	10	20	30	40	50	60	70	80	90	100
SACRIFICE	84	1	0	10	20	30	40	50	60	70	80	90	100
COMPLIANCE	34	5	0	10	20	30	40	50	60	70	80	90	100
CURIOSITY	60	7	0	10	20	30	40	50	60	70	80	90	100

This is what generates the need for a spotlight. You may have heard the term "spot lit leader" or maybe you haven't. The spot lit leader has surpassed the *desire* to be seen as unique and has entered the danger-zone of personal *need*. Personal sovereignty emphasizes the *need* for both freedom and autonomy. Free to do as they please and free to do it the way they want to. This is the two-fold prong to this style. When one enters the need zone, above 75 on the bi-axial scale in this case, something takes place within the psyche of the individual.

Wants are much different than needs. If I desire a great wife then I will put in the right amount of effort and make sure I find the traits and temperament that works with my style. I will spend a fair amount of time doing whatever I must in order to ensure I find the best wife possible. This might mean taking more time to find someone suitable rather than settling for the first person who comes along. Because I want to find the right person, certain actions must take place to ensure it happens the right way. To *want* is to desire. It's about what I believe is necessary. It may also reflect a requirement. When requirements are in play, only *certain* outcomes will be acceptable. But if I *need* someone, my emotions will exceed my rationale. Need oriented decisions never go well. If I *need* a wife, I will settle for what I can get because my insatiable "need to have a wife" will supersede wanting for the right one to come along.

This same dynamic plays about within our IMO's. Each value element has a "need zone" associated with it. It doesn't matter which element is under discussion; if the element is in a need zone according to its consistency level, the desire degree will supersede any rational minded approach to meeting the need. The individualistic element will have specific traits associated with a need zone.

Fig. 2

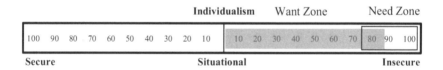

When an individual enters the need zone within the individualistic value element, the need for attention will increase beyond what is necessary for normal human development. Depending on my behavioral framework, my emotions that structure that framework will determine how this will play out publicly.

Fig. 3

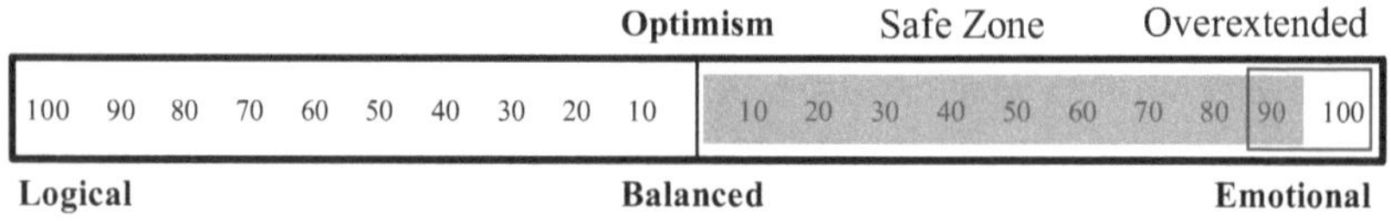

Consider figure 3 above. This is a measurement of the consistency level within the optimistic emotion (I in DISC and A in TARP). Because it has increased above 89 on the emotional scale, the emotion is now overextended. Depending on how much anger is in play will determine the level of logic there will be to offset the emotion. If the anger level is equally intense, although logical as an emotion, the logical piece will diminish if patience and fear are not playing along.

Although this may seem complex, it simply means that each emotion, just like the value elements has a specific part to play. Think of your emotional makeup and your IMO; they are an orchestra made up of many instruments. When an emotion is considered "in play," the psychic energy associated with that emotion is both a trusted and relied on as a primary source for decisions, directions, and deeds. It becomes our primary approach to situations, people, and things. These primary emotions act in concert with each other to produce a variety of personality and behavioral traits with which we are familiar.

For example, think of four different instruments working in concert to play a variety of songs. Each instrument differs in its prominence depending on the song choice. In one song, one instrument may take center stage while another is indistinct in the background. Our emotions operate in the same way. But don't let prominence fool you; emotions that become front and center may not be the responsible emotion[s] for the decisions we ultimately make.

The emotions that *hang back* may have a more significant influence on our decisions than we care to admit. Often, emotions of lower consistency carry a heavier weight of influence when collaborating with emotions encompassing higher consistencies. Emotional patterns work together, not in part when determining the actions spawned by each configuration.

Whether it's horns, woodwinds or stringed instruments, each instrument plays in unanimity with the other instruments to form melody and tone, but a solo instrument can perform without the assistance of other instruments before being joined by the remaining orchestra. Your brain's emotional make-up is similar. As a whole, it is responsible for the different varieties or *types* of music we all represent as individuals. Behaviorally speaking, some people play jazz while others might prefer rock, thrash, or easy-listening.[67]

If we examine the above examples in unison, the overextension in the optimistic emotion combined with the danger zone in the individualistic value element will cause a critical need to be seen as unique and important. It will be so powerful that the need will move far beyond the norm of most people. This will cause this person to stand out like a sore thumb when in public. We're not talking about right or wrong or good or bad here, but rather acceptable or unacceptable behavior depending on the environment.

When these performance-based, active styles have a strong limbic bent (higher influence), they will tend towards *need oriented* behaviors and relationships—this is the classic attention getter—they make friends with their children rather than parent them and they tend to make poor people decisions when in groups. The need for personal sovereignty goes beyond its limits. In an effort to *stand out* from the group, decisions will be made to make that happen.

Remember, standing out from the group is not an option here; it's now an emotional requirement. The emotional over-valuing of independence and uniqueness requires it. I need you to believe I'm more unique than anyone else. If you do not understand this then I am forced by the need machine to prove it and nearly always this will be at one's personal expense.

---

[67] Steven Sisler, *The Angry Brain: A Contemporary View of the Anger Emotion and How it Relates to Human Behavior, Character, and Temperament*, The Focus media group, p. 11. Published 2018.

Rand's Objectivism

Ayn Rand's *objectivism,* generally speaking, regards every human as an independent, sovereign entity who possesses an inalienable right to his or her own life, a right derived from his or her own nature as a rational being. Individualism and Objectivism hold that a civilized society, or any form of association, cooperation or peaceful coexistence among humans, can be achieved only on the basis of the recognition of individual rights. That any group, as such, has no rights other than the individual rights of its members.[68]

Every human being will have a personal sense of individuality, but not every human being needs to put it on display. Many people, when in groups of other people, will blend in with the group and find a place of belonging that does not draw attention to its functional presence. This is when cooperation has its greatest chance of happening. Cooperation is about self-diminishment and the promotion of others through an unbalanced mechanism.

We cooperate when we do not over-regard our individuality. We are able to merge to the extent of a loss of self. This works best when "I'm okay—you're okay." When I'm not okay unless you recognize my independence from you, then the idea of outstanding begins to take root. Recognizing our individual rights as an objective part of being human is where we begin, but to push this idea too far will create problems and challenges.

As each individual is combined to make a whole group, the combined qualities and characteristics will determine how a group will function. Consider a team at work. Think about your part on that team. To what degree do you need others to know what part you bring to the table? Those who sport high consistencies in the individualistic value element will desire others to not only recognize

---

68 *Objectivism* is a philosophical system developed by Russian-American writer Ayn Rand.

them as a unique player but provide them the freedom and autonomy to do things in their own creative way.

If you've been paying attention the last five years you will have likely heard someone mouth the words "*my truth*." This isn't anything new in a general sense, but it's brand new in a corporate sense.

My Truth

This new term, *my truth* is about having our own unique take on life and it must be respected above whatever anyone else thinks is right or wrong. It's a personal permission slip to do whatever we want to do regardless of what others think. I understand that we as sentient beings have personal rights that others should not condemn, but this is moving beyond this fundamental idea and it's being hailed by those who have a high individualistic mindset coupled with a lower regulated thinking mind.

Systems Judgment and Individualism

There's a big difference between independence and subversion. Being independent is one thing, but when we use our independence to subvert a system that others share in united existence then our freedoms are no longer restricted to ourselves—they affect others. This idea plays to the "systemic" value system in all of us.

Systems Judgment is an analytical observation, a structured, ordered or consistency in thinking. It encompasses theoretical or conceptual organization and planning; valuing what "ought to be" in an *ideal* sense. This is the ability to see and appreciate systems, order, structures, conformity, and authority for what they're worth.

When a person has a crystal clear view of systems, this person has an excellent capacity for seeing and appreciating systems, order, and conventional thinking and planning. They can see the proper place for systems and the order and consistency which systems impose. They can both see and appreciate the importance of authority, which maintains the orderliness of systems and the need for conformity to organizational rules, ideas, ideals, concepts, and conceptual and imaginative planning.

Both conceptual meaning and meaning created by our mind is important. It's actually the most important means of generating proper understanding. People with very clear systems judgment can also see and appreciate the need for structuring a frame of reference which integrates the present and the future; preserving the meaning of a situation. Moreover, this person will believe in commitment, duty, and trust their expectation that the world should act as it ought. This being said, we will also bring personal biases into this equation. Our level of clarity is one thing, but personal brain bias is another.

Consider having clear systems judgment and a positive bias. In other words, when it comes to what I think "ought to be," I tend to think about it in positive terms; I look for what ought to be in line with what would be a positive influence "if it was so." It's like looking for what is good about a new rule—what makes this a good rule?

For example, a new rule has been put in place. I remember when airline flight attendants would take cash for drinks purchased on the plane. Now they only take plastic. Why this change? The first time I experienced this, the voice went over the speaker like this; "We no longer take cash for in-flight purchases. We will be happy to take your Southwest card or any credit or debit card for inflight purchases." Now, after hearing this for the first time, what was my *next* thought?

I'll tell you exactly what it was because I remember it like it was yesterday even though it was many years ago. I thought, "oh, people must be pocketing the cash and it's costing the airline money. It's a *good* rule." Now, I don't know if that was the reason or not, but I remember thinking this is a good way to stop folks from grabbing a few bucks when nobody's looking.

This is a clear process of systems judgment with a positive bias. I value good systems for all the right reasons—so what ought to be can continue being what it should be without interruption. The airline ought to continue to make money uninterrupted.

Fig. 4 The S-1 dimension within formal axiology

Transition	Visible	Unconventional	Clear	Crystal Clear
100 90 80 70 60 50 40 30 20 10			10 20 30 40 50 60	70 80 90 100

Negative Bias			Positive Bias
100 90 80 70 60 50 40 30 20 10		10 20 30 40 50 60	70 80 90 100

What happens when we have a negative bias?

When having a clear understanding of systems value with a negative bias, an individual will:

- Overtly or covertly question the authority of rules, norms, and institutions, especially if they believe them to be ineffective or in their way.
- Feel uncomfortable in a rigidly controlled environment.
- Determine whether or not established rules and protocols are worthy of their obedience.
- Be inattentive to inconsistencies in plans and ideas, to imperfections in things or people and to disorder in the world in general.
- De-emphasize conformity to rules, structures, and beliefs.
- Lack a sense of urgency to order and structure the world; to conceptually structure their thinking and planning.

The Systemic Dimension in formal axiology is a dimension of formal concepts. It's ideas of how things *should be*. This dimension is one of definitions, ideals, goals, structured thinking, policies, procedures, rules, laws, ought's and should's. It is one of perfection if you will. If a person values something or someone systemically, then that person must fulfill their idea of how they *should be* perfectly or completely. In other words, you either have obeyed the law (a mental idea of how we should act) or you have not obeyed the law (the non-fulfillment of the idea). This is an either/or dimension.

It is for this reason that this dimension fits nicely with the regulatory value element. The regulatory value element is strongly associated with the individualistic value element. They are the "freedom and autonomy" leg of the three-legged motivational orientations stool. We are either motivated towards freedom and autonomy or rule dependence.

To further explain this black and white mindset, a woman is either pregnant (a mental definition of a state of being) or she is not pregnant (does not perfectly fulfill all the aspects of the definition of pregnant). Here the valuation is based on total and complete fulfillment of an idea—you can never be sort of pregnant. There is no middle ground or partial fulfillment in the systemic value—no grey. You either perfectly fulfill the concept (ideal, definition, law, policy, etc.) or you do not perfectly fulfill the concept.

Another example of systemic valuing is displayed by the definition of a geometric circle: "A plane closed curve equidistant from a center point." If an object fulfills this definition, then it is a geometric circle. If it lacks only one element of the definition, then it is not a geometric circle. Every definition is an "idea." To value something is to give it systemic valuation.[69] Furthermore, our levels of clarity can differ to a great extent. This begs the question; how clearly do I see and understand how something should be in no uncertain terms?

---

69 Zeke Lopez, Axiologist, Granule; Irvine, California.

Can I walk into any given situation and immediately see and understand how something should be? Would I see and understand that when painting a bedroom, you should cut the wall in with a paintbrush first and then fill in the larger areas with a roller once the framing of the ceiling and baseboards is complete? Or do I not clearly see and understand that and pick up the nearest roller and randomly start rolling the wall wherever is most convenient or expedient for me? Or maybe it's my way or the highway if you're working for me.

In the 1980's I watched a painter get fired his very first day because the painter was bent on using a pot-liner in his paint pail. The new painter said to the owner, "I don't work without a pot-liner." The owner replied, "then get your stuff and go home." Each had opposing ideas with very strong biases on what one should do when painting with a paint pail.

It is either total fulfillment or non-fulfillment of the idea. The systemic dimension is the world of Yes/No, black/white, and should's. There are no possible shades of maybe or partially. The concept is either fulfilled or not fulfilled. The mathematical properties of this dimension are finite sets and finite elements (that is, a limited number of choices and a limited number of properties for the object in question).

This dimension is the major aspect of geometry, physical science, law, dogmatism, long range planning, policies and procedures, doing things right, ideals, principles, personal attainment of one's goals, schematic thinking, order, prejudice, and perfection. When a person pays too much attention to this dimension the resultant behavior is an overemphasis on doing things by the book, an excessive preoccupation with planning and having things be done perfectly, a strong tendency to measure everything and everyone against a preset idea of how they should be, and an inability to be comfortable with changes and surprises—a loss of individuality.

When a person does not pay enough attention to this dimension, the resultant behavior is an unwillingness to submit to policies and rules imposed from the outside, a skepticism about the value of spending time and money planning for the future, and an uneasiness when systems are in place and running smoothly—a stronger bent towards personal freedom to make one's own choices, live by one's own truth about the matter, or become independent of any truth other than one's own altogether.

Often, people with a negative bias in systems judgment will have a higher consistency in the individualistic value element, but not always. I call it "holding hands." Individualistic mindsets hold hands with low regulated value interests because they are non-contradictory.

Individualism and the 6 Value System

Some assessment companies use a six-value interest set. These are usually described as Utilitarianism, Aesthetic, Social, Individualistic, Traditional, and Theoretical. These are based on the work of Eduard Spranger in 1928. We use a model that reflects seven value elements and here's why.

We added a "power" element whereas some other groups only use the "individualistic" value. While the Individualistic element in these other tools does reflect a sense of authority, it does not fully express individualism and power needs directly. We have chosen to address both individualism and power needs separately in order to bring the greatest amount of definition possible. The "traditional" element is also not the same as our regulated or compliance orientation.

The traditional orientation denotes a soulish or more religious or spiritual dimension whereas our regulated or compliance orientation denotes structure and systemic values. Therefore, the combination of the individualistic and regulated value sets is what create the best sense of freedom and autonomy needs or regulation and rule dependence.

Duel Individualistic Convergences

Duel convergences are a combination of two separate value elements. I already talked about these so I will not further elaborate on how these factors work. You may reference the former if you need to brush up on convergences.

IND/H–AES/L (Self-Directed): This value factor associates *freedom and autonomy* with *real-world thinking*. When the individualistic value is high, and the aesthetic value is low you will have no inner conflict. This will create a strong real-world and autonomous approach to solving problems, challenges, and finding opportunities. This will cause an *innovative* rather than a creative approach. Innovation is more purposeful while creativity is more experiential.

IND/H–AES/H (Imaginative): This value factor associates *freedom and autonomy* with *unconventionality*. These two forces are married when competing. When the individualistic value is high, and the aesthetic value is high you will have harmony. This will create a strong need to diverge while creating paths forward. The process to this end can be euphoric when the need to *experience* the world with an unrestricted sense of self takes president. This is what I call the desires of a "unicorn." I often refer to this as a "gypsy spirit" depending on how low the economic interest is.

IND/H–ECO/L (Aloofness): This value factor associates *freedom and autonomy* with *self-satisfaction*. When the individualistic value is high, and the economic value is low you will have no inner conflict. This will create a need to experience freedom while center stage. This style values freedom over financial security and may enjoy innovative thinking, presenting and assisting others by sharing their ideas openly.

IND/H–ECO/H (Opportunistic): This value factor associates *freedom and autonomy* with *self-mastery*. These two forces are semi-conflictive. When the individualistic value is high, and the economic value is high there's an innovative and clever response to the world. One will use their out-of-the-box ideas and stage presence to attract opportunities and secure their future endeavors.

IND/H–POW/L (Compromising): This value factor associates *freedom and autonomy* with *submission*. These two forces are non-conflictive when both are in play. When the individualistic value is high, and the power value is low you will have some inner conflict. This individual will desire to maximize personal freedom but may lack the fortitude to fight for it when necessary.

IND/H–POW/H (Domination): This value factor associates *freedom and autonomy* with *power*. These two forces are maximized when both are in play. When the individualistic value is high, and the power value is high you will have maximum leverage. This individual desires to maximize personal freedom and independence while determining how and when it can happen. They will desire to independent of others' agendas.

IND/H–ALT/L (Self-Focused): This value factor associates *freedom and autonomy* with *being guarded*. These two forces are disassociated (conflictive) when both are in play. When the individualistic value is high, and the altruistic value is low you will have no inner conflict. This individual will desire to prioritize personal freedom and opportunities at the expense of others who may suggest another way.

IND/H–ALT/H (Wavering): This value factor associates *freedom and autonomy* with *sacrifice*. These two forces are conflictive when both are in play. When the individualistic value is high, and the altruistic value is high you will have inner conflict. This individual will prioritize personal wants and opportunities in line with their personal agenda while struggling with a need to meet the needs others may have. This creates a me-me conflict response; should I do it or give not do it?

IND/H–REG/L (Defiant): This value factor associates *freedom and autonomy* with *independence*. These two forces are maximized when both are in play. When the individualistic value is high, and the regulated value is low you will have no inner conflict. This individual will insist on multithreaded and subversive approaches to solving problems and meeting personal needs. They will desire to march to the beat of their own drum.

IND/H–REG/H (Two-Faced): This value factor associates *freedom and autonomy* with *systemic thinking*. These two forces are conflicted when both are in play. When the individualistic value is high, and the regulated value is high you will have inner conflict. This individual may insist on specific ways of doing things and may hold others and *not themselves* to the same standard of operation.

IND/H–THE/L (Instinctual): This value factor associates *freedom and autonomy* with *intuition*. These two forces are neutralized when both are in play. When the individualistic value is high, and the theoretical value is low you will have no inner conflict. This individual will rely on intuition, instinct, and past experiences for learning what to do next. They will study to pass rather than learn to know.

IND/H–THE/H (Instructive): This value factor associates *freedom and autonomy* with *fact-finding*. These two forces are neutralized when both are in play. When the individualistic value is high, and the theoretical value is high you will have no inner conflict. This individual will rely on interesting facts for leveraging how to maximize their current position in the world. These types can be very innovative.

IND/L–AES/H (Creative Confidence): This value factor associates *support* with *unconventionality*. These two forces are not in conflict when both are in play. When the individualistic value is low and the aesthetic high you will have no inner conflict. This will create unconventionally imaginative and original approaches to tasks.

IND/L–AES/L (Pragmatic): This value factor associates *security* with *realism*. These two forces are maximized when both are in play. When the individualistic value is low, and the aesthetic value is low you will have no inner conflict. This will create a practical yet supportive style.

IND/L–ECO/H (Self-Reliant): This value factor associates *security* with *self-mastery*. These two forces are semi-conflictive when both are in play. When the individualistic value is low, and the economic value is high you will have no inner conflict. This individual desires to cooperate in an effort to get what they want. They will display confidence and will not need to be center stage.

IND/L–ECO/L (Abetting): This value factor associates *accommodation* with *satisfaction*. These two forces are semi-conflictive when both are in play. When the individualistic value is low, and the economic value is low (rare) you will have no inner conflict. This individual resists responsibility and will yield their position to avoid controversy. Passive by nature, they may seek to diminish their personal worth.

IND/L–POW/H (Self-Confident): This value factor associates *security* with *authority and power*. These two forces are neutralized when both are in play. When the individualistic value is low, and the power value is high you will have no inner conflict. This individual desires control over their surroundings and will exude confidence that may create anxiety in insecure people types.

IND/L–POW/L (Self-Effacing): This value factor associates *accommodation* with *submission*. These two forces are neutralized when both are in play. When the individualistic value is low, and the power value is low you will have some inner conflict. This individual resists responsibility and will yield their position to avoid controversy. Passive by nature, they may seek to diminish their personal worth.

IND/L–ALT/H (Supporting): This value factor associates *support* with *sacrifice*. These two forces are not in conflict when both are in play. When the individualistic value is low, and the altruistic value is high you will have no inner conflict. This individual will endeavor to support and cooperate with others without the need of excessive attention or the spotlight.

IND/L–ALT/L (Apprehensive): This value factor associates *security* with *self-protection*. These two forces are in harmony when both are in play. When the individualistic value is low, and the altruistic value is low you will have no conflict. This will create guarded style who expects others to qualify before entering into their private space. They may over-focus on what is missing in other people.

IND/L–REG/H (Amendable): This value factor associates *apprehension* with *black and white thinking*. These two forces are in conflict when both are in play. When the individualistic value is low, and the regulated value is high you will have no inner conflict. This individual is rigid and may be punitive in nature. They could to be cause driven or missional. May be strict or *narrow* in thinking.

IND/L–REG/L (Passive-Resistant): This value factor associates *security* with *subversion*. These two forces are in conflict when both are in play. When the individualistic value is low, and the regulated value is low you will have no inner conflict. This individual may be passive-resistive. In other words, they may covertly seek to do things their own unique way.

IND/L–THE/H (Apprentice): This value factor associates *security* with *curiosity*. These two forces are neutralized when both are in play. When the individualistic value is low, and the theoretical value is high you will have no inner conflict. This individual will cooperate with instructions and will desire to learn while taking directions well.

IND/L–THE/L (Guesstimating): This value factor associates *security* with *dis-interest*. These two forces are neutralized when both are in play. When the individualistic value is low, and the theoretical value is low you will have no inner conflict. This style is intuitive and resists over-working their cognitive mind. They may be subject to errors in judgment or may scan material without reading it all.

Situational Individualistic Consistency

To reiterate, these are values *not* behaviors. Values speak of our *desires* and what moves us in a directional effort. Keep also in mind that this list is associated with a single value element and not the *integrated motivational orientation*, which includes all seven value elements. I'm going to say this again because it bears repeating; what we desire can often conflict with what we will actually do.

Keep in mind that this list is in no way exhaustive. Individuals with a *general* or situational (situational/midpoint) consistency and direction within the *single* motivational element of individualism will likely desire to:

1. Have a non-invasive or controversial infringement within the realm of ideas.
2. Not be extreme in their need to be unique or set apart from the crowd.
3. Be balanced between being and individual and a team player.
4. Not need to be in the limelight or to attract special attention to their contributions.
5. Have the ability to identify with and understand individuals who have both high and low satisfaction rates.
6. Be happy to yield their position if warranted in an effort to give others a chance at their ideas and contributions.

7. Be able to both lead and follow depending upon the circumstances involved.
8. Be flexible and free flowing without an excessive need to be number one or not at all.
9. Take a stand or sit quietly depending on what is necessary for accomplishing the task.
10. Be more stable than unpredictable when influencing decisions that belong to them or someone else.
11. Mediate all available ideas as opposed to only focusing on their own.
12. Not be bent on having to win in everything.
13. Be very flexible when deciding to lead or support; it's not one or the other.
14. Be a stabilizing force within a variety of environments involving people.
15. Provide input without pushing for your own personal agenda and even step back when you recognize someone else's solution.

Very High Individualistic Consistency

Remember, these are values not behaviors. Values speak of our *desires* and what moves us in a directional effort. Keep also in mind that this list is associated with a single value element and not the *integrated motivational orientation*. What we desire can often conflict with what we will actually do. Keep in mind that this list is in no way exhaustive.

Individuals with *very high* (situational/midpoint) consistency and direction within the *single* motivational element of individualism will likely cause them to:

1. Seek their own personal niche where they can be seen as unique and unbelievable.
2. Be the red penny in a jar of 500 pennies.
3. Have out-of-the-box ideas.

4. Be very different, but not necessary valuable when it comes to creative ideas.
5. Enjoy doing their own thing their own way.
6. Take the necessary risks to ensure their freedom and autonomy.
7. Feel "jailed" and desire to be free and unfettered.
8. Seek situations that will place the spotlight on their efforts and creative outcomes.
9. Present their ideas to groups who are interested in what they know.
10. Seek out situations to teach others or expose their imaginative thinking.
11. Feel overly insecure about what others are thinking about what they are doing or saying.
12. Want a forum to share their ideas out loud.
13. Innovate rather than create.
14. Associate with out-of-the-box thinkers.
15. Bend the rules to ensure things work to their favor.
16. Do things very differently to ensure they stand out when in groups.
17. Seek unconventional approaches to common problems.
18. Seek to be independent of others so they can make their own decisions.
19. Determine which rules should be followed and which rules can be ignored.
20. March to the beat of their own drum.

Very Low Individualistic Consistency

Individuals with *very low* (situational/midpoint) consistency and direction within the *single* motivational element of individualism will likely:

1. Not seek the limelight.
2. Hang back and support someone else's ideas rather than promoting their own.

3. Be left feeling like a ghost for failure to draw proper attention to themselves.
4. Feel overlooked for failure to make enough noise.
5. Support other with their tasks and be left fending for themselves when it's their turn.
6. Lack the energy to fight for what they want.
7. Not care about getting the credit for contributions made.
8. Not need to control all outcomes.
9. Think some people are outrageous or attention hogs.
10. Not like it when people force others to do things.
11. Be supportive when others feel pressure.
12. Respect other people's ideas without over-promoting your own no matter how good they are.
13. Be the unsung hero of any team project.
14. Be able to lead from the back.
15. Yield their position power when others have not shown enough participation.
16. Feel very secure in their ability to do things.
17. Display quiet confidence.
18. Work behind the scenes with vigor.
19. Possibly rely too heavily on others for answers.
20. Share the stage.

As you may have noticed, the individualistic value element is the part of the whole value structure that represents our desire to be the star of the show. It's our desire or need to be autonomous, free, and independent of others. It's our sense of personal uniqueness. When combined with the other value elements, it brings a healthy balance to human interactives and the need to depend on other people for our success. We will now focus our attention on authority and power.

7
AUTHORITY AND POWER

Not everyone needs to be in charge. Moreover, the idea of "taking the reins," or "taking over" may feel a bit harsh for some and many may experience negative feelings when they hear words like authority, power, control, or leadership. Separating the ideas between social sympathy and social subordination can be difficult. Differences between helpful interest in the lives of others and forcing others to do what we think they should is a stark contrast.

Power, as it relates to the authority and power element is about domination and control. I may refer to this element as the "political" element in this chapter. This is the original descriptor as theorized by Eduard Spranger in 1928. The counterpart to this value is dependence. As we move through this next value element we will decipher the full quality of this value and help you grasp as many nuances associated with it as we can in this short chapter.

When speaking of the power element, I don't want you to think about *superiority*. One can have superior knowledge of some issue, but at the same time not exercise power-to or power-over another concerning it. One may have technical superiority but may not "supervise" another with their expertise. Having superior qualities does not translate into authority or control on its own. The *power* value as it relates to the seven value elements under discussion in this book is about leadership, authority, and control.

Control

What do you feel when you hear that someone is controlling? This may be an indication as to where you are personally on this value scale. Control is about positing our own value system on another either as a permanent or transitory motive.[70] Power and control lacks all service and altruistic motive. Spranger's "political attitude" is understood in a more religious or spiritual sense that lacks a connection with what most of us experience in the world.

The political attitude by nature sees all else as subject to it. Like the anger emotion, the power value is an *active* value. Passive values include theoretical, aesthetic, and altruism. Active values impose; they establish and imply. While passive values *assist*, active values *insist*. This is what is behind control; an insistence. Think of the state "imposing" a tax on you.

The power element thus contains an authoritarian element. This authoritative element begins with the *self* and moves outward to the outer-world. Superior self-power is the engine that drives this desire to control one's self, surroundings (space), and future destiny. Those who experience a desire for personal power want authority *equal to* or *greater than* personal or delegated responsibilities. In other words, if I'm in charge of it, then I am the one who makes all the decisions concerning it. This is what self-control is about.

The person with the power makes the rules and often enforces them. Those with a strong service intension *support* them. Power types take the hill while altruistic types hold the fort. Power and service are completely unrelated. Those who enter politics never enter to serve; they enter to control. Never forget this. The power value is not a service intention; it's an authority intention. If you want to control a social system and have the power to generatively conceive a particular outcome that suits your value system or worldview, enter politics. If you want to serve your country, join the military.

You don't enter congress and "serve" for 30-years and wind up worth 139 million because you're altruistic and sacrificial. I'm not

---

70 Eduard Spranger, Types of Men (1928) p. 189.

talking here about self-control as defined by an inability to control one's poor behavior or the impulses that cause one to be inconsistent with decisions or actions. The power value orientation represents, in its positive state, "power-to" whereas in its negative state it represents "power-over."

Positive Control (Power-to)

According to Fromm, the ability of an individual to make productive use of his or her powers is their "potency." Having the power *to* do something equates to one's ability to *influence* something or someone that can be influenced. Having influence is a positive form of control. Desiring control is much different than *doing* control. The power element is a passion or desire—a value if you will. It's about "wanting" to steer a thing or perform an action according to one's own values or standards.

For example; let's say I desire to fill a different role in my work as I have just been informed that a new position is available. Do I have the *power to* initiate this process? Do I *desire to* initiate this process? And if I desire to initiate an action, what amount of "controlling force" do I need to implement in order to ensure it has a chance of happening? Wanting something to happen that fits my value system is one thing; making something happen that fits my value system is another thing.

Am I thinking:

1. I believe I have the *power*-to initiate this process and make something happen; we'll see what happens.
2. I wish I had the *power*-to initiate this process and make something happen, but I don't know if I do or not.
3. I don't have the *energy* for this, so I'm going to pass on the opportunity. I'm probably not qualified anyway.
4. I've got this. I'll talk to John in the morning. There's no way I'm passing this up.

5. Yes! I was waiting for this! This position is mine! I'll call my wife Joanne and tell her that the position has finally opened up! I'm so glad I spoke with John a month ago anticipating this might be available.

You may see yourself in one of these above scenarios. To the degree that we *desire* power will be the degree that our "power potential" is present. Power and control is always in a position of potential energy. Having a desire to control "what happens to us" is a sign that we are in a potential position to influence what happens to us. Power is our active form of influence capacity. Numbers 4 and 5 in the above scenarios speak of someone who not only desires to control their own space and destiny, but also believes they have the emotional fortitude to "make" it happen.

Scenario number 5 is a bit different as this person "needs" to control their own space and destiny. They were expecting something to happen and began influencing long before the opportunity presented itself. They were not only aware of the future, but they were ensuring the future went a certain way. He was influencing the decision maker a month earlier in an effort to ensure he attained the position he wanted. The power orientation is clearly in play in numbers 4 and 5. Number 1 has potential, but low efficiency drive and possibly low self-worth. These are examples of a positive "power to" influence.

Negative Control (Power-Over)

Negative "power-over" is a perversion of positive "power-to." With the power of reason one can penetrate the surface of phenomena and understand their essence. With the power of love one can break through a wall that separates one person from another. With the power of imagination we are enabled to visualize things that have not yet happened. Because of this we can create from a new plan. But when a person's potency is lacking, their relatedness to the world is *skewed* into a wrongful desire to dominate.[71]

Erich Fromm relates dominance with death and potency to life. Domination springs from impotence and in turn reinforces it, for if an individual can force somebody else to serve him, his own need to be productive is increasingly paralyzed.[72] Some of the most dominant people are the most impotent. In fact, those who are excessive in force perceive themselves as having the least amount of control. Excessive control needs are typically born out of a sense of having no control at all.

If one feels they have no control during formative years or during adolescence, they may have an increased desire to be *in* control during their adult years. Domination occurs when an individual is emotionally stripped of their personal powers and their relatedness to the world is distorted. If a person is experiencing an atrophy of their generative capacity, they will be able to recognize things as they actually are, but they will be unable to envision what they *could* be.

Fig. 1

Motivational Direction and Consistency Graph
Authority and Power

			0	10	20	30	40	50	60	70	80	90	100
ORIGINALITY	26	3	0	10	20	30	40	50	60	70	80	90	100
EFFICIENCY	40	4	0	10	20	30	40	50	60	70	80	90	100
INDIVIDUALITY	80	6	0	10	20	30	40	50	60	70	80	90	100
POWER	37	2	0	10	20	30	40	50	60	70	80	90	100
SACRIFICE	84	1	0	10	20	30	40	50	60	70	80	90	100
COMPLIANCE	34	5	0	10	20	30	40	50	60	70	80	90	100
CURIOSITY	60	7	0	10	20	30	40	50	60	70	80	90	100

---

71 Erich Fromm, Man For Himself: an Inquiry Into the Psychology of Ethics, 1947, p. 68.
72 Ibid.

Their ability to enliven their internal perception is diminished. Control begins with the ability to see below the surface of what *is* in order to experience what is essential and not yet apparent. This is akin to Dr. Hartman's theory of Practical Attention clarities and biases. This is the dimension of comparisons relative to practical thinking and value.

Practical thinking includes the elements of the real, material world, comparisons of good/better/best, and seeing things as they compare with other things in their class. This is the dimension of seeing things and their properties as they apply in different contexts. Lacking generative capacity limits one to surface analysis. Reality is only what has materialized. This is a realist—they believe you can't fight city hall.

Therefore, normal human beings relate to the world in two ways; *Reproductively* by *perceiving* it as it is, and *Generatively* by *conceiving* it; by altering it and enriching it by his or her own powers. Conceiving the world is to give birth to new and broader definitions of it and to enrich existing perceptions to the level of making changes through a creative effort. This is how human beings *expand* their horizons. To expand one's horizons one must affect the existing world and change it through an expenditure of psychic energy. This can be done in a positive way through power-to or a negative way through power-over.

If you cannot see into what already is or perceive past its surface to what *could be*, you are left with a feeling of impotence; unable to alter existing frameworks for a lack of perception or imaginative relatedness to the world. It is for this reason that one could either yield to the world in a submissive stance and surrender to their lack of perception positively, or they will overpower and dominate the existing system through excessive strength of force, authority, and control.

There are three types or levels of control. Control is the need to force outside stimuli to submit to one's sense of security. When those who experience (feel) a loss of impotence become insecure in their sense of loss, they will enact emotional energies in a way that brings balance to their instability in the world.

3 Types of Control

We are either:

- In control (power)
- Out of control (lack of power)
- Under control (restrained power)

The best use of control really depends on the circumstances, but being out of control is never advantageous. There are times when we need to be in control of a situation much like driving a car. Whether you are a manager, wife, mother, or ambulance driver, maintaining control is essential. But some folks need to be in control *all the time*. That's a problem. Wanting to be in charge is positive, needing to be in charge is negative and produces negative results. If I want a wife I'll find a good one; if I *need* a wife I'll marry anyone.

High Power Consistency

This authoritative value element is about being seen as a leader. It's about having influence and control over one's own environment or success. Competitiveness and control are often associated with those scoring high in this motivational dimension. Highly politically/power driven styles will only listen for two reasons:

1. They listen to direct and control
2. They listen to agree or disagree with the individual[s] they are conversing with

They rarely listen in an effort to understand. They are not usually interested in where others are emotionally or where they're coming from strategically. The politically or power minded individual doesn't want to get into the vehicle (metaphorically speaking) unless they're the one driving it. Winning is everything: there's typically no plan B with this style—they like to be large and in charge. If you're like this, you're likely a fixer. You may feel at home when ramming your ideas through to a conclusion while discrediting the ideas of those you don't respect. You may also create relationships just to advance your own position—this is because power driver's always need a ladder to climb.

These styles believe they deserve a shot. They believe victory is theirs. They will always be looking for respect. Advancement must be available or they will be highly dissatisfied. They will expect respect for the personal gains they make or the problems they have solved. They will be looking for rewards and recognition for a job well done. And they will need signs of personal authority, such as their name on their parking space, business card, or desk. They believe others must know they're in charge and will find ways to let them know.

They will seek position power and influence everywhere they go. They must call the shots within their area of knowledge or expertise. They will also need to direct and control subordinates, as opposed to letting them control themselves, because they believe the buck stops with them. Controlling types don't like moochers. They are likely a *survivor* style if especially intense, and will need difficult problems to overcome in order to feel important or satisfied. They will own their roles within the workplace and handle everything associated with it. When working for others they will act like they own the business and borrow their building.

If you are like this you are likely going to accept responsibility for both successes and failures. You will never quit trying, especially if you have a high dominant behavioral style (+D in DISC and +T in TARP). The high anger emotion is supportive (married) of the high Political attitude when they are both consistent. When this happens they fight for what they want. If an individual has a high Political mindset and a *low* anger emotion, they may pout or become passive-aggressive. If the anger emotion is absent from the equation it leaves them with no sense of urgency. This can be very frustrating for someone who experiences this—it's an internal me-me conflict between personal values and emotions.

Intense political styles believe they will be victorious before they even start the race or else why start at all? They are also direct like the dominant behavior and because of the high consistency within this value will likely be overpowering to those who are timid or passive. If you are like this you should allow others the same freedom to make decisions that you want.

You should recognize that some people want to own their own environments as well. You should be willing to share victories and not hog them all for yourself. You should understand you come across stronger than you think. It's important to empower others with the same power you want to have.

In the work world, high political types need hyper flexibility and freedom to create when learning new things. They need their own space when working with teams and must link the benefits of learning new things to their personal ability to make them happen. They'll likely create an environment that encourages others to follow them. They also need a wide variety of nuclear options available to them. They need the freedom to come up with their own agenda and options. Sometimes their extreme need to be in control will stifle others' abilities. Their potential value can clash with aesthetic people types who think in irrational terms.

This style needs to allow others to fail, and then assist them in becoming better when they do, as opposed to gloating when others can't keep up. They can also get caught up in selling themselves instead of their idea. Those with high political impulses need to be aware of the fact that being in charge may be all too important to them and may turn certain people types off.

They typically will have no time for slower moving people when their sense of urgency is high and may be annoyed by them; seeing them as in the way. When dominating, they lack humility and diplomacy as a rule. They might think in terms of crush, kill, and destroy when thinking about adversaries. Again, the power of this style is supremely evident when accompanied by high dominance and anger, but can lay undetected for long periods of time when they are less dominant and more passive.

If their economic attitude is higher, they may be overly decisive and less contemplative. People tend to get in the way of this style and will feel more like a hindrance than a help to the dominant political oriented mind. understanding that a larger than life attitude can be overpowering for some, an individual like this needs to be cognizant of their behavior.

Curbing this behavior can be done by simply using more commas and question marks and less periods an exclamation points when conversing. This invites people in as opposed to forcing them out. When people feel like they are involved with the conversation as opposed to being the brunt of it, they will open up and experience more emotional looping, communication, and honesty.

Passive-Aggression

Passive people types that have a higher consistency in the power value will be passive-aggressive. Aggressive in their desire to control and passive in their behavioral display. This is what I call the *rip-tide*. Unlike waves crashing on the shore, you cannot perceive a rip-tide. You wade out into the surf only to realize you have bitten off more than you can chew but it's too late.

Remember, human behavior is separate from human desire. Desiring authority and power can be largely undetectable. If an individual operates from a high patience or fear platform in their character base, it's even less detectable. It's better to have active emotions in play when you have high power needs because they work together well. Passive people types are unreadable. Because of this dynamic, aggression is only seen while it's happening but you will not see it building. A passive person's sullen response to losing power will be the only indicator that provides the evidence they desired it.

Low Power Consistency

The lesser intense political impulse will not like high-pressure environments with excessively driven people types. They will excel when in situations that require a maintenance mindset over high drive and control. They usually prefer slow and steady to fast and faster. They'll want to watch others lead more than they'll want to lead the charge—they are behind the scenes people. They don't want to shoulder all the responsibility that accompanies being in charge. Another reason is because they will not have the energy for conflicting matters or leadership disputes, especially with lower drive in the anger emotion and greater consistency of patience.

They may not volunteer for positions of great responsibility, but will hang back in the shadows helping someone else. They typically feel out of place on teams where people jockey for position. When problems and challenges arise they will "play dead" as opposed to "wait to pounce." Their approach to difficulty is to sneak in through a back window with a jack-knife as opposed to kicking in the front door with a shotgun. They are less deliberate and more responsive when facing problems, challenges, and opportunities, thus ensuring nearly nothing happens.

In work settings, lower consistencies in power types create or translate into maintainer types rather than obtainer types—they will maintain the status quo as opposed to pushing for the impossible or what they want or need. If this sounds like you, you will not seek lime lit roles, preferring to stay back and support those you feel have the backbone to carry it. Because you don't seek attention for your efforts, you may be left feeling like a ghost, much like the lower individualistic impulse. You may never make the necessary noise surrounding important issues and therefore will set yourself up for being overlooked. Seeing that the squeaky wheel gets the grease, you'll never get any—especially if your drive (anger emotion) is out of play. You will support others while never gaining the personal support you want or need.

These styles are far more mission-minded as opposed to being control and authority driven. These styles avoid conflicts and abrasive people. They will be a target for aggressive people who may want to take advantage of their willingness to help. All in all, lower power styles are unobtrusive, serene, and emotionally helpful rather than boastful.

When associated with anger they'll feel conflicted because they won't take the roles they desire and they won't bother with positional manipulation even though they may think about it often or appear like they could shoulder the responsibility that comes from ownership. Many times lower political mindsets are accompanied by lower economic mindsets. The power value and the economic value always act as a team and are usually the driving force behind the majority of entrepreneurs.

If this is you I suggest you embrace who you are and not covet dominance. Many believe the more dominant one is the better, but this isn't true. Capitalize on your creativity and you strong unconventional and original style. Look for supportive roles with less responsibility or places to volunteer your talents. This style is necessary even though it doesn't explode onto the scene making demands with wild fanfare. Think of all your body parts—which ones do you think are most significant?

Now image working without your fingernails or mowing the grass on a hot day without your eyebrows. Although these parts seem more meager than the others, they are extremely necessary.

Self-Power Conflict

But what happens when our desires are in conflict with our actions? My emotions are "low-keyed" but my desires are driven; now what? The anger emotion contains a strong "taking" orientation and when it's integrated with a power orientation there's a greater flow of energy. In other words, what they desire they do. But not everyone does what they desire to do.

Fig. 2

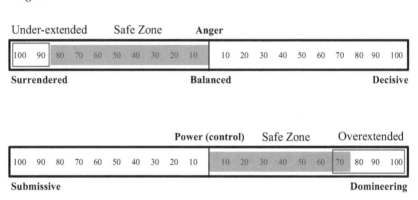

Using the graphs above, consider what happens when we desire to "be in charge" (domineering) but have a diminished capacity to "take" charge because we do not have the emotional energy to do it (surrendered). This is a classic me-me conflict. The conflict restricts the energy flow. We therefore do not have sufficient energy to fulfill our desire. Being in flow is what creates the clearest path forward. No flow creates obstacles—hurtles that sap our energy system.

Duel Power Convergences

I already talked about duel convergence so I will not further elaborate on how these factors work. You may reference the information in an earlier chapter if you need to brush up on convergences.

POW/H–AES/L (Pragmatic): This value factor associates *authority and control* with *real-world thinking*. When the power value is high, and the aesthetic value is low you will have no inner conflict. This will create a strong real-world and directive approach to solving problems, challenges, and finding opportunities. This will cause a *realistic* rather than an unconventional approach to leadership. This person may be direct and time-sensitive.

POW/H–AES/H (Creative-Control): This value factor associates *authority and control* with *unconventionality* and it's not very common. These two forces are contrary when competing. When the power value is high, and the aesthetic value is high you will likely have an unorthodox leader. This will create a strong need to diverge while leading forward. There's a need to *experience* the surroundings with a sense having to control the experience.

POW/H–IND/L (Self-Assured): This value factor associates *authority and control* with *security*. When the power value is high, and the individualistic value is low you will have no inner conflict. This will create a strong real-world and directive approach to solving problems, challenges, and finding opportunities. This will cause a *realistic* rather than an creative approach to leadership. This person may display strong confidence and appear frightening to insecure people.

POW/H–IND/H (Autonomous-Control): This value factor associates *authority and control* with freedom and *autonomy* and it's not very common. These two forces are not contrary when competing. When the power value is high, and the individualistic value is high you will likely have an autonomous leader. This will create a strong need to be themselves while leading forward. There's a need to *express* and *prove* their independence to the world.

POW/H–ECO/L (Passive-Aggressive): This value factor associates *authority and control* with *satisfaction*. When the power value is high, and the economic value is low you will have some inner conflict. This will create a strong need to control one's environment while lacking urgency and vision for the future. This can create a need to be in charge without a sense of proper timing.

POW/H–ECO/H (Supremacy): This value factor associates *authority and control* with *self-interest*. These two forces are powerful when in play. When the power value is high, and the economic value is high you will likely have a dominant leader. This will create a strong need to control surroundings while leading forward. There's a need to *own* the surroundings with a sense having to control all outcomes for personal gain.

POW/H–ALT/L (Suspicious): This value factor associates *authority and control* with *being guarded*. These two forces are compatible when both are in play. When the power value is high, and the altruistic value is low you will have no inner conflict. This individual will desire to prioritize personal freedom and opportunities at the expense of others who may suggest another way. They will be guarded and suspicious of others motives. These types are difficult to know.

POW/H–ALT/H (Levelheaded): This value factor associates *authority and control* with *personal sacrifice*. These two forces are conflictive when both are in play. When the power value is high, and the altruistic value is high you will have inner conflict. This individual will prioritize personal wants and opportunities in line with their personal agenda with a need to meet the needs others may have. This can create a me-me conflict response; should I do it or not do it? This person will likely divide the needs between self and others evenly.

POW/H–REG/L (Insubordinate): This value factor associates *authority and control* with *subversion*. These two forces are maximized when both are in play. When the power value is high, and the regulated value is low you will have no inner conflict. This individual will insist on multithreaded and subversive approaches to solving problems and meeting personal needs. They will desire to march to the beat of their own drum and will reject unwanted constraints.

POW/H–REG/H (Commanding): This value factor associates *authority and control* with *systemic thinking*. These two forces are conflicted when both are in play. When the power value is high, and the regulated value is high you will have inner conflict. This individual may insist on specific ways of doing things and may hold others and *not themselves* to the same standard of operation.

POW/H–THE/L (Instinctual): This value factor associates *authority and control* with *intuition*. These two forces are neutralized when both are in play. When the power value is high, and the theoretical value is low you will have no inner conflict. This individual will rely on intuition, instinct, and past experiences for learning what to do next. They will cram to pass rather than learn to know.

POW/H–THE/H (Supervisory): This value factor associates *authority and control* with *fact-finding*. These two forces are neutralized when both are in play. When the power value is high, and the theoretical value is high you will have no inner conflict. This individual will rely on interesting facts for leveraging how to maximize their current position in the world. These types can be innovative and will use facts and evidences to advance their position.

POW/L–AES/H (Creative-Support): This value factor associates *submission* with *unconventionality*. These two forces are not in conflict when both are in play. When the power value is low and the aesthetic high you will have no inner conflict. This will create unconventionally imaginative and original approaches to assisting with what needs to be done.

POW/L–AES/L (Pragmatic): This value factor associates *submission* with *realism*. These two forces are maximized when both are in play. When the power value is low, and the aesthetic value is low you will have no inner conflict. This will create a practical yet supportive style that may lack an agenda.

POW/L–IND/H (Yielded): This value factor associates *submission* with *independence*. These two forces are in semi-conflict when both are in play. When the power value is low, and the individualistic value is high you will have no inner conflict. This will create independent, imaginative, and original approaches to assisting with what needs to be done.

POW/L–IND/L (Accommodating): This value factor associates *submission* with *cooperation*. These two forces are maximized when both are low. When the individualistic value is low, and the power value is low you will have no inner conflict. This will create a supportive style that yields to avoid potential controversies.

POW/L–ECO/H (Frustrated): This value factor associates *submission* with *self-mastery*. These two forces are not in conflict when both are in play. When the power value is low, and the economic value is high you will have inner conflict. This will create a need to get what you want but a diminished ability to take the necessary approaches to control and realize outcomes.

POW/L–ECO/L (Surrendered): This value factor associates *submission* with *satisfaction*. These two forces are maximized when both are in play and out of play. When the power value is low, and the economic value is low you will have no inner conflict. This will create a style that surrenders to circumstance and settles for less than what is optimal.

POW/L–ALT/H (Supporter): This value factor associates *apprehension* with *sacrifice*. These two forces are not in conflict when both are in play. When the power value is low, and the altruistic value is high you will have no inner conflict. This individual will endeavor to support and cooperate with others without the need of excessive attention or the spotlight.

POW/L–ALT/L (Apprehensive): This value factor associates *submission* with *self-protection*. These two forces are in harmony when both are in play. When the power value is low, and the altruistic value is low you will have no conflict. This will create guarded style who expects others to qualify before entering into their private space. They may over-focus on what is missing in other people.

POW/L–REG/H (Amendable): This value factor associates *apprehension* with *black and white thinking*. These two forces are in conflict when both are in play. When the power value is low, and the regulated value is high you will have no inner conflict. This individual is rigid and may be punitive in nature. They could to be cause driven or missional. May be strict or *narrow* in thinking.

POW/L–REG/L (Passive-Resistant): This value factor associates *submission* with *subversion*. These two forces are in conflict when both are in play. When the power value is low, and the regulated value is low you will have no inner conflict. This individual may be passive-resistive. In other words, they may covertly seek to do things their own unique way.

POW/L–THE/H (Apprentice): This value factor associates *submission* with *curiosity*. These two forces are neutralized when both are in play. When the power value is low, and the theoretical value is high you will have no inner conflict. This individual will cooperate with instructions and will desire to learn while taking directions well.

POW/L–THE/L (Browsing): This value factor associates *submission* with *dis-interest*. These two forces are neutralized when both are in play. When the power value is low, and the theoretical value is low you will have no inner conflict. This style is intuitive and resists over-working their cognitive mind. They may be subject to errors in judgment and might scan material without reading all of it.

Situational Power Consistency

To reiterate, these are values *not* behaviors. Values speak of our *desires* and what moves us in a directional effort. Keep also in mind that this list is associated with a single value element and not the *integrated motivational orientation*, which includes all seven value elements. I'm going to say this again because it bears repeating; what we desire can often conflict with what we will actually do.

Keep in mind that this list is in no way exhaustive. Individuals with a *general* or situational (situational/midpoint) consistency and direction within the *single* motivational element of power will likely desire to:

1. Lead or follow depending upon the circumstances involved.
2. Be flexible and free flowing without an excessive need to be number one.
3. Take a stand or sit quietly depending on what is necessary within a leadership role.
4. Drive the car or sit in the back seat; no extremes in either mindset.
5. Mediate all available ideas as opposed to only focusing on their own.
6. Not be fully in charge and shoulder everything, but to be willing to take initiative within an area of expertise if necessary.
7. Be a stabilizing force in normal team operations and to lead if necessary, but won't *need* to.
8. Be both cooperative and competitive depending on the situation at hand.
9. Bring balance to a team of power hungry people.
10. Understand both aggressive and passive leaders.
11. Share leadership needs when those with greater experience are available.
12. Be both team and individual oriented as the needs arise.
13. Cherry pick the control options available.

14. Exercise authority or yield a position depending on the situation.
15. Provide input without forcing an agenda or over-controlling outcomes

Very High Power Consistency

Remember, these are values not behaviors. Values speak of our *desires* and what moves us in a directional effort. Keep also in mind that this list is associated with a single value element and not the *integrated motivational orientation*. What we desire can often conflict with what we will actually do. Keep in mind that this list is in no way exhaustive.

Individuals with *very high* (situational/midpoint) consistency and direction within the *single* motivational element of power will likely cause them to:

1. Only listen to direct and control or agree or disagree.
2. Rarely if ever listen in order to understand where others are coming from.
3. Not get into the car unless they're driving it.
4. Believe winning is everything: there's typically no Plan B.
5. Want to be large and in charge.
6. Be a fixer.
7. Feel at home when ramming their ideas through to a conclusion.
8. Secretly believe that they are "all that."
9. Create relationships for the sole purpose of advancing their own position.
10. Need a corporate ladder to climb.
11. Believe the sky is the limit.
12. Feel like they always deserve a shot.
13. Believe victory is theirs.
14. Always look for respect.
15. Believe advancement must be available or they will be highly dissatisfied.

16. Look for respect for personal gains made.
17. Look for rewards and recognition for a job well done.
18. Desire signs of personal authority such as their name on their parking space or a big desk.
19. Believe others must know they are in charge and will find ways to let them know.
20. Need authority equal to or greater than their responsibility.
21. Call the shots within their area of knowledge.
22. Direct and control subordinates as opposed to letting them control themselves.
23. Believe the buck stops with them.
24. Not like moochers or people who take the credit for another person's ideas.
25. Be a survivor needing difficult challenges to overcome.

Very Low Power Consistency

Individuals with *very low* (situational/midpoint) consistency and direction within the *single* motivational element of power will likely:

1. Not like high-pressure environments with excessively driven people types.
2. Excel when in situations that require a maintenance mindset over high drive.
3. Prefer slow and steady to fast and faster.
4. Want to watch others lead more than they'll want to lead things themselves.
5. Not want to shoulder all the responsibility that accompanies being in charge.
6. Not have the energy for conflicting matters or leadership disputes.
7. Not volunteer themselves for positions of great responsibility.
8. Feel out of place on a team where people jockey for position.

9. "Play dead" as opposed to "waiting to pounce" when confronted with challenges.
10. "Sneak in through a back window with a jack-knife" as opposed to "kicking in the front door with a shotgun."
11. Be less deliberate and more responsive when facing challenging opportunities.
12. Be more of a maintainer than they are an obtainer.
13. Not seek lime lit roles but would rather stay back and support someone else.
14. Not seek attention for their efforts, they may be left feeling like a ghost seeing they never draw attention to taking charge.
15. Not make the necessary noise surrounding important issues and therefore will set themselves up for being overlooked.
16. Seeing the squeaky wheel gets the grease, they'll likely never get any.
17. Support others while never gaining the personal support they want or need.
18. Be tempted to stay out of leadership roles for the sake of it.
19. Not have the energy to fight for what they really want.
20. Not likely care about getting credit.

As you may have noticed, the power value element is the part of the whole value structure that represents our desire to be in control. It's our desire or need to be in charge of our personal space and destiny. Unlike personal sacrifice, which we will discuss next, the power mindset is rooted in a strong self-concept. It is these types who desire to drive their emotional and behavioral vehicles to their desired locations and take control of it.

8
PERSONAL SACRIFICE

What do you think of when you hear the words personal sacrifice? Does it excite you? For some, the idea of sacrificing your own needs in order to encourage someone else is irresistible. This value element is an expression of the need or *energy* to benefit others at the expense of the self through self-sacrificing. There are five levels of consistency within this element just as there are five levels of consistency in every individual element. Each level of consistency determines the normalcy or severity of need.

We will first examine the moderate level of consistency, which describes where many will sit on the scale but keep this in mind; it's the combination of all seven elements that determine how each element will *desire* to respond to circumstances and then the whole of our value system must receive "permission" from our behaviors fueled by our primary emotions in order to make our desired outcomes a reality.

At times there's genuine sincerity in this dimension to help others. Every human being has a level of empathy that acknowledges how we desire to be treated by someone else and we will reciprocate this feeling toward others. This is normal behavior and it's expressed by a good majority of people. Those who extend much higher or lower in this dimension will experience clear differences from the norm. Ultimately, it is the many variables and consistencies associated with behaviors, emotions, and worldviews that will determine if extensions will be easily detected or not.

What amount of psychic energy do we decide is warranted when it comes to sacrificing our own personal needs for the needs of another?

Self-Preservation and Self-Sacrifice

What is normal Self-preservation? Self-preservation is a behavior that ensures the survival of an organism. Self-preservation urges animals to collect the energy and resources required to prolong life as well as resources that increase chances of survival. Basic needs are available to most humans (roughly 7 out of 8 people), and usually for a low cost. The same instinct that drives us to gather resources also drives some to over-consumption or to patterns of collection and possession that essentially make hoarding resources the priority.[73] Everything is open to overextension.

According to social analysis, the desire for self-preservation has led to a myriad of laws and regulations surrounding a culture of safety in society.[74] Seat belt laws, speed limits, airbags, texting regulations, and the 'stranger danger' campaign are familiar examples of social guides and regulations to improve survival, and these laws are largely influenced by our natural drive for self-preservation.[75] Self-preservation is what the economic value represents. This is why the economic value is opposed to the altruistic value. When each is opposing the other, a natural *flow* exists between them.

High consistencies in the economic value hold hands with lower consistencies in the altruistic value. High consistencies in the altruistic value hold hands with the lower consistencies in the economic value. But social scientists have discovered some interesting nuances deep within this sacrificial element that should be discussed. This begs the question; is self-sacrifice really sacrificial? Altruism is an individual performing an action which is at a cost to themselves (e.g., pleasure and quality of life, time,

---

[73] Bush, Ronald F.; Hunt, Shelby D. (2011-10-15). Marketing Theory: Philosophy of Science Perspectives. Marketing Classics Press. ISBN 9781613112281.
[74] Lyng, Stephen (1990). 'Edgework: A Social Psychological Analysis of Voluntary Risk Taking." American Journal of Sociology. 851–886.
[75] Self-preservation: Wikipedia.org.

probability of survival or reproduction), but benefits, either directly or indirectly, another individual.

These actions are without reciprocity-driven expectations or a need for equal compensation in return for these actions. David Steinberg[76] suggests a definition for altruism in the clinical setting; "intentional and voluntary actions that aim to enhance the welfare of another person in the absence of any quid pro-quo external rewards." But according to research, there are some *hidden* rewards that follow sacrificial acts.

The International Encyclopedia of the Social Sciences defines psychological altruism as a "motivational state with the goal of increasing another's welfare." Moreover, psychological altruism is juxtaposed to psychological egoism, which refers to the motivation to increase one's own welfare.[77] But to what degree is this true? The idea of whether or not humans are truly adept to psychological altruism has come under scrutiny by some.[78] Some definitions do specify a "self-sacrificial" nature to altruism and a lack of external rewards for selfless behaviors.[79]

Nevertheless, because altruism has its own benefits, meaning, we feel good and have a greater sense of worth when enacting an altruistic action, the selflessness of altruistic acts is brought into question. Social exchange theory postulates that true altruism *only* exists when benefits to the self are greater than the costs to the self.

It is the push and pull between psychological egoism and psychological altruism that leaves some researchers to determine that egoism has the greater energy. So, rather than benefitting

---

76 Steinberg, David (2010). 'Altruism in medicine: its definition, nature, and dilemmas." Cambridge Quarterly of Healthcare Ethics. 249–57.
77 Altruism. International Encyclopedia of the Social Sciences. Ed. William A. Darity, Jr. 2nd ed. Vol. 1. Detroit: Macmillan Reference USA, 2008. 87-88. Gale Virtual Reference Library. Web. 10 April 2012.
78 Batson, C. (2011). Altruism in humans. New York, NY US: Oxford University Press.
79 Batson, C. (2012). A history of prosocial behavior research. In A. W. Kruglanski, W. Stroebe, A. W. Kruglanski, (Eds.), Handbook of the history of social psychology (pp. 243–264). New York, NY US: Psychology Press.

another at personal expense, it appears that humans are *exchanging* actions for positive feelings. This in my opinion is one of the two axiomatic principles of altruism.

I'm reminded of the first century prophet Jesus who said, "Be careful not to practice your righteousness in front of others to be seen by them. If you do, you will have no reward from your Father in heaven."[80] This warning gives us a glimpse into the mind of the prophet who obviously saw humanity as those operating on the *social exchange* program.

In other words, there's a personal reward for sacrificial behaviors. The prophet continues, "So when you give to the needy, do not sound a trumpet before you, as the hypocrites do in the synagogues and on the streets, to be praised by men. Truly I tell you, they already have their full reward...."[81]

I agree with the prophet. There are several social and emotional rewards associated with true acts of altruism. Social exchange theory is a sociological and psychological theory that considers the *natural* social behaviors that develop between the interaction of two parties that implement a cost-benefit analysis to determine risks and benefits.

Also, the theory involves economic relationships that occur when each party has goods that the other party may consider valuable. These calculations occur within romantic relationships, friendships, professional relationships, and ephemeral relationships that may be as simple as exchanging words with a customer at the cash register.[82]

---

80 Matthew 6:1. NIV.
81 Matthew 6:2. BSB.
82 Mcray, Jeni (2015). "Leadership Glossary: Essential Terms for the 21st Century". Credo Reference. Mission Bell Media. Retrieved 21 October 2018.

How often do males tell females what they want to hear in an effort to gain a sexual favor in return?

Him: "Will you come home with me?"
Her: "Do you love me?"
Him: "Oh, yes! How could I love anyone else?"

Daniel Batson is a psychologist who surveyed this question and argues against the social exchange theory. He identified four major motives for altruism: altruism to ultimately benefit the self (egoism), to ultimately benefit the other person (altruism), to benefit a group (collectivism), or to uphold a moral principle (principlism). Altruism that in due course serves our self-interests is therefore distinguished from selfless-altruism, but the general conclusion has been that empathy-induced altruism can be *genuinely* selfless.[83] This is likely true, but I would consider it rare.

Fig. 1

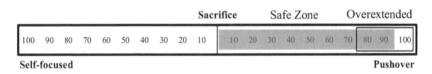

The empathy-altruism hypothesis declares that psychological altruism does exist and is induced by a genuine empathic desire to help someone who is suffering. Feelings of concern are contrasted with feelings of personal distress, which compel people to reduce their own brain tensions brought on by their emotions. People with a greater degree of empathy will help others in trouble even when avoiding the situation is an option. Those lacking in empathic

---

[83] Batson, C., Ahmad, N., & Stocks, E. L. (2011). Four forms of prosocial motivation: Egoism, altruism, collectivism, and principlism. In D. Dunning, D. Dunning (Eds.), Social motivation (pp. 103–126). New York, NY US: Psychology Press.

concern will usually avoid helping others in distress related circumstances unless it is too difficult or impossible to avoid it.[84]

But what does this look like emotionally? I'm suggesting that selflessness that comes from a true state of empathetic concern originates when there's a balance between economic values and altruistic values. This would also include individualism when in a lesser state. Lower consistencies in individualistic value create a cooperative attitude when we are willing to make a sacrifice.

When I'm not thinking about what I'm getting in return for an action, I'm more willing to lose personal pleasures. When I'm in no need of the spotlight, I'm more inclined to cooperate and less driven by the need to be the star of the show. A true state of altruism can be seen in the direction and consistency graph below. This is not the only graph depicting this, but it's an example of a balanced value set.

Fig. 2

Motivational Direction and Consistency Graph
Sacrifice

			0	10	20	30	40	50	60	70	80	90	100
ORIGINALITY	26	3	0	10	20	30	40	50	60	70	80	90	100
EFFICIENCY	40	4	0	10	20	30	40	50	60	70	80	90	100
INDIVIDUALITY	80	6	0	10	20	30	40	50	60	70	80	90	100
POWER	28	2	0	10	20	30	40	50	60	70	80	90	100
SACRIFICE	91	1	0	10	20	30	40	50	60	70	80	90	100
COMPLIANCE	34	5	0	10	20	30	40	50	60	70	80	90	100
CURIOSITY	60	7	0	10	20	30	40	50	60	70	80	90	100

---

84 Altruism." International Encyclopedia of the Social Sciences. Ed. William A. Darity, Jr. 2nd ed. Vol. 1. Detroit: Macmillan Reference USA, 2008. 87-88. Gale Virtual Reference Library. Web. 10 April 2012.

In conclusion, each set of values will stand on their own when determining where one sits on the sacrificial scale. While exchanging favors with others is a natural means of emotional negotiation, there's nothing inherently wrong with it. We all make choices in line with what *feels* good to our brains. In this next section I want to address sacrificial overextensions. What happens when we are out of balance in the area of self-sacrifice? What does it look like when there's an emotional dysfunction associated with our need to serve?

Very High Altruistic Consistency

This impulse is associated with giving and caring, but there's a caveat; it must be at the expense of the self. This is why I call this a sacrificial motivation. The sacrificial style always places others before themselves. They are very cognizant of the underdog and may lean toward "stray dog" people types in society. They won't feel empowered unless they are *disempowered*. I want you to think about this—the need to be disempowered.

My mother passed 1 in 2018. She was a wonderful mother. I believe she gave away eight cars to others in need during her married life. She was a servant. My memories of her growing up are fond and encouraging. During the cold winter months there was always a fire in the fireplace and hot cocoa for consumption. She made sure I was wearing my mittens and hugs were available 24-hours a day. The best way to describe my mother is she felt like a big human hug. But there was something amiss deep in my mothers brain. I wouldn't discover it until I was well into my 30's.

My father is a mild sociopath.[85] He lives alone and is eighty-one years old now. He was unable to be faithful to my mother for who knows how many days in a row for well over 50 years. His secret life is sordid and blasphemous; it has been this way since he was a teenager. He's a pathological liar, a thief, expert manipulator,

---

[85] This means "sociopathic traits" (not full blown) such as limited empathy, chronic lying, excessive denial, crystal clear clarity with diminished brain bias (negative) towards people.

peeping tom, and somewhat of a stalker (relentless pursuit). He was a minister for many years before getting kicked out for his insane and devious sexual behavior.

Sociopaths are drawn to the clergy like a magnet. I won't say anything more here about him, but I want to turn my attention to my mother. She's the one who bore the brunt of his psychopathic existence for more than 50 years before my father kicked her "fat ass" (his words) out of the house at around age 70. My mother, like many mothers, was an *extreme* altruist. God rest her eternal soul.

As I move through this next section, understand that my mother was an *extreme* version of the sacrificial mind. As you read these next few paragraphs, understand that there are levels of consistency within all the motivational elements. My mother was as about as high on this consistency measurement as you can get and she's not the only one in my family like this.

My mother knew of my father's behavior in the 1970's but never left him. This is where I will explain how the power of sacrifice can take an ugly turn leading one down a road of self-deprecation, deception, and misery. I'm an avid viewer of the ID channel. ID stands for Investigation-Discovery. The channel is made up of shows depicting the worst of society; psychopaths, sociopaths, and serial killers who are one in the same. More often than not these psycho's are married to women of intense sacrifice. Unfortunately, psychotic men can sniff them out like a bloodhound.

One of the shows that depicts these family scenarios perfectly is called; "Evil Lives Here."[86] This program is made up of reenactments blended with police footage, family photographs, videos, and interviews that give the audience a view of the psychopath as told through the eyes of someone close to them. Let's examine a few traits associated with the sacrificial motivational

---

[86] *Evil Lives Here* is an American documentary television series on Investigation Discovery that debuted on January 17, 2016. This 60-minute true crime show spends each episode interviewing a family member of the highlighted murderer.

element; not in its extreme form, but simply as a value element. We will examine the extreme form in the coming paragraphs.

Those with a high altruistic impulse can work long and hard at someone else's project and not their own. They believe it's better to give than it is to receive and will give their time and talent freely to others who need them. They are sincere and open to listening to the problems and challenges of others. Very high altruistic styles, as a rule, will often experience low self-worth. Although behind a genius mask of benevolence, their good deeds are typically a sign of their view of self—they always see others as more important than themselves.

Fig. 3   Motivational Direction and Consistency Graph
Sacrifice

ORIGINALITY	51	6	0	10	20	30	40	50	60	70	80	90	100
EFFICIENCY	26	4	0	10	20	30	40	50	60	70	80	90	100
INDIVIDUALITY	15	3	0	10	20	30	40	50	60	70	80	90	100
POWER	15	2	0	10	20	30	40	50	60	70	80	90	100
SACRIFICE	96	1	0	10	20	30	40	50	60	70	80	90	100
COMPLIANCE	34	5	0	10	20	30	40	50	60	70	80	90	100
CURIOSITY	61	7	0	10	20	30	40	50	60	70	80	90	100

Humans naturally focus on what they believe to be important. Sacrificial styles never focus on the self. Busy with the lives of others, their own life and mission becomes lost in the life and mission of others. This is known as being *swallowed* by others. My father swallowed my mother. This is hard to hear. The altruist finds this impossible to see. This is partly due to the fact that everyone sees them as a genuine helper and partly due their view of themselves in the world.

Their generosity and their selfless attitude could not possibly reflect personal low self-worth now, could it? The answer is; absolutely! Low self-worth is the underpinning of excessive benevolence. Altruistic styles believe saying "I can't" is more like saying "I won't." It feels wrong to focus on personal needs. This will have an impact on them later on, but when they are young and full of energy, it's hard to fathom. These are the compulsive caregivers—they always lose while those they associate with always win. This is called "the lose-winner."

Eduard Spranger sees the altruistic mindset as one who "takes the place of another." This is a dominant impulse. The sympathetic spirit is the driving factor. Do not confuse the sacrificial value for love. It is not love. It is rooted in pity and self-abasement. One cannot deny that the attitude that honors another life is special and significant, but let's not see through an opaque glass here.

The sacrificial attitude cannot be confused with empathy. While empathy "feels into others" and can *feel* their pain, sympathy is rooted in our ability to "understand" someone's pain. Excessive sympathy is associated with a misunderstanding of someone's pain. This misunderstanding is the crux between a healthy and unhealthy response mechanism.

The misunderstanding relates to the differences between self- and social-understanding. If I misunderstand my own worth I run the risk of misunderstanding someone else's worth—it can become exaggerated.

Why Rescue Baby Jessica?

Jessica McClure Morales, born March 26, 1986 became famous on October 14, 1987, at the age of 18 months after she fell into a well in her aunt's backyard in Midland, Texas. Between that day and October 16, rescuers worked for 56 hours to free her from the eight-inch well casing that dropped 22 feet below the ground. It was a nightmare. But why did anyone bother to rescue baby Jessica?

"McClure's rescue proved to be a much more difficult ordeal than was first anticipated. Within hours of beginning the emergency procedure, the Midland Fire and Police Departments devised a plan that involved drilling another shaft parallel to the well and then drilling a tunnel at a right angle across to it. Enlisting the help of a variety of local (often out-of-work) oil-drillers, the Midland officials had hoped to free McClure in minutes. However, the first workers to arrive on the scene found their tools barely adequate to penetrate the hard rock around the well.

It took about six hours to drill the shaft and longer to drill the tunnel, because the jackhammers used were designed for drilling downward, rather than sideways. A mining engineer eventually arrived to help supervise and coordinate the rescue effort. TV viewers watched as paramedics and rescuers, drilling experts and contractors worked tirelessly to save the baby's life. Meanwhile, they were reassured when they heard Jessica singing "Winnie the Pooh" from deep in the well. As long as she was still singing, they knew she was still alive. Forty-five hours after McClure fell into the well, the shaft and tunnel were finally completed."[87]

Rescuers worked tirelessly for over 55 hours to free the child for one reason. Empathy. Empathy is an intrinsic dimensional part of the human value system. The *intrinsic* value dimension of life is its *feeling and emotional* "unifying" components.[88]

Empathy understands and sees other people as unique individuals with intrinsic value. The spiritual, irreplaceable worth of others, or the value of any 'thing' as it exists in itself, are all part of this intrinsic empathetic outer-world position. The ability to see and appreciate the inner worth of others and to see and accept others *as they are* without placing any stipulations or expectations on them, defines this view.

---

[87] Jessica McClure; Wikipedia, 2019
[88] PTSI Remedial Strategies & Exercises: David Mefford Ph.D. and Vera Mefford, MA., 2007.

This innate ability to place oneself in another person's shoes without passing judgment on them is what makes the empathetic value and viewpoint possible. Empathy can be measured in two areas; clarity and bias. Empathy encompasses seeing other people as unique individuals in and of themselves without comparison to outside objects—the value of a person as they exist *outside* of time.

Fig. 3

Baby Jessica's Rescuers (Oct 17, 1987)[89]

Furthermore, self-esteem is the exact same thing but as intrinsic value relates to our own self. It's seeing the self as infinitely valuable; the unique individuality of our self; the understanding of "who I am" with all my strengths and limitations. To be authentic, honest, and sincere considering who I actually am. It's the act of accepting yourself "as is" without judgment or comparison.

The image (fig. 3) above is an amazing picture of human empathy and sacrifice. I want to revisit my former question; why rescue baby Jessica? She wasn't able to contribute a whole lot to society only being 18 months of age. She was more consumer based than she was

---

89 Image source: Rescuers prepare to lower a volunteer into a well parallel to the one 18-month-old Jessica McClure fell into, during rescue efforts in Midland, Texas, Oct. 17, 1987. (Anonymous/ASSOCIATED PRESS)

contribution based at such a young age; you see my point. Human beings have intrinsic worth in and of themselves. We never have to fret over the choice between the baby or the car. Which one should I get rid of?

It doesn't matter whether you have a Ph.D. or a pacifier; your worth as a human being never diminishes. Our human worth is measured on a constant not an instant. Instant measurements as they relate to value fall into the "extrinsic" realm of practical thinking—now.

Ah, but why do we tend to diminish our own worth? Those with 1. excessive altruistic intensions, 2. less self-value interest, and 3. high empathy, are always self-diminishing. They believe that their worth can get better or become worse. They do not understand that their worth as a human being is set within a constant. If they do not perform to the out-of-sync idealistic standard that they place on themselves, their brain, as if seeing themselves as a worthless baby Jessica, says, "get back in the well where you belong."

There's a misappropriation, which is a misunderstanding of "who they are" in relationship to "what they do." If they perform well, they see themselves as a better person—they have a greater sense of worth. If they perform poorly, they see themselves as having less worth, which translates into worthless. They compare themselves with those around them and find themselves lacking—always.

They do not see their personal human worth as in a *fixed*, constant position. This is the one idea that makes Christianity so attractive to those who have given themselves over to its ideology. The Christian experience tells you that you are "worthless" in your own strength. You have no moral judgment and your "good" deeds are as filthy *menstrual* rags (Greek Septuagint).[90] According to the

---

[90] "We are all infected and impure with sin. When we display our righteous deeds, they are nothing but filthy rags. Like autumn leaves, we wither and fall, and our sins sweep us away like the wind." Isaiah 64:6, NLT.

Christian philosophy, only in Christ are you clean and pure. I'm not going to argue the morality of this idea or take this away from those who emotionally benefit from the philosophy, but you can see the attraction to its premise.

Their "good deeds" are an exercise in futility. They live as an Olympic skater waiting for their scores. They never get a 10. Benevolence is their penance. If complimented, their brain's first instinct is, "really? You think so?" They never think, hell yes! That would be a sign of pride or self-conceit. They're so busy trying not to think of themselves "more highly than they ought to think"[91] that they fail to think of themselves as highly as they should. Although you could argue the benefits to this philosophy (and I would not stop you), you could also argue the emotional backlash.

The Thin Line Between Servant and Slave

There's a hair width line between being service-oriented and being a slave. Some move back and forth across it while others set on one or the other side more frequently. Excessive styles are a mile away in the wrong direction. My mother was a slave. My father would be caught cheating on her and the following week my mother is serving him potato chips and ice cream in his lazy-boy in hopes that he won't leave. Her thinking was, "who will take care of him?"

An unfortunate memory I have is my father's infamous 3-word phrase after every dinner my mother prepared and served. "What's for desert?" Many times my mother would slave in the kitchen for hours. My father knew good and well that she didn't have the time nor the energy to make a desert, but after wiping his used lips with a napkin after the meal, my siblings and I would wait for the depressive question. He was a first class jerk in those days and still is. Rather than knocking his ass of the chair with a frying pan, my

---

91 Paul the apostle; Romans 12:3, NIV.

mother would feel bad, inept, unqualified, and shameful. This is the slave.

There's nothing wrong with serving dinner. And theirs nothing wrong with going the extra mile once in a while. But if you are servicing other people in an effort to feel better about who you are in the world you're heading in the wrong direction. It's not something you will see at a glance; you have to think about it—deeply.

It runs much deeper than your conscious mind where we might plan and organize the kitchen table. It's deep in the unconscious mind where your belief that your worth is based on how much you can sacrifice and diminish yourself or what other people will think of you if you don't is on automatic pilot.

Don't Shit on Me

I heard a story once. I don't remember the name of the woman in the story, but she was a psychiatrist. She had a small wooden desk and behind it on the wall was a large sign that read; "Don't shit on me." She's my hero. High sacrificial styles get shit on a lot—too much for that matter. When their economic values are low and their power values are lacking, they are easily shit on by the world. They wipe it off in silence and keep sacrificing their own energy for those ungrateful bastards who see them coming from a mile away.

I watched the ID Channel the other night and this woman was living with a serial killer for 15 years in the 1980's. He removed the telephone from the house (this was before cell phones) so she would be disconnected from the outside world. He beat her and the kids for years. 15 years into the marriage one of her children went to a neighbor and had them call the police. Her youngest daughter did what she could not bring herself to do. In the interview she kept saying while looking downcast, "I thought it was my fault."

These are extreme cases but they are everywhere. Don't let people shit on you. You are not a bad person because you don't have time to help. Overextensions within the sacrificial value framework are emotionally diminishing. Balance is the key to life. When this is heavy in the wrong direction we suffer for it. You *feel* like a loser. This is a subtle happening and it builds over time without formal notice. People like this don't realize that their actions, although generous, are unhealthy over time if unbalanced. Feelings of unappreciation will creep in and feelings of low self-worth will be bolstered because of these continued actions.

You may be tempted to ask; is it bad to help others? The answer is of course not. But many are helping others to the point of emotional exhaustion. Again, these attitudes can be very high, high, average, low, and very low. Depending upon where your consistency is will determine how well your bents are working for you or whether or not they may be working against you in life. If this is you, even though you may not realize it, you're celebrating defeat. Your brain celebrates defeat. You don't celebrate victory because you're too busy celebrating everyone else's victories. You need to change your brain.

A simple brain exercise can fix this. Next time you accomplish any simple task, pinch or hug yourself and say, "well done—Insert your name. That's another win for us"[92] You must say this aloud. This is because we are more committed to what we *say* than we are to what we *think*. It's why we say wedding vows rather than have wedding thoughts. Thoughts unspoken die unborn. By doing this several times a day you will build new neural networks that spell "victory" in your brain.

Low Altruistic Impulses

The lower this impulse the more one is distrusting of others and protective of their own space. Lower altruistic people types will see

---

92 Greg Smith, Mauianalysis.com. Greg's an expert in his form of Axiology.

others as guilty before seeing them as innocent, which is in stark contrast to the higher impulse. These people are tough to take advantage of whereas the higher sacrificial types are easier to take advantage of—they never see it coming because everyone is presumed innocent.

With the lower value, people are more in your way, as opposed to the higher value where you will feel like you may be in other people's way. Higher sacrificial types will be walking down the street and be run into by someone who isn't looking, but will apologize as it was their fault the collision happened. Lower and less driven altruists will instinctively say (or *think* depending on their +D and -S line in DISC), "Watch where you are going!"

Because these people are not moved by emotional appeals, they will see such actions as manipulation and can be turned off by them. These folks have a low tolerance for people who complain, whine, or rant about their problems—low altruists typically don't want to hear it. You can understand why these styles are able to do the harder things when it comes to difficult people decisions.

They will not appreciate people who don't carry their own weight or who capitalize on other people's efforts. Many times others are simply seen as a means to an end. When accompanied by high political and economic drives, the lower altruistic person can come off as extremely self-centered, which they are. These styles can separate out their individual emotions and not allow them to distort their decision making. They have a no-nonsense approach to people and things, especially when they sport a low influence (optimism) emotion. All outcomes are connected to practical needs rather than people needs.

Lower altruistic styles have no problem saying "no" to those whom they disagree with, especially if they are high-task oriented. We must understand that this is not personal. People's behavior is always a reflection on how they see the world around them and that reflection is based upon their experiences throughout their lifetime.

If their experiences were difficult, they will have made the proper adjustment in order to get through the circumstances. If their circumstances were not difficult, then they would not have had to build up resistance against incoming arrows.

People's skin is either thick or thin based on the atmospheric conditions during the formative years. Low altruistic impulses are not bad, but rather necessary for some people. Because of this, they will have different approaches to working with others in the business world. These styles will likely enjoy group activities that have less personal agendas. They may not enjoy cooperative learning activities as opposed to activities that require directing and controlling.

They also may not feel at home when working emotionally with teams and likely will be quiet and in the background when involved in training activities. If you are one of these styles you may need to step back and realize your strength when working with passive types. Being forceful isn't bad, but sometimes it scares people if it's too strong, so be aware of your no nonsense approach to other people.

Because of your style, emotional "feeler" types will likely avoid you. Some may think you are selfish and self-absorbed so you must remind yourself that helping others also helps yourself. Many will see you as reserved and closed to their emotional appeals if you are much lower than the national mean within this impulse. People will misunderstand your motives.

Even though you may care about people, some will think you have a funny way of showing it. You may be cutthroat when competing with others if you're dominant and logic based, but not if you are a people person. If you have a high theoretical mindset and you are dominant you will have little patience for stupidity.

If you're like this make sure the person is at least trying before passing judgment. Remember that some people simply take longer to learn. I don't want you to get the idea that all lower Altruistic styles are hard to get along with or that they are difficult people because that would be a tragic conclusion. Working with others can feel like they are working in spite of you, as opposed to working with you in a friendly, open, meaningful way.

What I'm saying is that most of the time, when people measure far below the national norm within this attitude, they are distrusting and protective of their space as a rule—there are always exceptions.

Altruism Vs. Empathy

I have found that although an individual may not be so willing to sacrifice what is there's for someone else, it has little to do with their level of empathy. It is for this reason that I have discovered that you cannot confuse the two. Some people are highly outgoing and often willing to lend a hand but they only see what is missing in other people. Conversely, I have seen those who do not like giving up their time and energy to others except when they qualify and yet they display a higher level of empathy.

Altruism is largely based on sharing time and energy through social exchanging while empathy is rooted in one's ability to *feel into* another and usually at great expense. Empathy is associated with "intrinsic value." When a person sees into another and recognizes they have value in and of themselves and without comparison. An empathetically driven person will always be willing to sacrifice, but not all people who are willing to sacrifice are empathetic. This is why it's important to understand the difference. Empathy is seeing other persons as unique individuals; the emotional, spiritual, irreplaceable worth of others.

It's about understanding the value of a *person* as they exist outside of time. It's the ability to see and appreciate the inner worth of others; to see and accept others "as they are" without placing any stipulations or expectations on them outside of what they already have. The best way to describe it would be "the ability to see and accept others as is."

Sacrificial: "I'll not loaning you the money. I told you last time that if you do not fix your spending problems you'll have to find someone else to fund you through your problems."

Empathetic: "But honey; he doesn't have any money. Let's just get him through this rough spot and he'll be back on his feet."

Sacrificial: "Money doesn't grow on trees! I've given him roughly 12,000 dollars over the last three years! Isn't it time he learned?"

Empathetic: "But he's our son!" (crying)

Sacrificial: "He's playing us!"

Duel Altruistic Convergences

Again, I already talked about duel convergence so I will not further elaborate on how these factors work. You may reference the information in an earlier chapter if you need to brush up on convergences.

ALT/H–AES/L (Beneficial): This value factor associates *selflessness* with *real-world thinking*. When the altruistic value is high and the aesthetic value is low you will have no inner conflict. This will create a strong real-world and directive approach to solving other people's problems and challenges. This will cause a *realistic* rather than a unconventional approach to others. This person may be direct and time-sensitive.

ALT/H–AES/H (Creative-Supporter): This value factor associates *selflessness* with *unconventionality*. These two forces are not contrary when competing. When the altruistic value is high and the aesthetic value is high you will likely have an unorthodox helper.

There's a need to *experience* the surroundings with a sense having to share the experience.

ALT/H–ECO/L (Lose-Winner): This value factor associates *selflessness* with *satisfaction*. These two forces are in conflict when both are in play. When the altruistic value is high and the economic value is low you will have no inner conflict. This individual will endeavor to support and cooperate with others at the expense of self. Helping others win is a win for the self.

ALT/H–ECO/H (Conflicted): This value factor associates *selflessness* with *selfishness*. These two forces are in conflicted when both are in play (rare). When the altruistic value is high and the economic value is high you will have a me-me conflict. This will cause a vacillation between helping others or helping one's self. The outcome will largely depend on the soft skill emotions and their consistency levels. High optimism and patience will lend towards assistance. Lower consistencies will not.

ALT/H–IND/H (Star-Supporter): This value factor associates *selflessness* with *independence*. These two forces are not in conflict when both are in play. When the individualistic value is high and the altruistic value is high you will have no inner conflict. This individual will endeavor to support and cooperate with others with a need for excessive attention or the spotlight.

ALT/H–IND/L (Team-Player): This value factor associates *selflessness* with *security*. These two forces are in harmony when both are in play. When the individualistic value is low and the altruistic value is high you will have no conflict. This will create a cooperative team player. Assisting others comes easy to this style for a lack of a need for attention.

ALT/H–POW/L (Pushover): This value factor associates *selflessness* with *submission*. These two forces are not usually conflicted when both are in play. When the altruistic value is high and the power value is low you will have no conflict. This will create a style that surrenders to challenges and settles for the road of least resistance.

ALT/H–POW/H (Passionate): This value factor associates *selflessness* with *control*. These two forces are conflicted when both are in play. When the altruistic value is high and the power value is high you will have some conflict. This will create a style that expels a lot of controlling energy when assisting others. They may force others to do things differently for others' benefit.

ALT/H–REG/L (Teachable): This value factor associates *selflessness* with *defiance*. These two forces are maximized when both are in play. When the regulated value is low and the altruistic value is high you will have no inner conflict. This individual will insist on multithreaded and subversive approaches to solving other people's problems and will be open to new ideas.

ALT/H–REG/H (Missional): This value factor associates *selflessness* with *compliance*. These two forces are strengthened when both are in play. When the altruistic value is high and the regulated value is high you will have no inner conflict. This individual may insist on specific ways of doing things and may hold others to the same standard of operation they hold themselves to. They are missional and believe in doing the right thing at any cost.

ALT/H–THE/L (Street-Smart): This value factor associates *selflessness* with *intuition*. These two forces are neutralized when both are in play. When the altruistic value is high and the theoretical value is low you will have no inner conflict. This individual will rely on intuition, instinct, and past experiences for helping others grow.

ALT/H–THE/H (Instructive): This value factor associates *selflessness* with *fact-finding*. These two forces are neutralized when both are in play. When the altruistic value is high and the theoretical value is high you will have no inner conflict. This individual will rely on interesting facts for leveraging how to maximize others in the world. These types can be very complex.

ALT/L–AES/H (Creative-Avoidance): This value factor associates *distrust* with *unconventionality*. These two forces are not in conflict when both are in play. When the altruistic value is low and the aesthetic value is high you will have no inner conflict. This will create unconventionally-imaginative and original approaches to avoiding those who do not fit your ideals.

ALT/L–AES/L (No-Nonsense): This value factor associates *distrust* with *real-world thinking*. These two forces are maximized when both are in play. When the altruistic value is low and the aesthetic value is low you will have no inner conflict. This will create a practical no-nonsense style who will not usually tolerate shenanigans.

ALT/L–IND/H (Independent): This value factor associates *distrust* with *autonomy*. These two forces are not in conflict when both are in play. When the altruistic value is low and the individualistic value is high you will have no inner conflict. This individual will endeavor to meet their own needs and find their own way regardless of what others think.

ALT/L–IND/L (Self-Assured): This value factor associates *distrust* with *security*. These two forces are in harmony when both are in play. When the individualistic value is low and the altruistic value is low you will have no conflict. This will create guarded style who expects others to qualify before entering into their private space. They may over-focus on what is missing in other people.

ALT/L–ECO/H (Gainer): This value factor associates *distrust* with *self-mastery*. These two forces are in conflict when both are in play. When the altruistic value is low and the economic value is high you will have no inner conflict. This individual will endeavor to support self without attention others. Some may see them as cold or unconcerned about others. They believe in eating their own kill and not sharing it with everyone who wants it.

ALT/L–ECO/L (Internalized): This value factor associates *distrust* with *satisfaction*. These two forces are conflicted when both are in play. When the altruistic value is low and the economic value is low you will have conflict. This will create a guarded style who keeps to themselves. This style may over-focus on what is missing in other people.

ALT/L–POW/H (Authoritarian): This value factor associates *distrust* with *authority*. These two forces are in conflict when both are in play. When the altruistic value is low and the power value is high you will have no inner conflict. This individual will endeavor to control others and tell them what to do. They will distrust those they know little about and may show disdain for those who don't carry their own weight.

ALT/L–POW/L (Tentative): This value factor associates *distrust* with *submission*. These two forces are in minimal conflict when both are in play. When the altruistic value is low and the power value is low you will have minimal conflict (rare). This will create a guarded style who keeps to themselves and hangs back in groups.

ALT/L–REG/H (Imposing): This value factor associates *distrust* with *systemic thinking*. These two forces are not in conflict when both are in play. When the altruistic value is low and the regulated value is high you will have no inner conflict. This individual is rigid and may be punitive in nature. They are strict or *narrow* in their thinking. They may impose their rules or ideas on others.

ALT/L–REG/L (Felonious): This value factor associates *distrust* with *subversion*. These two forces are not in conflict when both are in play. When the altruistic value is low and the regulated value is low you will have no inner conflict. This individual may have a criminal mind. In other words, they may covertly seek to do things their own way at the expense of others. Rules are determined worthy only when they work in their best interest.

ALT/L–THE/H (Know-It-All): This value factor associates *distrust* with *factual*. These two forces are neutralized when both are in play. When the altruistic value is low and the theoretical value is high you will have no inner conflict. This individual will see those of lesser intelligence as stupid and uninformed.

ALT/L–THE/L (Ill-Considered): This value factor associates *distrust* with *street-smarts*. These two forces are neutralized when both are in play. When the altruistic value is low and the theoretical value is low you will have no inner conflict. This style is intuitive and resists over-working their cognitive mind. They may be subject to errors in judgment and might scan material without reading all of it. They may resist others help and see them as nosey or intrusive when questioned.

Situational Sacrificial Consistency

To reiterate, these are values *not* behaviors. Values speak of our *desires* and what moves us in a directional effort. Keep also in mind that this list is associated with a single value element and not the *integrated motivational orientation*, which includes all seven value elements. What we desire can often conflict with what we will actually do.

Keep in mind that this list is in no way exhaustive. Individuals with a *general* or situational (situational/midpoint) consistency and direction within the *single* motivational element of altruism will likely:

1. Be a stabilizing force between givers and takers without having an extreme view of either one.
2. Both help and hold back depending on the situation at hand.
3. Think clearly and logically about the needs of others while keeping things in perspective.
4. Understand the poor and the affluent without passing judgment on either one.

5. Have a balanced outlook when assisting those who may be scamming the system.
6. Be able to pitch in when necessary and also say "no" when you've had enough.
7. Be able to take a stand for injustice while letting some seemingly unjust situations ride.
8. Understand when helping becomes a hindrance to someone's long-term success.
9. Not be moved by every sob story that comes down the pike.
10. Be able to appreciate giving a helping hand and doing hard work while understanding the differences between the two clearly.
11. Be pragmatic in your efforts to assist others.
12. Be a good judge as to how often you should "bail" someone out of an existing pattern.
13. Be uncomfortable with those who are taken advantage of or give to others in excess.
14. Be uncomfortable with those who over-focus on themselves.

Very High Sacrificial Consistency

Remember, these are values not behaviors. Values speak of our *desires* and what moves us in a directional effort. Keep also in mind that this list is associated with a single value element and not the *integrated motivational orientation*. What we desire can often conflict with what we will actually do. Keep in mind that this list is in no way exhaustive.

Individuals with *very high* (situational/midpoint) consistency and direction within the *single* motivational element of sacrifice will likely cause them to:

1. Put others first while placing themselves last.
2. Be overly cognizant of the underdog.
3. Feel compelled to assist the unfortunate.
4. Believe it's better to give than to receive.

5. Believe "you can't take it with you."
6. See others as more important than yourself.
7. See the value in others much sooner than they can see the value in themselves.
8. Be sincere to a fault.
9. Find greater value in doing for others while resisting when others want to do for them.
10. Give things away as opposed to selling them.
11. Believe losing is good when the loss is beneficial to others who do not win regularly.
12. Connect personally before connecting professionally.
13. Appreciate kind and good-hearted people types.
14. Look for purpose and meaning in everything they do.
15. Be always willing to volunteer their time and efforts.
16. Treat others with respect and care.
17. Be compulsive in care-giving.
18. Exaggerate the needs of others while minimizing their own.

Very Low Sacrificial Consistency

Individuals with *very low* (situational/midpoint) consistency and direction within the *single* motivational element of sacrifice will likely:

1. Be able to do the harder things when it comes to people decisions.
2. Be able to separate emotions from necessary actions.
3. Be difficult to take advantage of.
4. See certain people coming from a mile away.
5. Be less likely to put up with nonsense.
6. Have a no nonsense approach to horse-sense.
7. Not be afraid to say "no."
8. Avoid "stupid" people.
9. Make decisions that will benefit their future.
10. Take problems and challenges seriously.
11. Be able to stop an intruder dead in their tracks.
12. Not shy away from difficult decisions.

13. Have a low tolerance for wasted time and energy.
14. Have little to no patience for ignorance.
15. Connect all outcomes to practical needs as opposed to people needs.
16. Have little tolerance for those who are wishy-washy.
17. Have a suspicious view of others whose motives may be unclear.
18. See others as intruders.
19. See others as guilty until proven innocent.
20. Be distrusting of others as a rule.
21. Be emotionally detached from others be keeping an emotional distance.

As you may have noticed, the altruistic value element is the part of the whole value structure that represents our desire to better others at personal expense. It's our desire or need to be on the losing end. Unlike ambition and power elements, it's getting lost or potentially swallowed by those around us. Let's now take a look at the regulatory element. This value is what gives us our sense right and wrong ways of doing things.

9
COMPLIANCE AND REGULATED THINKING

What is regulated thinking? We'll get in to that in a moment, but I first want to get us familiar with what this attitude was all about when Eduard Spranger first brought it to the public's attention. This was formally known as a "religious" attitude.[93] I refer to the current model as compliance, which is another way of expressing a regulated thought pattern. We will discuss this in the section on regulated thinking.

According to Spranger, "Life is an alternating play of experiences whose content depends upon two factors; fate, in the broadest sense of the term, and the soul structure of the experiencing subject. These experiences contain values in varying degrees, in other words, the meaning of each experience sounds a value-tone in the mind of the individual experiencing it. But this does not imply that the value experience is always adequate to express the objective content of the mental context in question.

For, it may be relatively isolated, unconnected either by feeling or reflection with the total life. If, on the other hand, an isolated value experience, no matter how subjective, is grasped in its significance for the total meaning of life, it has a *religious* emphasis."[94] Spranger goes on to postulate that these religious values accumulate into what he calls the "highest value experience." The religious value element is thus defined by the condition, instinctive or rational, in which a single experience is either positively or negatively related to the "total value of life."

---

93 Eduard Spranger; Types of Men, 1928, p. 210.
94 Ibid.

Some currently call this value a "traditional" value. A tradition is a belief or behavior passed down within a group or society with symbolic meaning or special significance with origins in the past. In this context, traditions have life-altering *meaning* which is why they have been cherished and passed down through the ages. In this sense, a tradition therefore, is associated with a high value experience as defined by Spranger.

The concepts of tradition and traditional values are frequently used in political and religious discourse in hopes of establishing the *legitimacy* of a particular set of values. In the United States in the twentieth and twenty-first centuries, the concept of tradition has been used to argue for the centrality and legitimacy of conservative religious values.[95] It is for this reason that those who score high on a traditional value index will likely have strong beliefs based upon a "wright and wrong" set of ideas.

Those who score high in this traditional element are usually black and white thinkers when it comes to what they *believe* and how they believe people should conduct themselves. Because of the either/or nature of this mindset, and because in its root there are imaginary penalties for violating boundaries, they leave no wiggle room for themselves or others when boundaries are crossed. The one unfortunate trait associated with this value element is that they hold those outside of themselves to the same iron clad rules they hold themselves to.

Black and White Thinking

First of all, do not associate black and white thinking with Borderline Personality Disorder (BPD). Borderline Personality Disorder is associated with a psychological term known as "splitting." Traditional thinking has nothing to do with this. Whereas BPD needs professional treatment, a traditional value

---

95 Bronner, Simon J. "Tradition" in International Encyclopedia of the Social Sciences. Ed. William A. Darity, Jr.. Vol. 8. 2nd ed. Detroit: Macmillan Reference USA, 2008. p420-422.

mindset does not. Borderline Personality Disorder is a mental illness marked by an ongoing pattern of varying moods, self-image, and behavior. These symptoms often result in impulsive actions and problems in relationships. People with borderline personality disorder may experience intense episodes of anger, depression, and anxiety that can last from a few hours to days.[96] Black and White Thinking as it relates to Spranger's religious or *traditional* value element hypothesizes that there's one way to do a thing—the right way.

If you're a high traditional thinker then you likely think, "It's tight but it's right." This style is what I call the OTP or the Old Testament Parent—"I brought you into this world, I can take you out." They believe, "If it isn't broken, we shouldn't try to fix it." To really place this idea into a workable context, think of living up to an ideal. Traditional thinkers view the world through a particular lens. They "receive" their marching orders from a higher value system than their own; they believe that they answer to a *higher* authority.

Traditional Concepts in Religion

Although traditional religions are designed to encourage the individuals through communal activities, tribalism, solidarity, and conversion processes that hopefully unite them with the gods and ensures their safe passage into eternal life, it has a fundamental flaw at its root. Religion acts as a seemingly necessary framework for positive self-maintenance, self-esteem, role-awareness, self-direction, and communal benevolence. Unfortunately, it creates the very thing it's designed to destroy—performance initiatives.

Granted, many religions support a positive-self and generally bring better self-awareness and self-esteem to most people who might lack it, but the process typically begins on a negative, as it must in order to warrant its imposition. The idea of a negative-self

---

[96] National Institute of Mental Health.

was likely birthed through the theory of the *fall of man* within the garden myth, which speaks of the "disobedience of *all* mankind" early on in the Hebrew narrative found in the Genesis account. This is an ancient Hebrew attempt at understanding the *duality* within us all through the power of story.

Religion thus provides a traditional based framework for people to live *within* that allows for creating distinctions between what many see as right and wrong behaviors. In other words, the role of religion is to create a cosmic "standard" for mankind to fall short of while ensuring a roadmap for living up to it along with boundaries upheld by rewards and punishments to guarantee one stays within it. At first glance, it appears to be somewhat successful, but is it really?

Fig. 1

Motivational Direction and Consistency Graph
Compliance

			0	10	20	30	40	50	60	70	80	90	100
ORIGINALITY	26	4	0	10	20	30	40	50	60	70	80	90	100
EFFICIENCY	40	5	0	10	20	30	40	50	60	70	80	90	100
INDIVIDUALITY	64	6	0	10	20	30	40	50	60	70	80	90	100
POWER	86	2	0	10	20	30	40	50	60	70	80	90	100
SACRIFICE	84	1	0	10	20	30	40	50	60	70	80	90	100
COMPLIANCE	69	3	0	10	20	30	40	50	60	70	80	90	100
CURIOSITY	61	7	0	10	20	30	40	50	60	70	80	90	100

I have come to a startling realization; most traditionally minded people need an *external* reference point in order to make the many distinctions regarding their self-worth and their intrinsic value as it relates to the world. This, I suggest, is a phenomenon. But there's a fundamental difficulty; people's perceptions differ widely based upon cultural norms, individual knowledge bases, life experiences, upbringing, and geographies—not all people feel the same way, nor do all have the same mind.

Unfortunately, there's a guaranteed singularity that seems to persist among traditional minded humans; it's never enough to simply believe something for one's self and enjoy that belief in private—we must create a solicitous in-group forcing everyone else to believe it *with* us if it's going to have any real meaning or evidential merit. The larger the in-group, the truer the associated beliefs become.

Religion appears to do for us what we cannot *allow* ourselves to do *for* ourselves. In other words, if God says I'm good then I'm most definitely good, but if I alone say, "I'm good apart from what God might think," there will inevitably be another person somewhere in space-time who could announce that I may *not* be as good as I originally thought I was and therefore may influence others to believe it as well.

As a matter of fact, if I say I am good without any God saying so, then those within the traditional system may deny my claim altogether. Furthermore, this idea of God declaring we are good or not good not only trumps our behaviors in regards to how we think about our behaviors (in light of what we believe God and people think about us behaving badly), it ultimately modifies our behaviors.

When the traditional either/or attribute is applied to this model, a black and white mindset accompanies it. Ideas become right or wrong and good or bad—there's no wiggle room. Our values become more instinctive because they tend to run on auto-pilot. We don't really consciously think about them; we simply believe them in the unconscious background.

Thinking does not have to be the enemy of belief; it can also help support or discourage a bad belief. Thinking mustn't always be subject to belief as if the belief has more enormity. Both thinking *and* believing are done within the same mind—they cannot be separated so easily. People's beliefs differ in that people and what they value are fundamentally different just as our fingerprints differ. Thinking is an essential part of being human—we have the capacity to think for a very good reason—it keeps us safe.

For example, one male mindset might believe it is a good thing to physically and brutally beat a woman into submission because of cultural standards, religious fundamentalism, and acceptances within their personal religious frameset; however, another male mindset may believe that it's good to support the "weaker vessel" because he believes it was the woman who was first deceived and not the man as the Genesis narrative suggests and St. Paul affirms.

One believes a woman to be completely inferior, while another believes many women to be *silly*[97] or gullible (weaker) as St. Paul believed. Judaism is a shame-based culture with a patriarchal frame of mind—men are in charge. Good is therefore subject to an individual's perception, which can differ enormously between people and is based upon one's personal interests, attitudes, worldview, culture, or upbringing. In other words, without an outside influence (outside of this physical world system or planet) establishing a standard rule of conduct, people tend towards what appears to be right in their own eyes.

In other words, while one believes it's okay to have a glass of wine, another believes it to be a sin. Both should respect their own beliefs without passing judgment on the other, but because of the traditional mindset it becomes increasingly hard not to judge. Unfortunately, many with strict *traditionally* driven mindsets cannot allow others to participate in whatever they themselves believe to be wrong.

If it's wrong for me to do this and such, it's wrong for you to do it as well. This can be harmful to a society if those who are at the top

---

2 2 Timothy 3:6: "They are the kind who worm their way into homes and gain control over gullible women, who are loaded down with sins and are swayed by all kinds of evil desires" NIV.

administer authority *over* others in harmful ways through ego-driven behaviors, encouraged by a poor sense of self and supported through a religious effort. Otherwise we settle for doing what seems right based on worldviews, community norms, education, or perhaps natural instinct.

These imposed rules are a human phenomenon and are prevalent in not just a few religious communities. The Torah, the Koran, the Bible, the Book of Mormon, the Apocrypha, and other works of standard rules for conduct, provide a peripheral scaffold for emotional reliance and stability and behavioral modification. But if these rules are to be followed, there must, unfortunately, be introduced into the system a process of rewards and punishments to ensure its celestial weight and continued enforcement by the people that preside over it. Do *this* or else *thus* becomes the driver.

All religions offer traditional rules of conduct that if violated spell dread and punishment in some form for all offenders. Christianity for example, offers hell for those in rebellion against the guidelines of conduct or to the unbeliever, whom they believe to be living outside the clearly drawn lines. Hell, by definition, is the naughty step—forever. Hell is believed to be where the violators will reside for all eternity after transition.

Flames of fire, torture, screaming regret, and pain are a few descriptors that are designed to thwart unwanted behaviors into following the religious orders set in stone by traditional texts and leaders. Spranger doesn't go as far as I am with these ideas around the religious value element, but these are its consequences regardless. I'm not saying religion is bad, I'm saying this is how religion works. This is how the religious value element functions. An inside and outside dimension is created within this value component. Folks are seen by very high traditional thinkers as either *in* or *out* of the celestial system. In is good, out is bad.

That being said, those perceived to be living outside of any system designed around traditional operating procedures can be harmful to the customarily-minded community and are typically expelled. It is these distinguishing trademarks within all traditional religious institutions that perpetuate the prison of performance and enable those to follow hard after the correct behaviors acceptable to both the community as a whole and the deity who smiles upon them when they properly perform within the valued guidelines.

People must understand this fundamental truth; behavior is modified best by what we believe to be the best reason for its correction. The claim that behavioral modification is the authentic sign that one has found the true faith or the one true God is both irrational and fallacious. For example, obnoxious persons will alter their behavior for the simple reason that they are in a library.

A suitor will alter his behavior in order to get the girl, and so on. Any religious in-group will be filled with converts who have aligned behaviorally with what is expected by the traditionally set code of conduct handed down in order to ensure membership within the coveted tribe. Behaving well is necessary for inclusion within any religious system.

Regulated Thinking

Regulated thinking is not the same as religious or traditional thinking although it's vaguely similar. Regulated thinking is based on the same principle but is associated with how things *should* be. Religion is how things are—on earth as it is in heaven. Much like the systemic dimension in formal axiology, it's a dimension of formal concepts—ideas of "how things should be." This dimension is the one of definitions, ideals, goals, structured thinking, policies, procedures, rules, laws, ought's and should's.

It is one of perfection. If a person values something or someone systemically, then that person must fulfill the idea perfectly or completely. In other words, you either have obeyed the law (a mental idea of how we should act) or you have not obeyed the law (the non-fulfillment of the idea). This is an either/or dimension much like traditional thinking, but it has no religious connotations.

For example, a woman is either pregnant (a mental definition of a state of being) or is not pregnant (does not perfectly fulfill all the aspects of the definition of pregnant). You cannot be sort of pregnant. Here the valuation is based on total and complete fulfillment of an idea. There is no middle ground or partial fulfillment in the systemic—no grey.

You either perfectly fulfill the concept (ideal, definition, law, policy, etc.) of pregnancy or you do not fulfill the concept at all. Another example of systemic or regulated valuing is displayed by the definition of a geometric square. If a square is not a square then it's not a square. A square is a regular quadrilateral, which means that it has four equal sides and four equal angles (90-degree angles, or (100-gradian angles or right angles).

Fig. 2

Motivational Direction and Consistency Graph
Compliance

ORIGINALITY	26	4	0	10	20	30	40	50	60	70	80	90	100
EFFICIENCY	40	5	0	10	20	30	40	50	60	70	80	90	100
INDIVIDUALITY	64	6	0	10	20	30	40	50	60	70	80	90	100
POWER	36	2	0	10	20	30	40	50	60	70	80	90	100
SACRIFICE	68	3	0	10	20	30	40	50	60	70	80	90	100
COMPLIANCE	85	1	0	10	20	30	40	50	60	70	80	90	100
CURIOSITY	61	7	0	10	20	30	40	50	60	70	80	90	100

If an object fulfills this exact definition, then it is a geometric square. If it lacks only one element of the definition, then it is not a geometric square. Every definition is an *idea*. To value something in this way is to give it *systemic* valuation. It is either a total fulfillment or a non-fulfillment of the idea. The systemic valuing dimension is the world of Yes/No, black/white, and should's. There are no possible shades of maybe or partiality. Again, the concept is either fulfilled or it is not fulfilled.

"The mathematical properties of this dimension are finite sets and finite elements (that is, a limited number of choices and a limited number of properties for the object in question). This dimension is the chief aspect of geometry, physical science, law, dogmatism, long range planning, policies and procedures, doing things right, ideals, principles, personal attainment of one's goals, schematic thinking, order, prejudice, and perfection.

When a person pays too much attention to this dimension or over-values the concept the resultant behavior is an overemphasis on doing thing by the book. There becomes an excessive preoccupation with doing things a *certain* way; a strong tendency to measure everything and everyone against a preset *idea* of how they should be, and an inability to be comfortable with changes and surprises that do not reflect certainty.

When a person does not pay enough attention to this value dimension, the resultant behavior is an unwillingness to submit to policies and rules imposed from the outside, a skepticism about the value of spending time and money planning for the future, and an uneasiness when systems are in place and running smoothly."[98] Overtly or covertly doing things in their own creative way is the result.

High Regulated Value Impulses

An individual with an intensified valuing of regulation wouldn't do certain things for a million dollars. They're very strict on themselves and are very traditionally-minded although not

---

98 Zeke Lopez; axiologist. Granule.

necessarily religious. The odds are usually against the breaking of rules because these people are enforcers. Does this mean no rules are ever broken? No, it does happen. And when it does, they will justify (to themselves) the breaking of these moral codes. If they break one—they always have a reason they believe makes them justified in doing so. Others often see those with this consistency as narrow-minded because they believe there's only one-way to skin a cat; their way. They will usually stick with traditional means that they know work or fulfill their conceptual idea and reject everything else.

This is a black and white thinker. If you fall into this category, you are likely very hard on yourself and others. You'll hold others to your standards. In your family, you're likely the "bad cop" if you score higher in the value index. You're looking for a cause and a purpose and will want others to have the same purpose you have—if it's wrong for me to breastfeed in public, it's wrong for you to breastfeed in public as well.

This style also understands and appreciates authorities and figureheads. They will strive to *convert* others to their own way of thinking; and it's very hard to change their mind. Taking commands from someone else is like swimming in handcuffs for this style. They'll struggle with those who are too open-minded and will see them as careless and untidy. For this person, using someone else's method may feel like wearing a strait jacket.

High regulatory driven people believe certain things for a long time without updating their ideas, especially when engaged in religion and politics. They want to color within the lines and expect others to do the same—if it's wrong for them it's wrong for everyone. These styles create a system around their actions if one isn't present.

Their ideas tend to be reliable, but even when they're not, they won't likely give up on those ideas anytime soon. They will feel the need to reign others in, especially their children or their mate when they wander outside the lines. They like to think for themselves *and* for everyone else. They'll remind everyone of the rules they forgot. These styles will likely take things seriously while others are goofing off believing they should hold themselves to a higher ideal. They rarely give people three chances—they're either in or out. Once these styles decide, it's decided. They like to be standing while everyone else is falling. These people are very black and white thinkers and will therefore have very strong views and opinions.

My mother was a very high regulated thinker. I was arguing with my mother when I was 24 years old because I disagreed with something she believed. Her response was, "Listen Steve, I have forgotten more than you will ever know." I suppose that was meant to silence me. I had hit an invisible wall; there was no changing her mind.

Seeing they won't cross certain lines, they rarely give others permission to cross their own lines. Enforcing their ideas on others, these people believe they are correct. If not copiously convinced, their mind will not likely change. This style works well with the scared thinker because not only do they believe they are right, they will look diligently for the proof of their rightness.

Other people will see this style as rigid, unbending, and dogmatic. Typically found in the military, law enforcement, and in the clergy, those with a high regulatory impulse desire to call the moral shots. If you are like this you may want to expand your horizon a bit and take a few risks. You may also want to realize that others could be highly put off by this dogmatism and tight/right mindset.

Of course, all these styles vary in their consistency, but when this style is very high on the values index, they become increasingly difficult to work with on all levels, especially if they're highly political/controlling. Plusses include systematic thinking, systems management, and systems creation if none are present, holding to standards, and either/or thinking.

Power Needs and Regulation

When one sports a high power value and a high regulated value things take another turn. This creates an Enforcer. When these value elements are very high, the style can be difficult to work and live with. Adding a high dominant emotion increases this dynamic to a fevered pitch. Imagine the strong black and white thinking element combined with a need to control one's space and destiny. This can be highly restrictive in what one allows another person to do in their space.

Law enforcement officers, ministers, judges, school principals, and military leaders may have this dynamic within their value base. These types do not feel at home in the body unless they have full control of their surroundings and everybody in them. Others become *subjects* as opposed to peers or subordinates. People are subject to their wants and needs. Without strong behavioral tendencies such as directedness or optimism, these types can become extremely passive-aggressive.

Of course, when the regulated value is much lower, the restrictions cease and the need to do things according to strict guidelines is highly diminished. They will want to control the environment but will be open-minded as to the available options for moving through that same environment. Low regulated or low compliant thinkers are multithreaded in their approach to solving problems, meeting challenges, and creating opportunities.

Lower Regulated Impulses

You march to the beat of your own drum when your passion is low in this dimension. You believe nothing is in stone. You will likely hate it when people refuse to believe things they don't fully understand. Coming up with inventive ways for getting things done is like pulling a rabbit out of a hat for these types. They will not like being constrained or restricted to certain protocols if their consistency is lower.

Akin to the low compliant in a behavior context (-C, -P), they are in need of freedom from the rules and regulations that *stifle* creative flow or independent thinking. They may think about and imagine jumping off a precipice and building their wings on the way down and will feel bogged down when forced to do things a "certain" way. They'll likely do things "by the book," but it's their book and not *someone else's* book.

The lower regulatory mindset works well with low compliance— it flows but will feel conflicted with a fear emotion in play (above the energy line). If their individualistic element is consistent with fear, they will feel inner conflict and will experience a block in flow. It will be like wanting to buy a Hummer but returning home with a Jeep—they will only *imagine* taking bold chances but will often error on the side of caution (fear) in the end.

Fig. 3

Motivational Direction and Consistency Graph
Compliance

ORIGINALITY	26	3	0	10	20	30	40	50	60	70	80	90	100
EFFICIENCY	40	5	0	10	20	30	40	50	60	70	80	90	100
INDIVIDUALITY	75	4	0	10	20	30	40	50	60	70	80	90	100
POWER	68	6	0	10	20	30	40	50	60	70	80	90	100
SACRIFICE	84	1	0	10	20	30	40	50	60	70	80	90	100
COMPLIANCE	17	2	0	10	20	30	40	50	60	70	80	90	100
CURIOSITY	61	7	0	10	20	30	40	50	60	70	80	90	100

Having your dreams "relegated" only to your imagination can be grueling for some. Lower regulating elements when coupled with individualism will be looking for freedom, independence and autonomous actions—free from unnecessary restrictions. Not wanting to be controlled by others or by the rules, this style (like the low fear emotion) wants to be *independent of* as opposed to being *dependent on* anything. The individualism creates a strong independent person who is looking to do things their own unique way.

This will also work with lesser systemic outlooks within the HVP model of Axiology (how their choices work with established systems, rules, and protocols—see above). Even though these levels are within the value framework, behavior will always find a way to trump or overpower the outcome.

In other words, an intense fear emotion in behavior will not likely succumb to a low regulatory value need. Neither will a low anger orientation succumb to a high power value need. This is very important to know. In other words, although they may fantasize about driving a Hummer (+IND, -REG), they may very well end up purchasing a Jeep (+S, +C).

The high fear emotion will always contradict the value impulse to entertain risk thus creating risk-avoidance. This is known as a *me-me* conflict response.

Fig. 4

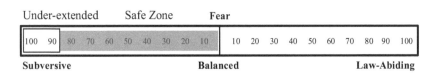

Duel Regulated Convergences

Again, I already talked about duel convergence so I will not further elaborate on how these factors work. You may reference the information in an earlier chapter if you need to brush up on convergences.

REG/H–AES/L (Structured): This value factor associates *compliance* with *real-world thinking*. When the regulating value is high, and the aesthetic value is low you will have no inner conflict. This will create a strong real-world and structured approach to the world. This will cause a *realistic* rather than an unconventional approach to challenges. This person may be direct, controlling and time-sensitive.

REG/H–AES/H (Creative-Structured): This value factor associates *compliances* with *unconventionality*. These two forces are contrary when competing. When the regulating value is high, and the aesthetic value is high you will likely have an unorthodox enforcer. There's a need to *experience* the rules with a sense having to solicit others to follow them.

REG/H–ECO/L (Missional): This value factor associates *compliance* with *satisfaction*. When the regulating value is high, and the economic value is low you will have no inner conflict. This individual will endeavor to support and cooperate with others while maintaining compliance and following protocols.

REG/H–ECO/H (Efficient): This value factor associates *compliance* with *efficiency*. When the regulated value is high, and the economic value is high you will seek to comply with expected operating procedures for gaining the best outcomes. Rules are seen as the most effective and pragmatic means to an end.

REG/H–IND/H (Self-Structured): This value factor associates *compliance* with *independence*. These two forces are in conflict when both are in play. When the individualistic value is high, and the regulating value is high you will have inner conflict. This individual will endeavor to maintain individualism through self-disciplinary actions and structured processes.

REG/H–IND/L (Teacher): This value factor associates *compliance* with *security*. When the individualistic value is low, and the regulating value is high you will have no conflict. This will create a cooperative rule follower. Assisting others with the proper way of doing things comes easy to this style for a lack of a need for attention.

REG/H–POW/L (Passive-Aggressive): This value factor associates *compliance* with *accommodation*. These two forces are not in conflict when both are in play. When the power value is low, and the regulating value is high you will have minimal inner conflict. This individual will endeavor to desire more than they may be willing to do. They will be more suggestive than confrontive when following procedures.

REG/H–POW/H (Enforcing): This value factor associates *compliance* with *control*. These two forces are not in conflict when both are in play. When the power value is high, and the regulating value is high you will have no inner conflict. This individual will endeavor to control those within their space and exercise authority over them. They will be more aggressive and enforcing when pushing others to follow procedures.

REG/H–ALT/L (Constraining): This value factor associates *compliance* with *suspicion*. These two forces are not in conflict when both are in play. When the sacrificial value is low, and the regulating value is high you will have no inner conflict. This individual will endeavor to control through establishing rules and protocols for others to follow with little concern to how it makes them feel.

REG/H–ALT/H (Missional): This value factor associates *compliance* with *sacrifice*. These two forces are not in conflict when both are in play. When the sacrificial value is high, and the regulating value is high you will have no inner conflict. This individual will endeavor to follow a cause and create a mission. They believe others will be better off if they follow their guidelines.

REG/H–THE/L (Intuitively-Structured): This value factor associates *regulation* with *intuition*. These two forces are neutralized when both are in play. When the regulating value is high, and the theoretical value is low you will have no inner conflict. This individual will rely on intuition, instinct, and past experiences for maintaining and rule following.

REG/H–THE/H (Corrective): This value factor associates *compliance* with *fact-finding*. These two forces are neutralized when both are in play. When the regulating value is high, and the theoretical value is high you will have no inner conflict. This individual will seek ways to control others by using their ignorance against them and pointing out their lack of knowledge.

REG/L–AES/H (Revolutionary): This value factor associates *defiance* with *creativity*. When the regulating value is low, and the aesthetic value is high you will have no inner conflict. This will create a strong out-of-the-box and revolutionary approach to the world. This will cause a an unconventional approach to challenges. This person may be direct, insurrectionary and less time-sensitive.

REG/L–AES/L (Pragmatic): This value factor associates *defiance* with *reality*. These two forces are contrary when competing. When the regulating value is low, and the aesthetic value is low you will likely have real-world rebel. There's a need to *defy* the rules with a sense having to be conventional.

REG/L–ALT/H (Undisciplined): This value factor associates *defiance* with *sacrifice*. When the regulating value is low, and the altruistic value is high you will have no inner conflict. This will create a missional style that sees any available means for assisting others.

REG/L–ALT/L (Free-Wheeling): This value factor associates *defiance* with *suspicion*. These two forces are maximized when both are in play. When the regulating value is low, and the sacrificial value is low you will have no inner conflict. This will create a more dangerous style that may pull out all the stops at the expense of others to gain what one wants.

REG/L–IND/H (Autonomous): This value factor associates *defiance* with *autonomy*. These two forces are in conflict when both are in play. When the regulating value is low, and the individualistic value is high you will have no inner conflict. This individual will seek freedom, autonomy, and any means to an end.

REG/L–IND/L (Measured-Down): This value factor associates *defiance* with *security*. These two forces are not in harmony when both are in play. When the individualistic value is low, and the regulating value is low you will have minimal conflict. This will create a casual approach to the world with a possible undercurrent of unsuspecting subversive behaviors.

REG/L–ECO/H (Triumphant): This value factor associates *defiance* with *self-mastery*. These two forces are not in conflict when both are in play. When the regulating value is low, and the economic value is high you will have no inner conflict. This individual will endeavor to support self by any means. Some may see them as risky or defiant at times.

REG/L–ECO/L (Care-Free): This value factor associates *defiance* with *satisfaction*. These two forces are not conflicted when both are in play. When the regulating value is low, and the economic value is low you will have conflict. This will create a defiant style that reaps the whirlwind by neglecting standards with little energy to fix it.

REG/L–POW/H (Unrestricting): This value factor associates *defiance* with *authority*. These two forces are nor in conflict when both are in play. When the regulating value is low, and the power value is high you will have no inner conflict. This individual will endeavor to control others and tell them what to do. They will not follow the rules they hold others to. "Do as I say, not as I do" is the usual mantra.

REG/L–POW/L (Malleable): This value factor associates *defiance* with *submission*. These two forces are not in conflict when both are in play. When the regulating value is low, and the power value is low you will have minimal conflict. This will create a malleable style that may be easily influenced to break the rules.

REG/L–THE/H (Inventive): This value factor associates *defiance* with *factofinding*. These two forces are neutralized when both are in play. When the regulating value is low, and the theoretical value is high you will have no inner conflict. This individual will be resourceful and may find original and ingenious ways to solve problems.

REG/L–THE/L (Instinctual): This value factor associates *defiance* with *street-smarts*. These two forces are neutralized when both are in play. When the regulating value is low, and the theoretical value is low you will have no inner conflict. This style is intuitive and resists over-working their cognitive mind. They may be subject to errors in judgment and might scan material without reading all of it. They may resist standards, rules, and protocols at every opportunity.

Situational Regulative Consistency

To reiterate, these are values *not* behaviors. Values speak of our *desires* and what moves us in a directional effort. Keep also in mind that this list is associated with a single value element and not the *integrated motivational orientation*, which includes all seven value elements. What we desire can often conflict with what we will actually do.

Keep in mind that this list is in no way exhaustive. Individuals with a *general* or situational (situational/midpoint) consistency and direction within the *single* motivational element of regulation will likely:

1. Challenge rules that do not make any sense.
2. Fall generally in the middle when it comes to protocols and having to do things a certain way.

3. Accept authority but will not do it blindly especially if the authority figure does not obey their own rules.
4. Appreciate details to a point but will likely not depend on them.
5. Understand structure but will not be bound by another's idea if it does not work for them.
6. Be able to work with both leaders and followers and will bring something to the table with either one.
7. Fall in the middle when it comes to uniformity needs.
8. Have no extremes when it comes to regularity and dependence on methods that work.
9. Have no extremes when it comes to desiring an organized and stable environment.
10. Be a stabilizing member when necessary but can also do their own thing if required.
11. Be able to moderate those who may challenge established authorities while understanding both sides.
12. Be a situational doer, being able to work within established structures or within arenas that may lack guidelines.
13. Be able to challenge the establishment as long as you believe you have a better method of accomplishing a particular task.
14. Be both judgmental and merciful, depending on the situation.
15. Not be so closed that they can't see things in multiple dimensions.
16. Have both open and narrow views on many things.
17. Appreciate regularity and structure, but you are not controlled by this need.
18. Understand logical sequence but will be able to move things around when necessary.

Very High Regulative Consistency

Remember, these are values not behaviors. Values speak of our *desires* and what moves us in a directional effort. Keep also in mind that this list is associated with a single value element and not the *integrated motivational orientation.* What we desire can often conflict with what we will actually do. Keep in mind that this list is in no way exhaustive.

Individuals with *very high* (situational/midpoint) consistency and direction within the *single* motivational element of regulation will likely cause them to:

1. Think, "It's tight but it's right."
2. Be considered an Old Testament parent (OTP).
3. Think in terms of, "I brought you into this world, I can take you out," when dealing with their unruly children.
4. Believe "if it isn't broke, don't fix it."
5. Not do certain things for a million dollars.
6. When breaking a moral code, justify it.
7. Be seen by others as narrow-minded.
8. Believe there's only one-way to skin a cat: the right way.
9. Stick with traditional means that work.
10. Be a black and white thinker.
11. Be very hard on themselves and others; holding them and themselves to strict standards.
12. Act like the "bad cop."
13. Seek a cause and a purpose.
14. Understand and appreciate authority.
15. Strive to convert others to their way of thinking.
16. Find it difficult to shift positions or to change their mind.
17. Feel like taking commands from someone else is like swimming in handcuffs.
18. Struggle with those who are too open-minded.
19. Feel like using someone else's method may feel like wearing a strait jacket.
20. Believe certain things for a long time without updating their ideas.
21. Color within the lines and expect others to do the same.
22. Believe if it's wrong for them it's wrong for everyone.
23. Create a system if one isn't present.

Very Low Regulative Consistency

Individuals with *very low* (situational/midpoint) consistency and direction within the *single* motivational element of regulation will likely:

1. Look for freedom and autonomy.
2. Believe there's always another way to do it.
3. Believe there's more than one way to skin a cat.
4. Think in terms of "whatever it takes."
5. Have many questions.
6. Pull the trigger when things are clear.
7. Not want to wait for permission.
8. Always find a way.
9. Be very open-minded.
10. Think like an innovator.
11. Believe in freedom to express ideas.
12. Believe mistakes are normal and part of the learning process.
13. Not be narrow-minded.
14. Always have an opinion.
15. Try anything once.
16. Believe there's always another way when the current situation changes.
17. Pick and choose the rules that match their desired outcome.
18. Believe a yellow traffic light means go faster.
19. Have an active imagination.
20. Want to be the red penny among many plain ones.
21. Be highly adaptive.
22. Be able to loosen up when necessary.
23. Believe the ends justify the means.

As you may have noticed, the regulated value element is the part of the whole value structure that represents our need to march to the beat of our own drum. It's our desire or need to be the author of our own rule book. Unlike highly complex and compliant thinkers, the lower regulated thinker cherry-picks the rules that make the most sense.

On the other hand, higher regulated thinkers live within a structured world. Like Hartman's structured thinking dynamic; analytical observation, structure, order and consistency in thinking, theoretical or conceptual organization and planning, and valuing what "ought to be" in an *ideal* (future) sense, all contributes to the ability to see and appreciate systems, order, structure, conformity and authority.

How clearly do we see and understand what is defined in no uncertain terms. Do we understand the rules to the game? What about important protocols, procedures, authorities, forecasts, budgets, fixed rules and standards? Are you self-regulated? Do you walk a chalk-line? Or do you tend to undermine the rules or find a work-around? Do you resist what *should be* done and attempt to do things in your own unique way despite what is expected?

Do you color within the lines? Do I think in terms of black and white or gray? Are your lines strictly drawn or blurred? Answering these questions will help you discover how you think and value regulation.

10
CURIOSITY AND THE NEED TO KNOW WHY

It has been said that the person who knows *how* has a job but the person who knows *why* is the boss.

"On higher developmental levels, cognition is such an integral part of all other mental acts that it almost seems to be the essential achievement of mental life."[99] The theoretical mindset is all about uncovering, discovering, and recovering information—the facts. This is the itchy brain. If you experience value-consistency in this area you will need to get to the bottom of the things you need to know and won't likely give up easily until you find out the truth about any matter.

Others will view these people as experts in their field of interest. They learn everything there is to know about the subjects associated with whatever they believe they need to do in regard to both work and life. When accompanied by a consistent fear emotion (+C in DISC and +P in TARP), this can exaggerate the need to analyze and create analysis paralysis in a person. A friend to analytical problem solving, the higher theoretical thinker will need more information than necessary to solve the problems or meet the challenges at hand.

These styles are life-long learners. They may have forgotten more than some people know, especially if their consistency reaches 80 and above on the values scale. Having a high capacity for learning, they are machines at finding out what needs to be known. They will always educate themselves when necessary and will likely be well read. Vigorous at complex problem solving, these people enjoy making their brains work. Those with a high theoretical impulse are

---

[99] Edward Spranger, Types of Men; The Psychology and Ethics of Personality, 1928.

the same people most likely watching the History Channel. This is because they are driven by a need to learn things they never knew.

When logic driven, which is an individual who is less emotional and more matter-of-fact, these people can become socially inept or may find it difficult to converse with the "less cognitive" of society. High thinkers always feel challenged with low thinkers or what are known as "situational thinkers." When faced with tests, situational thinkers will study to pass, they don't study to know—this is known as cramming for the exam and moderate to lower theoretically driven styles will do this by default.

Preferring "logic and reason" over "feelings and emotion," these styles primarily operate out of their neocortex for decision making—they don't guess. Higher influencing styles with higher theoretical drives can surprisingly do both. Theoretical types continue educating themselves whether in or out of school—they never stop. With an insatiable need for gaining more information, they can often become hung up in details and endless rabbit trails. Usually driven by a fear of looking stupid, these types will follow every lead to see what else can be learned.

Power, Control, and Theoretical Thinking

When accompanied by higher economic impulses and higher power drives, these folks can come off like know-it-alls. Self-mastery value orientations are always pushing for the most practical, efficient, and incentivized way forward. When combined with higher theoretical drives, one can experience frequent knowledge bursts in an effort to maximize resources and personal outcomes.

Freedom and autonomy take a back seat to how and why. *I'm learning everything I need to know in an effort to get to where I need to be.* Power denotes authoritativeness. Efficiency denotes maximizing outcomes. Knowledge denotes understanding why something is the way it is.

Fig. 1

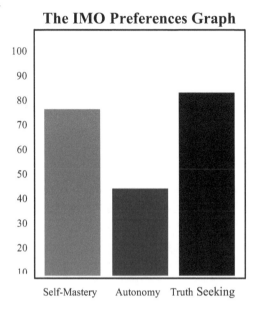

Knowledge becomes a means to a more efficient end. Combining knowledge with an authoritative and efficiency need can also represent a strong value towards practical attention. You might have an excellent capacity for seeing and understanding the functional worth, and usefulness of functional items. Strong knowledge drives in combination with an efficient mind might mean you understand how and when and how things should be done.

This can mean you have a great grasp on prioritizing activities, projects, and categorizing time and functional things. You could be exceedingly efficient when executing common sense, managing projects, and when thinking in terms of concrete organization. This can develop into keen insight and excessive attention towards knowing what to do and when to do it. Although you may not be fast acting in a behavioral sense (or maybe you are), you may value your time thus having a sense of when it's wasted.

People with clear clarity and insight into practical matters while focusing on what needs to be done next in order to be successful have a keen sense of what needs to be done and when it needs to be done. They can be very results oriented and extremely time conscious. They have a keen sense of material things of social, organizational status and appreciation. They may develop an overly sensitive mindset towards getting things done and being recognized for the accomplishment and the knowledge that was necessary to know it.

Such a one may have an excessive need to be recognized for their functional worth. Because they appreciate things looking good and being well-kept, they'll insist things be done in a timely manner once the knowledge of what to do materializes. Although one does not have to be dominant for these ideas to resonate, they will still do things with strong conscientiousness and attentiveness to time simply because they think in efficient ways. This is what Spranger called the *Economic Attitude*. Efficiency is not a behavior, it's an attitude. It's thinking quickly and efficiently—it's a *get-it-done* attitude.

You can be a passive brain type and still think efficiently. Although you will spend your available time building your knowledge bank because you value knowing why, your knowledge is maximized and trimmed down to fit the necessary bits and pieces into a workable framework.

Theoretical Unicorns

Like all combinations, there's always a unicorn among the styles. The most outlying unicorns are those who's theoretical consistencies are combined with high aesthetic consistencies. When the theoretical value is consistent and the aesthetic value is consistent you will have an excessive need to uncover, discover, and recover the truth/facts about uncommon concepts and/or philosophies. You will have a highly unconventional/analytical approach to problem solving deeply rooted in both logical and mystical/visceral instincts. An individual's capacity for useful insight and absorbing information will be one of their greatest strengths.

Although very rare, these unconventional thinking types are all around *alternative*-minded—they are "experimental" types. When overextended, they quickly drop into less than 1 percent of the population and will feel as though nobody understands them. As we covered earlier in chapter 3, aesthetic/theoretical combinations live in an alternate world. Add an individualistic component and things get even more interesting. If this combination of consistencies takes up residence in the brain of a musician, they may be drawn towards the banjo, the recorder, violin or the obo.

Fig. 2

Motivational Direction and Consistency Graph
The Unicorn

				0	10	20	30	40	50	60	70	80	90	100
ORIGINALITY	26	1		0	10	20	30	40	50	60	70	80	90	100
EFFICIENCY	40	5		0	10	20	30	40	50	60	70	80	90	100
INDIVIDUALITY	64	3		0	10	20	30	40	50	60	70	80	90	100
POWER	86	4		0	10	20	30	40	50	60	70	80	90	100
SACRIFICE	84	2		0	10	20	30	40	50	60	70	80	90	100
COMPLIANCE	69	7		0	10	20	30	40	50	60	70	80	90	100
CURIOSITY	61	6		0	10	20	30	40	50	60	70	80	90	100

Quirky and often feeling out of place and somewhere outside of time, these combinations will find it difficult to relate to *normal* people types. They are inventive, intuitive, and usually highly impractical. They may take the long way home simply because it's a better view or it *feels* better to the brain to be a part of *particular* surroundings. Highly sensitive to their surroundings, it has to *feel* right before their brain feels a green light to move ahead. When less dominant and more passive, time slows nearly to a stop. Life is lived or *experienced* in slow motion. Lessen the consistencies in power and efficiency and life comes to a dead stop—everyone is moving past you at a high rate of speed.

Does curiosity actually kill the cat? Why do people say such things? The origin of the modern variation of this phrase is unknown. It is however, found in an Irish newspaper from 1868: "They say curiosity killed a cat once."[100] Another early printed reference to the actual phrase "Curiosity killed the cat" is in James Allan Mair's 1873 compendium, *A handbook of proverbs: English, Scottish, Irish, American, Shakespearean, and scriptural; and family mottoes*, where it is listed as an Irish proverb on page 34. It was also printed in the 1902 edition of *Proverbs: Maxims and Phrases*, by John Hendricks Bechtel.[101]

This phrase was used to warn of the dangers of unnecessary investigation or experimentation. It is for this reason that people with unicorn profiles may experiment with alternative lifestyles (same sex relationships), alternative medicines, alternative foods, and hallucinogenic drugs. They may also be vegetarians, vegan's or could embrace out-of-the-box holistic living strategies. They can also be attracted to cults, fringe groups, and communal living if their altruistic consistencies are also very high.

The Insatiable Need to Know

What does the need to know why really look like? I love going to the Home Depot. That being said, as a profiler I'm always keen on the personality types whom I come in contact with, especially the floor help. Have you ever asked a service person if they sell a particular item? Often the service person simply stares at me like an aborigine staring at a Ferris Wheel.

"ah . . . I think that might be in the building department."

---

100 "Aunt Hetty's Strategem". Waterford Mirror and Tramore Visiter. Waterford: 4. 1868-10-28.
101 The phrase "Curiosity killed the cat" is the lone entry under the topic "Curiosity" on page 100.

Yet some never come with me to see if the item is actually there. At other times, I'll get, "Absolutely. Isle 8—all the way down on the left; bottom shelf. I think we have about 8 left." How did he or she know that? How did he or she remember that? The answer is simple. Whenever someone asks them a question about an item in the store, their brain will experience brain tension if they don't know the answer, so they find the answer in order to lessen the tension. This fuels the need to know.

This is what the theoretical mind is all about. This is what curiosity is all about. It's about the need to know. Some folks don't know and don't care that they don't know. Does this mean they lack intelligence? Absolutely not. It simply means they don't care to know. It doesn't mean they *can't* know. Not knowing has nothing to do with intelligence. "I won't find out" the answer is very different than "I can't find" the answer. I can't find the answer may not be a smart issue either. Maybe it's in the wrong place because someone moved it.

If you are not driven to dig deeper when it comes to knowing a thing it simply means you don't place a high value on knowing things. It doesn't mean you can't know them. My theoretical consistency score is about a 98. I'm currently listening to 7 audio books on several subjects pertaining to the brain, philosophy, behavior, and religion. I've always been curious. But as I grew older, my curiosity began to hone in on specific subjects.

In 1984, a friend told me I wasn't going to heaven because I didn't believe the right way. He was part of an offshoot of the Pentecostal cult. I was raised in a similar cult. He asked me to prove why I disagreed with him. It was a Friday night at about 10 O'clock. I didn't have the answer. The very next morning I opened my Bible to Genesis and started reading.

This one event started a journey that lasted 30 years and consumed over 20,000 hours of my time researching the Hebrew and Greek translations of the Bible. I needed to know—everything.

Fig 3.

My Bible from 1984

This journey ultimately led me to wanting to understand the power of belief and what causes us to place tremendous faith in ideas that cannot be proven. This led me to study human behavior; ultimately culminating into becoming a behavioral analyst. I have spent the last 16 years studying behavior, values, human consciousness, and human motivation.

I know some folks who don't read at all. Does this mean they're not smart? No. It means they don't care to know specifics. It means they'll rely more on their intuitive notions, past experiences, and what other people they respect think for moving forward and filling the *why* basin.

Low Theoretical Consistency

These types won't want to learn what they don't have to learn. Only when they love the subject matter does the subject matter. Because of their lack of investigation, these people will learn other ways—trial and error, intuition, asking someone else. They have a pragmatic approach to discovery and will pay more attention to one of the other 6 values. These people always think in terms of *something* as opposed to thinking in terms of *everything*.

With a brain that is easily satisfied, they may resort to visual or auditory learning and skip reading, thinking too much, or in-depth researching—they scan. This person is what we call a situational learning style—this is the *cram for the exam* style we already mentioned above. Learning on the fly or not at all works well for this style. Most people with this frame set will figure out a way to make up for it.

These are more hands-on people with less "light on" in the brain. This doesn't at all mean they are dumb or stupid, but rather that they have a different kind of intelligence. There are many people who hate school and sitting for hours listening to people speak—blah. They're usually active, outgoing, intentional, and emotionally combative. They can be dreamers, schemers, and horse thieves. This is the all too familiar street-smart style.

Having high street sense allows this style to skip boring and head on into doing. You will find these people in the construction trades, mechanical trades, and in the art world. Relying on intuition and life experience, the lower theoretical style can do a lot with a little. Each day is a learning experience and they all know what not to do because they have done it and experienced the results or the lack of results.

This style doesn't like waiting for information before starting a project, which may include reading the directions, but they always find a way. This could mean innovation and intuitive responses to problems and challenges. Always looking for the broader perspective, they are big picture driven and don't like details.

The ends will nearly always justify the means with lower theoretical styles. They may struggle to connect certain dots but will likely find a way to make up for it. They may prefer less paperwork, reading, and hypothesizing their way through to conclusions—"just do it" may be the battle cry. These people will prefer *experiences* over *explanations* and *images* over *words* all day long.

Creative Learning

What does it mean to be creative-smart or to learn in creative ways? It means you rely on instinctive imaginations and not logical reasoning when learning new things. If you're below 35 on the consistency scale within the theoretical dimension you're more intuitive and less instructive—you're likely *innovative*. This doesn't mean your answers will be right although they could be, because you probably won't want to spend an inordinate amount of time digging for the right answers.

If you don't value the use of your cognitive brain parts, your decision-making skills will have a much different outcome than those who do. Cognitive skills are the core skills your brain uses to think, read, learn, remember, reason, and pay attention. Working in tandem, these elements take incoming information through your senses and transfer it to the bank of knowledge you use every day whether you're at school, work, or living life.

The cognitive mind is a more reasonable mind. The emotional mind is more instinctive and imaginative. We don't formulate strategies with our emotions. The cerebrum, the larger, outer part of the brain, controls our reading, thinking, learning, speech, emotions and planned muscle movements like walking. It also controls our vision, hearing and other senses. The cerebrum is divided into two cerebral hemispheres (halves): left and right. The right half controls the left side of the body and the left half controls the right side of the body.

Each half has four sections called lobes; frontal, parietal, temporal and occipital. Each lobe controls specific functions. For example, the frontal lobe controls personality, decision-making and reasoning, while the temporal lobe controls, memory, speech, and sense of smell.[102] A group of psychology experts from Harvard, Yale, and a few other institutions of higher learning used MRIs to predict levels of creativity in participants with a high level of accuracy.

When comparing brain scans between participants engaged in creative work and those participants who were not employing creative tasks, "more connections" between the brains default network (inactive mode), the salience network (what the brain notices and doesn't notice), and the executive network (decisions and emotions) were discovered among those who were creating.[103]

When it comes to creativity, researchers hypothesize that these three networking centers operate as a team. According to Grant Hilary Brenner, MD, FAPA in a Psychology Today article,[104] the default mode network generates ideas, the executive control network evaluates them, and the salience network determines which ideas deserve to move to the executive control center. Brenner says, "Creativity is closely linked to what folks have called 'divergent thinking.'"

I hypothesize that this "divergent thinking" is measurable within our Integrated Motivational Orientation Report. Very low regulation scores on our consistency graph denotes *subversion* to compliant worthy concepts while aesthetic scores greater in consistency denote *divergence* and unconventional thinking. Independence, defiance, divergence, and unconventionality work as a team to create a more robust creativity. Taking into account a greater consistency within the theoretical framework produces what I have come to call the unicorn.

---

102 Johns Hopkins, Neurology and Neurosurgery Brain and Tumor Center.

103 *Robust Prediction of Individual Creative Ability from Brain Functional Connectivity*; Roger E. Beaty, Yoed N. Kenett, Alexander P. Christensen, Monica D. Rosenberg, Mathias Benedek, Qunlin Chen, Andreas Fink, Jiang Qiu, Thomas R. Kwapil, Michael J. Kane, and Paul J. Silvia; PNAS January 30, 2018 115 (5) 1087-1092; published ahead of print January 16, 2018.

104 Psychology Today; Feb 22, 2018, Your Brain on Creativity, Grant Hilary Brenner MD, FAPA.

These are those who's creativity overwhelmingly subverts their cognitive and analytical faculty. It's the difference between book-smart, street-smart, and creative-smart. We identify which one you are likely to be based on your personal IMO. One of the 27 styles I've identified within my Motivational Matrix is *The Story Teller*. There are 9 styles respectively but because the theoretical element stands alone within the matrix, I've associated 3 levels of curiosity and assigned each level to each of the 9 styles creating 27 (we are currently working on 37 styles).

Fig 4.

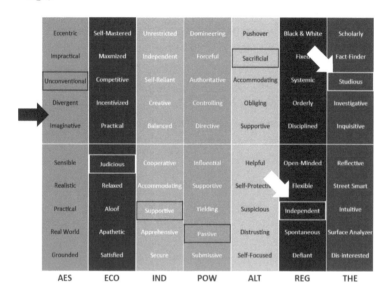

In the motivational matrix above (Fig. 4), word descriptors are highlighted in order to expose the motivational framework. This is a reflection of a story-teller style. Their basic desire is to seek knowledge and to cooperate with others through creative-expression while allowing some unconventional methods of doing it. Meeting others needs while not fighting for their own makes them feel accomplished and trustworthy.

They have an excessive need to uncover, discover, and recover the truth as well as interesting facts about many fascinating subjects. They will have a creative and highly analytical approach to problem-solving deeply rooted in *unconventional* thought. Their large capacity for useful and intuitive insight while absorbing large amounts of information will be one of their greatest strengths.

This style usually focuses on finding difficult yet creative solutions to thorny problems. Discovering creative and alternative solutions that produce a sense of purpose or support a meaningful cause is commonplace for this type. They're also interested in coming into contact with unconventional experiences involving the self and others. This is similar to the Non-Conformist but lacks consistency within the individualistic dimension.

Duel Theoretical Convergences

Again, I already talked about duel convergence so I will not further elaborate on how these factors work. You may reference the information in an earlier chapter if you need to brush up on convergences.

THE/H–AES/L (Fact-Finding): This value factor associates *investigation* with *real-world thinking*. When the theoretical value is high and the aesthetic value low you will have an excessive need to uncover, discover, and recover the truth/facts about anything. You will have a real-world/analytical approach to problem solving deeply rooted in logic and reason as opposed to reactive visceral instinct.

THE/H–AES/H (Unconventional-Thinking): This value factor associates *research* with *unconventionality*. When the theoretical value is high and the aesthetic value high you will have an excessive need to uncover, discover, and recover the truth/facts about uncommon concepts and/or philosophies. You will have an unconventional/analytical approach to problem solving deeply rooted in both analytics and mystical/visceral instinct.

THE/H–ECO/L (Casual-Thinking): This value factor associates *research* with *satisfaction*. When the theoretical value is high and the economic value low you will be more interested in the information itself than you will what the information can provide for you. Your brain is itchy and the only way to scratch it is to learn something you never knew before. This person is a life-long learner who can become absorbed into overthinking nearly everything just for the sake of thinking.

THE/H–ECO/H (Efficient-Thinking): This value factor associates *research* with *efficiency*. When the theoretical value is high and the economic value high you will be interested in information and what the information can provide for you. Your brain is itchy and the only way to scratch it is to learn something you never knew before. You're a life-long learner who can become absorbed into overthinking nearly everything just for the sake of thinking, but your thinking will always lead to improvements, shortcuts, efficiency, and personal gain.

THE/H–IND/H (Presenter): This value factor associates *research* with *independence*. When the theoretical value is high and the individualistic value high you will lack interest in boring information and seek out out-of-the-box ideas and philosophies. You may at times believe the ends justify the means. You will incorporate instinct and innovation when learning. You will want to share your *own* ideas publicly and will not shy away from the spotlight. You may be suited for presenting and will not mind speaking out when necessary—possibly insecure in what you don't know.

THE/H–IND/L (Team-Thinker): This value factor associates *research* with *security*. When the theoretical value is high and the individualistic value low you will be more interested in the information itself as opposed to a need to promote it. Your brain is itchy and the only way to scratch it is to learn something you never knew before. You can resist having to over-share your knowledge but may use what you know to assist others.

THE/H–POW/H (Aggressive-Thinker): This value factor associates *investigation* with *authority*. These two forces are not in conflict when both are in play. When the theoretical value is high, and the power value is high you will be interested in gathering information as well as using it to inform and control others. You will use your knowledge to gain authority and control over situations and people that affect your destiny. You won't have time for nonsense.

THE/H–POW/L (Submissive-Thinking): This value factor associates *investigation* with *submission*. These two forces are not in conflict when both are in play. When the theoretical value is high, and the power value is low you will be more interested in the information itself as opposed to using it to gain position power. You will not force others to change their thinking even if you disagree with them. You may remain in your head and enjoy solitude and quiet times of reflective thinking.

THE/H–ALT/H (Sacrificial-Thinker): This value factor associates *investigation* with *sacrifice*. Information is necessary for meeting the needs of those who are unable to meet their own. Sharing information in an effort to support necessary causes is likely. Information is for sharing not hording.

THE/H–ALT/L (Suspicious-Thinker): This value factor associates *investigation* with *suspicion*. When the theoretical value is high and the sacrificial value low you will be interrogative. Knowledge is necessary to ward off problematic people or circumstances.

THE/H–REG/H (Instructor): This value factor associates *research* with *regulation*. These two forces are not in conflict when both are in play. When the theoretical value is high, and the regulating value is high you will be interested in gathering information as well as using it to inform and constrain others. You will use your knowledge to create boundaries, ensure compliance, and create systems.

THE/H–REG/L (Alchemist): This value factor associates *research* with *defiance*. These two forces are not in conflict when both are in play. When the theoretical value is high, and the regulating value is low you will be experimental and multi-threaded in your approach to solving complex problems and inventive in your creations.

THE/L–ALT/H (Sacrificial-Thinker): This value factor associates *intuition* with *sacrifice*. When the theoretical value is low and the altruistic value high you won't likely want to wait for all the information before making choices. You'll learn as needed but won't seek knowledge for knowledge sake. You may spend more of your time using your imagination as opposed to your rational mind and you will see others as more important than yourself. You'll use what knowledge you have to make the world a better place.

THE/L–ALT/L (Suspicious-Thinker): This value factor associates *intuition* with *suspicion*. When the theoretical value is low and the altruistic value low you won't likely want to wait for all the information before making choices. You might focus on what is missing in other people. You may learn through trial and error or the school of hard Knox but will appreciate broader perspectives. You'll prefer less paperwork and minute details and may have little room in your life for know-it-all's.

THE/L–IND/H (Autonomous-Thinking): This value factor associates *intuition* with *autonomy*. When the theoretical value is low and the individualistic value high you will scan as opposed to dig. You may also believe the ends justify the means. You will rely on visceral instinct and innovative ideas for moving forward. You will want to share your intuitive ideas and will not shy away from the spotlight. You may be suited for presenting and will not mind speaking out when necessary—possibly insecure in what you don't know.

THE/L–IND/L (Complacent): This value factor associates *intuition* with *security*. When the theoretical value is low, and the individualistic value is low you will have a careless approach to important information and will likely learn by trial and error. You may resist established directions for getting things done or not do your homework. You may settle for less information as opposed to fighting for the information you need to know. Your casual approach to innovative learning may increase mistakes.

THE/L–ECO/H (Innovator): This value factor associates *intuition* with *self-mastery*. When the theoretical value is low, and the economic value is high you will have a careless approach to important information and may take shortcuts for quick gains. You may resist directions that waste your time or not do enough investigation. You may settle for less information as opposed to fighting for the information you need in an effort to speed up the process.

THE/L–ECO/L (Care-Free): This value factor associates *intuition* with *satisfaction*. When the theoretical value is low and the economic value is low you will have a careless approach to important information and will likely learn by trial and error and end up in the school of hard Knox because you may resist established directions for getting things done or not do enough homework. You may settle for the information you want as opposed to fighting for the information you need.

THE/L–POW/H (Authoritative): This value factor associates *intuition* with *authority*. When the theoretical value is low, and the power value is high you will lack interest in important information and will likely learn by trial and error. You may only scan your information before decision-making and may cram for exams. You will use your authority and ability to control others in place of your knowledge when getting things done.

THE/L–POW/L (Surrendered): This value factor associates *intuition* with *submission*. When the theoretical value is low, and the power value is low you will lack interest in important information and will likely learn by trial and error. You may resist established directions for getting things done or not do enough homework before decision-making. You may rely on instinct and innovative ideas for solving problems, but will not take charge, act as an authority or spearhead your ideas.

THE/L–REG/H (Forceful): This value factor associates *intuition* with *structure*. When the theoretical value is low, and the regulatory value is high you will lack interest in important information and will likely learn by trial and error. You may resist information you disagree with and not take the time to see other people's point of view before decision making. You will be narrow-minded and closed to most people's opinions if you disagree with their premise.

THE/L–REG/L (Instinctual): This value factor associates *intuition* with *subversion*. When the theoretical value is low, and the regulatory value is low you will lack interest in important information and will likely learn by trial and error. You will resist established directions for getting things done and not do enough homework before decision-making. You may rely on instinct and innovative ideas for solving problems but will resist the status quo and predictable choices. You will be flexible in your thinking and spontaneous.

Situational Theoretical Consistency

To reiterate, these are values *not* behaviors. Values speak of our *desires* and what moves us in a directional effort. Keep also in mind that this list is associated with a single value element and not the *integrated motivational orientation*, which includes all seven value elements. What we desire can often conflict with what we will actually do.

This list is in no way exhaustive. Individuals with a *general* or situational (situational/midpoint) consistency and direction within the *single* motivational element of curiosity will likely:

1. Learn what you need to learn in order to get to the next step.
2. Be a "situational" learner.
3. Have limited patience, you will "cram for the exam."
4. Need to know something, not everything.
5. Understand that investigation is necessary, but you will rarely over-investigate any issue.
6. Understand the big picture as well as the details of any subject and will alter your inquiry depending on the amount of time you have.
7. Be more of a broad brush minded person and less a minute detailed person when it comes to finding out why.
8. Want to know why but won't let it get in your way of getting things done.
9. Limit your technical prowess to the things you love.
10. Demonstrate awareness within your area of expertise.
11. Be both practical and theoretical depending on the subject matter.
12. Not get hung up in analysis paralysis.
13. Be curious to a point.
14. Have an average IQ.
15. School is great, but once you're done, you're likely done.
16. Bring stabilization to over-thinkers.
17. Be versed in a variety of subjects that you care about.
18. Pick up on new subjects rather easily.
19. Need some proof before you believe certain things.
20. Won't blindly believe or do things without at least some investigation.

Very High Theoretical Consistency

Remember, these are values not behaviors. Values speak of our *desires* and what moves us in a directional effort. Keep also in mind that this list is associated with a single value element and not the *integrated motivational orientation*. What we desire can often conflict with what we will actually do. This list is in no way exhaustive.

Individuals with *very high* (situational/midpoint) consistency and direction within the *single* motivational element of curiosity will likely cause them to:

1. Think, "It's tight but it's right."
2. Need cognitive challenges.
3. If you are not cognitively challenged, you'll quickly become bored.
4. Learn for the sake of it.
5. Spend a lot of time getting to the bottom of something.
6. Need to know everything about certain things may seem excessive to others.
7. Your intellectual capacity may seem limitless.
8. Be seen as an expert in your field of interest.
9. Need more information than necessary before making decisions.
10. Be a life-long learner.
11. Have an excessive need to uncover, discover, and recover the truth.
12. Need proof.
13. Have doubts about what you don't have ample evidence for.
14. Gravitate towards "knowing" and be uncomfortable with "believing."
15. Not like it when someone says, "trust me."
16. Get bogged down in the details of an idea if you are not careful.
17. Fear looking stupid.
18. Love learning things you never knew.
19. Enjoy analytical problem solving.
20. Steer clear of subjective matters and stick to what can be measured.
21. Have high focus and are likely research oriented.
22. Stick with it until you figure out what is wrong.
23. Act like a detective when it comes to discovering things.

Very Low Theoretical Consistency

Individuals with *very low* (situational/midpoint) consistency and direction within the *single* motivational element of curiosity will likely:

1. Spend time learning things that directly affect or impact your performance.
2. Prefer to work on many things with only partial importance rather than getting bogged down in only one function or role.
3. Appreciate technical support in areas where you have limited understanding.
4. Learn only what is necessary to complete a task.
5. Have an awareness of time management but will not let time be your boss.
6. Depend more on intuition than getting caught up in theory.
7. Learn more through trial and error.
8. Only learn what you have to.
9. Knowledge isn't the most important thing to you.
10. Be pragmatic and won't care if you don't know the details.
11. Be a MacGyver type individual.
12. Know something and not know why you know it.
13. Be more resourceful than you are a resource.
14. Not want to wait for all the information before deciding.
15. Always find a way.
16. Be open-minded to more options.
17. Be an innovative and practical thinker.
18. Believe in freedom to express progressive ideas.
19. Believe mistakes are normal and a learning process.
20. Not be narrow-minded and can think outside the box.
21. Have an opinion.
22. Try anything in your attempt to figure something out.
23. Believe there's always another way when the current situation changes.
24. Pick and choose your own rules instead of reading them.
25. Have an active imagination.

26. Be highly adaptive.

27. Believe the ends probably justify the means.

As you may have noticed, the theoretical value element is the part of the whole value structure that represents our need to know. It's our desire or need to be as informed as possible. Being consistently theoretical means, we desire to know the truth, find the facts and implement what we discover.

11
DUEL MOTIVATIONAL AND BEHAVIORAL INTEGRATIONS CREATING FLOW

Motivational integration associates differing desires with differing consistencies to produce conflictive emotions or integrative flow. When certain motivational elements team up, new strengths can emerge. Sometimes greater consistencies between elements create a dissociative sense generating inner conflict. These inner conflicts can actually *reduce* productivity within our motivational framework causing emotional lag or fatigue.

Emotional reduction may not appear to be conflictive or problematic because we are experts at maneuvering our minds to create emotional justifications. Rather than verifying personal conflict we will justify the outcomes created by it. How our primary emotions counteract with our value orientations determines the strength of our underlying motives.

Our primary emotions determine our temperament. Whether we are primarily introverted or extroverted will have a significant impact on our motivational framework. Our emotions will have the greatest impact on what we will ultimately do in any given circumstance. In other words, what we desire does not always translate into what we will do. Have you ever desired a raise but found it difficult to ask for one? This is an example of the many types of me-me conflicts we all can face at one time or another.

I will be using the TARP and DISC models throughout this chapter. TARP represents our behavioral orientations which correspond to our emotional *shifts* when bridging the gaps between what others expect and what we ourselves desire when in a shared space and DISC represents our character and temperament, which is our natural selves.

In this chapter we will look at a few examples of behaviors and motivational forces working with or against each other. The following combinations will selectively reflect a *consistent* element in response to an *inconsistent* element within the IMO framework. Although our behavioral orientations work with our motivational integrations it can be difficult to spot roadblocks when self-assessing. It is for this reason that self-assessments such as our IBO and IMO reports are so important for identifying potential blockers. Let's examine a few more duel convergences in order to give you a feel for how our motivational orientations work together to create motivational energies.

Aesthetic Orientations

+AES -ECO (Unconventional): This Value Factor associates a *creative* need, which is disassociated with personal returns. Individuals who score higher on this end will feel the need to experiment for the sake of *experiencing* the results as opposed to benefitting from them. Lower economic/efficiency drives lessen the need to "get ours" and increase the likelihood feel more satisfied with the status quo. This combination lends toward greater creative assets.

Aesthetic Element

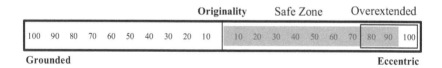

Lesser efficiency drives mean we are less focused on time and efficiency. Time ceases to be of the essence and the desire to experience the world (outside of time) overcomes the need to maximize utility—creativity replaces convenience. The primary emotions necessary to enhance this experience will be optimism and patience. Patience (+S, +R) plays nicely with a satisfied self (-ECO) as they both have plenty of time to engender experiences.

Optimism (+I, +A) also plays nicely with an imaginative (+AES) element because optimistic brain types are great at *imagining* things happening. Optimist's are "future feelers." For example; an optimist can imagine what the upcoming party will be like. These feelings will be primarily positive. Patient types do not imagine, they *hope*. "I hope the party goes well and that I didn't forget anything…" Because of the greater focus on people and experiences, the more motivational consistency associated with aesthetic/imaginative and satisfied/aloof motivational elements, the greater the flow within the human psyche.

Everything associated with the emotional consistencies, the resulting behavior, and the motivational elements is maximized. Potential disruptors could be impulsiveness, matter-of-factness, fear, or excessive anger orientations. These emotions can create dissonance when coupled with lower efficiency and higher aesthetic drives.

Behavioral and Motivational Combinations

+AES -IND (Inspirational): This Value Factor associates *creativity* and alternative thinking, which is more or less disassociated with a need to be seen as *uniquely* different. Individuals who score higher on this end will feel the need to deliver creative ideas and results for the common good. Patient (+S, +R) and optimistic (+I, +A) people types who have inspirational motivational patterns will experience the greater flow. This stems from the helping component that accompanies the patience emotion.

Because patient people types have a security need, working for the common good creates a flow with the desire to accommodate others thus enhancing people's personal security in the world (they know what it's like to need it). Both patient and lesser individualistically driven people types are accommodating by nature. The optimistic emotion has a greater sense of people awareness thus this emotion flows consistently with *cooperative* values (-IND/+ALT).

+AES -POW (Apprehensive): This Value Factor associates *creativity* and alternative thinking, which is disassociated with owning the rights to its benefits. Individuals who score higher on this end will feel the need to *share* experiences and creative outcomes within established groups and social structures. This combination also flows better with optimistic (+I, +A) and patient (+S, +R) types but will also work with scared types (+C, +P). Less consistency within the power (-POW) dimension produces a *yielding* of one's position to avoid controversies.

True believing types (-D, +T,+I, +A, +S, +R, +C, +P) accept information at face value and only pay attention to the good news or *what they want to hear*, which flows consistently with lesser consistency in the power and authority elements. Apprehensive people types want to avoid conflict and will yield their position when faced with the choice between being confrontational or acquiescent. Less power consistency translates into *accompaniment* as opposed to sole propriety. There's no need to own the space or the outcomes.

+AES -ALT (Precautious): This Value Factor associates *creative* experiences and alternative thinking disassociated with trust and shared existence. Individuals who score higher on this end will feel the need to explore and *experience* the world around them while being detached from others who might ruin it. Lower altruistic consistencies usually denote distrust and greater emotional distance between them and others.

Because getting to know these types is a bit more difficult, their creative expression tends towards a more solitary exercise. They will tend towards a precautionary attitude towards those whom their unfamiliar and possibly warm up after more information is realized (+S, +R, -I, -A). As you know, there are more factors to consider such as power, regulation, and individualism, but these two particular factors will give rise to a guarded attitude.

The emotional consistencies that will give greater flow to this style are patience and fear (+S, +R, +C) as these emotions are better at negotiating what could go wrong with logical reasoning. Optimism and anger (+D, +T, +I, +A) may also accompany the precautionary style but with limited flow in comparison to the former emotions.

+AES -REG (Unrestricted): This Value Factor associates *creative* experiences and alternative thinking with multi-threaded openness and subversive thinking. Individuals who score higher on this end will feel the need to explore and *experience* the world around them while being open to as many ways available for enjoying it.

While this style is usually accompanied by a higher consistency in the individualistic element, it may not be at all times. This unrestricted mindset finds greater flow when accompanied by the lest amount of fear and patience possible. Consistent fear and patience work against spontaneity (+I, +A, +D, -C, -P, -REG, +IND) and flexibility (-S, -R). Anger and optimism create a greater flow when mixing with an unrestricted thinker.

+AES -THE (Imaginative): This Value Factor associates *creative* experiences and alternative thinking with *intuitive* insights. Individuals who score higher on this end will feel the need to explore and *experience* the world around them while being detached from the necessary processes associated with the need to know everything about it.

Lower consistencies in the theoretical/curious element increase the chances of scanning and intuitive reasoning. Rather than taking the necessary steps to ensure one knows everything, this style will lean on past experiences and their own intuition for finding out what is necessary to know when learning new things. Greater flow is the result when this style has optimism (+I, +A), impulsiveness (-S, -R), carelessness (-C, -P), and individualism (+IND) on their side.

Economic Orientations

+ECO -AES (Conservative): This Value Factor associates *personal gains* with real-world attitudes built on common sense. Individuals scoring higher on this end will feel the need to use *conventional* and *reliable* means to gain personal security and self-sustenance without frills or nonsense. This conservative style finds more flow when emotional consistencies contain anger (+D, +T, -I, -A, +C)), logic, and fear. Both fear and logic are conservative emotions. Greater flow results when anger, fear, logic, and the desire for maximization combine forces.

Economic Element

Overextended		Efficiency	Safe Zone	Overextended
100 90 80	70 60 50 40 30 20 10	10 20 30 40 50 60 70	80 90 100	
Satisfied				**Self-Mastered**

Logic is built into dominance, fear, and lower influencing emotions. Cognitive realism takes precedent over emotion and imaginations. Angry brain's make things happen while emotionally charged brain's imagine things happening.[105] Making and maximizing are two orientations that hold hands.

+ECO -IND (Well-Adjusted): This Value Factor associates *personal gains* without a need to stand apart from others in gaining them. Individuals scoring higher on this end will feel the need to

---

[105] For more about these dynamics, see my book *The Angry Brain and How it Relates to Human Behavior, Character, and Temperament*, published 2018, Amazon.com.

gain within a shared existence with others while the possibly of *sharing* the spoils or how they got them. In other words, this individual does not need to be the star of the show. Although greater economic consistency does not auto-translate into sharing the wealth or blueprints, the lower consistency in individualism focuses on greater self-security, which *can* at times, translate into sharing the ball as opposed to hogging it.

Emotions that could bring greater flow within this dynamic are matter-of-factness (-I, -A), anger (+D, +T; 50-55), and patience (+S, +R). Pace-Setter styles tend to be more secure and therefore will find greater flow when their IMO is well adjusted.

+ECO -POL (Reasonable): This Value Factor associates *personal gains* without a need to over-control or influence others in the process. Individuals scoring higher on this end will feel the need to gain within a shared existence while yielding their position to more authoritative styles and possibly *sharing* the spoils or how they got them. The sharing is unlikely, but possible depending on the consistency of sacrifice.

Greater flow stems from being less dominant (-D, -T), more optimistic (+I, +A), and patient (+S, +R). This is a result of the *yielding* nature of the IMO framework.

+ECO -ALT (Self-Regarding): This Value Factor associates *personal gains* with greater self-interest while deciding who deserves their attention. Individuals scoring higher on this end will feel the need to gain while steering clear of freeloaders and those who don't pull their own weight. Emotions that will flow better with this value set will be logical thinking (-I, -A), impulsivity (-S, -R), and anger (+D, +T).

Suspicious minds tend to be guarded and tough to break into. Getting to know these types is not easy unless you qualify by passing their litmus test. And even then, it can be difficult to get into the inner sanctum. This is why there's better flow when the brain is more task oriented than people oriented. Brain types who believe all valuable assets lay outside the self and can only be gained by taking them by force will feel at home with this dynamic.

+ECO -REG (Precarious): This Value Factor associates *personal gains* without a need to follow established rules or protocols in the process. Individuals scoring higher on this end will feel the need to gain whatever way they can however they need to. They will observe rules in order to deem whether or not they are worthy of following. Greater flow comes when this type person is impulsive (-S, -R) and divergent (-C, -P). These emotions spawn independence and subversion.

Typically led by an individualistic attitude, this combination ensures freedom, autonomy, independence, and self-compliance. This means they will do things by the book but it's their book.

+ECO -THE (Situational): This Value Factor associates *personal gains* without a need to know or fully understand the process. Individuals scoring higher on this end will feel the need to gain within an experimental and unconventional experience that relies on intuition and experiences already learned. This is a situational learner. They don't have to know it all, they simply need to know enough. Flowing emotions include optimism (+I, +A) and stubbornness (-C, -P).

Individualistic Orientations

+IND -AES (Discrete): This Value Factor associates *freedom and uniqueness* within a practical, real-world environment. Individuals scoring higher on this end will feel the need to be their own person. Sharing their own unique ideas while not being an extremist or unorthodox in the process makes their brain feel good. Flow happens when this style is optimistic (+I, +A) and/or dominant (+D, +T). These types are grounded and usually somewhat pragmatic. They can be innovative and may be able to present well.

Individualistic Element

Overextended								Individualism		Safe Zone						Overextended		
100	90	80	70	60	50	40	30	20	10	10	20	30	40	50	60	70	80	90	100

Secure   **Unrestricted**

+IND -ECO (Freedom Seeker): This Value Factor associates *freedom and uniqueness* within an experimental environment where freedom trumps security or a vision for the future. Individuals scoring higher on this end will feel the need to be their own person by sharing their own unique ideas while not being bound by having to win in life. Easily satisfied, this style may settle for what they can get without feeling the need to win at all they do. The journey is more important than the destination.

Flow happens when this style is consistently optimistic (+I, +A), unobtrusive (-D, -T), and friendly (+S, +R). The other primary emotions may fall where they may without too much interference.

+IND -POL (Impartial): This Value Factor associates *freedom and uniqueness* within an easy-going environment where freedom trumps the need to control one's destiny or influence on others. Individuals scoring higher on this end will feel the need to be their own person by sharing their own unique ideas. This style will usually yield their position to avoid challenges or taking on too much responsibility.

Flow happens when they are less dominant (-D, -T), optimistic (+I, +A), peaceable (+S, +R), and self-willed (-C, -P). Higher independence needs without the responsibilities that accompany more authoritative roles allows for the necessary freedoms to enjoy life without being trapped by obligations and unnecessary assignments.

+IND -ALT (Disconnected): This Value Factor associates *freedom and uniqueness* within an environment absent from others' needs. Individuals scoring higher on this end will feel the need to be their own person by sharing their own unique ideas while avoiding the entanglements of others wants and needs. The goal is being independent of other people's entanglements. Flow begins when one has a greater emotional distance from others. The greater the emotional distance the more

Emotional distancing stems from a lack of empathy and not less consistency of optimism. One can easily be optimistic and extroverted while still maintaining emotional distance from others. The greater consistency in independence and freedom needs could also benefit from lower compliance (-C, -P).

+IND -REG (Rule-Breaker): This Value Factor associates *freedom and uniqueness* within an environment absent from established rules and structures. Individuals scoring higher on this end will feel the need to be their own person by sharing their own unique ideas while avoiding the entanglements associated with strict confinements, parameters, and established rules or boundaries.

Having greater influence emotions (+I, +A), dominance (+D, +T), compulsiveness (-S, -R), and a self-willed spirit (-C, -P) will ensure greater flow in this dimension. These combinations form a spontaneous and aroused behavior fit for unruliness and risk-taking. Lesser anger orientations will scale back the risky behavior.

+IND -THE (Resourceful): This Value Factor associates *freedom and uniqueness* within an environment absent from deep investigation. Individuals scoring higher on this end will feel the need to be their own person by sharing their own unique ideas while avoiding the morasses of having to follow strict instructions, established truths coming from others, or learning more than one has to about something. This style leans into their intuitive brain while relying on hunches and gut feelings. Innovative and whimsical, greater flow comes with greater consistency in optimism (+I, +A).

Power Orientations

+POW -AES (Authoritative): This Value Factor associates *ownership and control* over one's own space within a practical environment absent from nonsense. Individuals scoring higher on this end will feel the need to control their own destiny and influence their surroundings while maintaining common sense strategies and real-world approaches to problems, challenges, and opportunities. The anger emotion will ensure greater flow, especially when there's greater consistency from the economic element.

+POW -ECO (Possessive): This Value Factor associates *ownership and control* over one's own space within an environment absent from competitive attitudes. Individuals scoring higher on this end will feel the need to control their own destiny and influence their surroundings while being easily satisfied with current conditions. To ensure greater flow there needs to be more consistency of patience and personal sacrifice.

Power Element

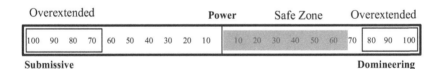

+POW -IND (Team leader): This Value Factor associates *ownership and control* over one's own space within an environment of shared existence. Individuals scoring higher on this end will feel the need to control their own destiny and influence their surroundings while also maintaining a cooperative attitude towards others. When greater dominance (+D, +T) enters the mix these styles can come off as scary to some. Higher anger emotions will cause one to appear very secure while lesser anger initiates cooperation. Greater influence (+I, +A) and patience (+S, +R) ensures a greater team spirit.

+POW -ALT (Apprehensive): This Value Factor associates *ownership and control* over one's own space within an environment of suspicion towards others. Individuals scoring higher on this end will feel the need to control their own destiny and influence their surroundings while avoiding being taken advantage of. Greater flow within this dimension requires more anger (+D, +T) and less optimism (-I, -A).

Lower consistencies in optimism allows for distrusting attitudes that pair nicely with logic, apprehension, and skepticism. These combined forces work in tandem to reinforce suspicious mindsets that lessen the chances of being taken advantage of, which is another attribute that accompanies anger.

+POW -REG (Open-Minded): This Value Factor associates *ownership and control* over one's own space within an environment of alternatives. Individuals scoring higher on this end will feel the need to control their own destiny and influence their surroundings while avoiding established rules and structures that could impede their creative processes.

Increased volume in this sphere will create multithreaded approaches to solving problems, challenges and creating more opportunities. Increased flow between these motivational elements and behaviors will require less fear (-C, -P) and increased optimism (+I, +A).

+POW -THE (Reactive): This Value Factor associates *ownership and control* over one's own space within an environment of trial and error. Individuals scoring higher on this end will feel the need to control their own destiny and influence their surroundings while taking chances, scanning surface information, and experimenting with new ideas. Increased flow requires more consistency in aestheticism, individualism, and less fear (-C, -P).

Sacrificial Orientations

+ALT -AES (Practical Assistance): This Value Factor associates *assisting others* through personal sacrifice and real-world solutions using practical means. Individuals scoring higher on this end will feel the need to assist others through practical processes that benefit others at a degree of personal expense. Greater flow requires a minor increase in consistency within the economic element and greater consistency of patience (+S, +R). Greater patience ensures a helpful attitude as patience engenders an attractiveness to personal loss.

In this case, the annoying cricket (hesitancy) allows for being more cautious for fear of arousing unnecessary challenges but may easily conflict with greater practical notions. This creates a battle between the need to lose one's self *into* another—being swallowed by another and maintaining an increased sense of self. Sociopathic persons can easily spot these people types when their economic factor is out of play and then swallow them whole.

+ALT -ECO (Considerate): This Value Factor associates *assisting others* with lessening the odds of personal gain or time for self. Individuals scoring higher on this end will feel the need to assist others while suffering personal losses associated with meeting the needs in others. Unlike the style above, in this case the annoying cricket (hesitancy) allows for being *exceptionally* lost *into* another and being swallowed aggressively.

The combination that creates the considerate type experiences flow when anger is absent (-D, -T) and patience is in play (+S, +R). Be aware that this style can be harmful to the self if unchecked or consistencies are overextended. I covered these issues in chapter 7. You may want to go back and reflect on these dynamics if you are experiencing similar outcomes.

+ALT -IND (Team-Player): This Value Factor associates *assisting others* with lessening the odds of personal freedom and autonomy. Individuals scoring higher on this end will feel the need to assist others and create teams while sacrificing personal gains in the process. This style will experience greater flow when patience (+S, +R) is increased. Patience is the emotion that allows our brains to give way to exterior strengths and difficulties pushing in our direction. Think of a bullfighter spinning out of the way of a charging bull by accommodating its power.

Altruistic Element

Overextended				Sacrifice				Safe Zone				Overextended		
100	90	80	70	60	50	40	30	20	10	10	20	30	40	50	60	70	80	90	100

Self-Focused   **Pushover**

This is a good picture of conflict avoidance. Team players avoid conflict and yield to assertive people and circumstances which is why they are beneficial to team synergies. "Getting along" is the necessary component that ensures team cohesiveness and comradery. Patience is part of what makes us *friendly* whereas optimism allows us to be *outgoing*. Optimistic types make many friends while patient people have fewer and keep them. Optimists play a short game while patient people are in it for the long haul. This is why some are better in an *instant* and others excel on a *constant*.

+ALT -POL (Easygoing): This Value Factor associates *assisting others* while avoiding challenges and lessening the odds of reaching personal goals. Individuals scoring higher on this end will feel the need to assist others while losing control and influence over others or within their own space. Achieving flow comes from having a low-dominant attitude (-D, -T) coupled with greater consistency in patience (+S, +R). easygoing types are conflict avoidant in nature and are more apt to assist people than resist them.

+ALT -REG (Carefree): This Value Factor associates *assisting others* through unconventional and lose-leafed means. Individuals scoring higher on this end will feel the need to assist others through unorthodox and carefree processes that push back against the system. Greater flow is achieved when fear emotions are out of play (-C, -P). Lesser "preserving" attitudes "let go" of structured paths forward and resist doing things the way they are "supposed to be done."

Believing there's more than one way to skin a cat, carefree people types are multithreaded in their approach to solving problems and challenges and creating opportunities. With an anything goes mindset, these types experience flow when all "resisting" brain agents are diminished.

+ALT -THE (Openhanded): This Value Factor associates *assisting others* with lessening the odds of understanding the full story. Individuals scoring higher on this end will feel the need to assist others without endeavoring to know everything concerning the situation. This could result in being taken advantage of.

Greater flow is realized when individualism (IND) is consistent and fear is less consistent (-C, -P). Lesser consistency within the theoretical element suggests a reliance on intuition and past experience for learning new things. An openhanded type can get bogged down in details or overwhelmed when forced to read the fine print.

Regulated Orientations

+REG -AES (Restrictive): This Value Factor associates the need to follow *established systems* and consistent rules with practical, common sense processes. Individuals scoring higher on this end will feel the need to live within a structured system devoid of creative influences, guessing, or unconventionality. Greater flow begins with higher economic consistencies, lesser optimistic tendencies (-I, -A) and greater fear consistencies (+C, +P).

Logical brain types are much more suited for greater regulation in thinking. Let's face it; we want our behaviors and emotions to work alongside our deepest desires. Having a regulated mind doesn't jive well with low-compliant behavior.

Regulatory Element

Overextended							Compliance	Safe Zone				Overextended			
100	90	80	70	60	50	40	30	20	10	10	20	30	40	50	60	70	80	90	100
Defiant															**Black & White**

+REG -ECO (Intolerant): This Value Factor associates the need to follow *established systems* and consistent *rules* without competitive attitudes. Individuals scoring higher on this end will feel the need to live within a structured system devoid of personal benefit. Flow occurs when greater consistency in altruism and lesser consistency in anger (-D, -A) takes place.

There are many other factors that may or may not be in play within all these dynamics but the specifics I point out are the hinges that assure a fluid relationship. For all these patterns, I'm only listing the most relevant consistencies and inconsistencies that will bring about the most uniform alliances between behavior and motivation.

+REG -IND (Traditional): This Value Factor associates the need to follow a black and white *established system* and consistent *rules* through shared existence. Individuals scoring higher on this end will feel the need to live within a community of structured systems with those of a similar mindset. Lower consistencies in individualism create a self-assurance or a cooperative mindset. When altruistic and empathetic impulses are in play, cooperation is the result.

When altruism is out of play and power is in its place, self-assurance is the result. Flow comes with higher patience and fear consistency (+S, +C, +R, +P) and lesser optimism (-I, -A). Systemic thinkers fair better when logic based. Fear creates an analytical approach to solving problems and allows for planning and strategic paths forward. Traditional thinkers appreciate specific outcomes that reflect preconceived ideas that are reliable.

+REG -POL (Backseat Driver): This Value Factor associates the need to follow a black and white *established system* and consistent *rules* without the need to control others adherence to the same. Individuals scoring higher on this end will feel the need to live within a community of structured systems established by higher authorities while *suggesting* others do the same.

These types struggle with authority and power while relying on established structures and systems. This is a me-me conflict of sorts. Desiring to enforce my rules upon you but lacking the authority to pull it off can be difficult. In order for this combination to flow, consistent anger (+D, +T) and/or optimism (+I, +A) is optimal.

+REG -ALT (Condescending): This Value Factor associates the need to dictate *established systems* and consistent *rules* through enforcement. Individuals scoring higher on this end will feel the need to establish the standards and control the actions of others as necessary. Maximizing flow between behavior and motivation entails greater consistency in logical thinking (-I, -A), dominant behaviors (+D, +T), and power positioning. These attributes make for an enforcer type. We see this among judges, law enforcement, and military leadership.

+REG -THE (Obtuse): This Value Factor associates the need to follow black and white *established systems* and consistent *rules* as they *believe* it should be done. Individuals scoring higher on this end will feel the need to establish order through beliefs rather than facts. Flow begins with consistent individualism and optimism (+I, +A). Optimism allows for instinctive action while individualism allows for intuition and creativity.

Strong imaginative processes overtake rationale in this case. These people would rather "cram for the exam" than "study for the test." They learn just enough to get by but will enforce their imaginative ideas on others whenever possible.

Theoretical Orientations

+THE -AES (Analytical): This Value Factor associates the need to uncover, discover, and recover the facts. Individuals scoring higher on this end will feel the need to establish the facts through analytical reasoning and rational thought. Flow comes when economic drives are in play and fear reigns supreme (+C, +P). This creates the "need to know why" coupled with a pragmatic sense of rationale. These types are effective planners and orchestrators.

+THE -ECO (Investigator): This Value Factor associates the need to uncover, discover, and recover the facts without a concept of time. Individuals scoring higher on this end will feel the need to establish the facts through analytical reasoning and rational thought while being unaware of the time it takes to accomplish it.

Flow comes from greater optimism (+I, +A) and patience (+S, +R). Patience and optimism, when combining forces, creates an agenda-less attitude that lacks urgency. This allows for the necessary time to dig deeper into rabbit holes without the need to conclude before all the facts are in. This will also work well with consistent fear emotions (+C, +P).

Theoretical Element

Overextended	Curiosity	Safe Zone	Overextended
100 90 80 70 60 50 40 30 20 10	10 20 30 40 50 60 70	80 90 100	
Dis-Interested			**Scholarly**

+THE -IND (Teachers Assistant): This Value Factor associates the need to uncover, discover, and recover the facts through shared existence. Individuals scoring higher on this end will feel the need to establish the facts through analytical reasoning and rational thought while not needing the credit for doing it.

Flow begins with greater altruism and patience (+S, +R). Cooperativeness is a hallmark of patience. Patience is the *helping* emotion. When individualism is out of play, focus on others begins. It is born along by self-sacrifice and nourished through patience.

+THE -POL (Innovator): This Value Factor associates the need to learn without needing to control the environment or the people in it. Individuals scoring higher on this end will feel the need to establish the facts through analytical reasoning and rational thought without the need to influence others with their outcomes or discoveries.

Innovative styles find greater flow when individualism and aestheticism are more consistent. Emotions can differ greatly with little effect on outcomes. This is because the theoretical component stands alone primarily and has a greater effect on discovery all by itself. For the greatest flow, consistencies must be above 75.

+THE -REG (Originator): This Value Factor associates the need to learn through whatever means. Individuals scoring higher on this end will feel the need to learn through unorthodox and unconventional means. Greater flow can be expected when aesthetic and individualistic elements are in greater play without economic drives. The lower regulation finds greater flow when fear is largely absent (-C, -P).

+THE -ALT (Know-It-All): This Value Factor associates the need to uncover, discover, and recover the facts while maintaining the need to control and distribute the information only to those worthy of it. Individuals scoring higher on this end will feel the need to withhold information from certain people and control others with what they know. Greater flow begins with greater power needs and consistency of anger.

Power is the controlling agent and anger (+D, +T) drives or *takes* it home. These are the elite thinker types. Large and in charge, they divvy up information selectively and disperse it to worthy subjects.

All these combinations are subject to minor changes based on intensities and consistencies coming from eleven elements. The four characteristic elements of emotion (The Primaries: Graph II), the changes made when in a shared space (The Orientations: Graph I), and the seven motivational elements (The IMO Style).

12
THE 37 MOTIVATIONAL STYLES

After 15 years of profiling thousands of people, I have come up with 37 styles of motivational orientation that dominate the motivational landscape. Our *IMO Preferences Measurement* identifies and describes our prioritized sources of motivational preference. It indicates how our brain organizes and prioritizes our approach to our unconscious desires or motivation. These different "approaches to organizing and prioritizing" the three areas of motivational importance create our differences. The three areas are self-mastery, freedom and autonomy, and truth seeking.

On the other hand, and as we have already discussed earlier in the book, our *IMO Consistency Measurement* reflects our direction towards two "opposing sources" of desire such as rule dependence and freedom and autonomy. It reflects how consistently our brain prioritizes a specific source of motivational preferences over others. The combinations created by these differing directions and preferences within our unconscious minds distill down to a very original motivational matrix that is assigned to us based on our gnome, DNA, and environmental influences. In other words, it could be said that this is what our brains have learned to *want*.

This chapter will cover the differing patterns of motivational orientation that I have discovered through many years of research, insight, and intuition. Each style has 3 dimensions based on the theoretical component. The theoretical component stands alone within the matrix and affects each style depending on how consistently one seeks to know more about a thing.

Theoretical consistencies are measured as 1, 2, and 3. Style-1 represents a lesser consistency and style-3 represents a much higher consistency, which leaves style-2 as an average consistency. These differing consistencies in the theoretical component will determine learning preferences. As well as which of the 3 versions of the styles one will be. There are 12 styles with 3 possible theoretical measurements each creating 36 styles. There's one style that holds a specific theoretical position bringing the total to 37 styles respectfully.

Greater consistency in style is predicated on greater consistency of flow between the motivational orientations and the behavioral orientations. When behavior flows with needs and desires, a maximization of consistency between the two bodies is realized. One may experience a subversive attitude within the desire framework but may error on the side of caution when the chips are down based on emotional consistencies. This is tantamount to *desiring* to purchase a Hummer but ultimately settling for a Jeep Cherokee in its place. The cautious action will emanate from greater consistency of fear.

Tension Reduction

It seems our brains are bent on reducing neurological tensions and embracing emotional flow. By this I mean diminishing inner and outer conflicts associated with what we desire. For example; sacrificial thinkers will experience brain tension if they are unable to make personal sacrifices associated with benevolent acts of service. It *feels* better to be overtaxed by the burden of abetting others than it does to be exempt from helping at all. In order to alleviate tensions, sacrificial thinkers will overextend themselves even while complaining about it—they don't want to be taken advantage of, their brain *needs* to be taken advantage of. This is why we have designated needs zones.

Another great example of tension reduction would be experiencing undo conflicts because one fails to receive the credit for a job well done. This was wonderfully displayed on a past episode of Seinfeld.[106] At Elaine's request, George purchases a "big

---

106 "The Big Salad" is the 88th episode of the NBC sitcom Seinfeld. This was the second episode for the sixth season. It aired on September 29, 1994

salad" to go for her from Monk's. When George asks Jerry, "What's in the *big* salad?", Jerry replies, "Big lettuce, big carrots, tomatoes like volleyballs." But George's girlfriend Julie (Michelle Forbes) unwittingly appears to take credit for the purchase when she hands Elaine the salad in Jerry's apartment. George is irritated that Elaine thanked Julie for buying the salad and mentions to Elaine that he was responsible for the purchase. George's revelation eventually leads to a rift between him and Julie when the truth comes out. The brain-tension is obvious and makes for great comedy.

The truth, in George's view, is not that Elaine thanked the wrong person, but that Julie accepted the thanks and robbed George of the personal security he needs to feel good about himself. As George makes loud and clear, "What I would like to know is, how does a person who has virtually nothing to do with the Big Salad claim responsibility for that salad and accept the thank-you under false pretenses?" Julie understands perfectly well, and says, "George, all I did was hand someone a bag." Semi-humiliated for exposing his insecurities, George vows never to buy Elaine lunch again.

George is clearly insecure. His IMO would likely sport a greater consistency in individualism and optimism and lesser consistency in his theoretical dimension and compliance. Individualism is not only about freedom and autonomy; it's also about the *need* to be seen as different and *unique—special*. George's girlfriend robbed him of his uniqueness and specialness by appearing to have purchased Elaine's lunch. Because George has an overextended optimistic emotion his insecurities ruled his reason.

Optimism flows with individualism and will have such an effect that it can highjack your rational mind, leaving you wishing you had kept your comments to yourself. Let's take a brief look at the 37 styles. I will explain just enough to give you the groundwork around how these styles operate. I will briefly touch on the three theoretical positions as they relate to each style. It will seem repetitive, but I believe it's necessary for remembering how these motivational orientations work and flow with our emotions. Some thoughts may seem repetitive, but this is because the patterns necessitate the same needs.

The Dominator

The dominator style-1 desire framework represents greater consistency in the power and economic elements (power is more consistent) and lesser consistency in the aesthetic, individualistic, and altruistic elements. The main objective for this style is to seek practical applications, authority equal to or greater than responsibility, position power, and control over one's own space as well as those who may find themselves within their space.

Their basic desire is to structure, direct, and to willingly take and maintain control of their space and destiny. These types are strongly self-interested and self-directed (not to be confused with selfish) and will work long and hard to gain what they believe belongs to them. They desire to own their personal work, space, life, and future.

Motivational Direction and Consistency Graph
The Dominator

	0	10	20	30	40	50	60	70	80	90	100
ORIGINALITY	0	10	20	30	40	50	60	70	80	90	100
EFFICIENCY	0	10	20	30	40	50	60	70	80	90	100
INDIVIDUALITY	0	10	20	30	40	50	60	70	80	90	100
POWER	0	10	20	30	40	50	60	70	80	90	100
SACRIFICE	0	10	20	30	40	50	60	70	80	90	100
COMPLIANCE	0	10	20	30	40	50	60	70	80	90	100
CURIOSITY	0	10	20	30	40	50	60	70	80	90	100

Their basic learning preference means they can strongly enforce the ideas and rules they may know little about. Rather than studying to know, they will quickly cram to pass. They may not like spending time in the part of their brain that methodically and painstakingly sifts through the unnecessary details or that solves difficult math problems or plans.

They will usually seek entrepreneurial groups, physical fitness activities that *prove* their winning side, status, structured environments, and leadership roles with upward movement. They desire to win their competitions and may see most people as opponents instead of allies.

They will likely focus on practical applications, structuring, systematizing, owning their ideas, building self-confidence, and fabricating relationships that will assist in advancing their position within the world and that meet their personal needs *first*. Structuring their surroundings by drawing hard, no-nonsense lines and functioning within them is commonplace with these types.

Although these ideas are desirable, they can be unexpectedly trumped by behaviors born out of their emotional consistencies and inconsistencies. Although a dominating style may desire to control their environment, little consistency in their anger emotion will not allow it to fully materialize.

Potential blockers are created when this style's only desire is to direct and control or agree or disagree with others rather than understand their plight. They tend towards self-interest and may meet their own needs first and then the needs of others after their own needs are met or others qualify for their costly attention or concern. Passive behavior types will enact these desirables in a very different way than a dominant type will.

Their strength lies in their unshakable confidence, their desire to own their own space, the need to direct and control their own destiny, and to manage difficult and complex situations. They are usually strong leaders who take personal initiative in an effort to climb the ladder within their work and personal life. They draw hard lines and tend to only work within real-world systems that function well.

Inner and outer conflicts associated with this style include overindulgence in practical matters without respect for others' creative imagination or intuition. Conflict responses include disregarding others creative opinions and ideas, drawing strict boundaries that carry harsh consequences when crossed, seeing others as intruders rather than partners, and overemphasizing personal needs over others. Emotions may be disregarded as trivial and actions may become the hero.

Style-2's main objective is the same as style-1 as it is to seek practical applications, authority equal to or greater than their responsibility, position power, and control over their own space as well as those who may find themselves within their space just like style 1. Their basic desire is to create structured environments that make sense, as well as to own their own life and destiny. The difference will be found in their learning preference.

Their basic learning preference means they can strongly enforce the ideas and rules you know only something about—not everything. Rather than studying to know everything, you may cram to know just enough to get themselves over the hump. Like style-1, they may not like spending too much time in the part of their brain that painstakingly sifts through unnecessary and boring details or solves complex math problems, but they'll be more apt to investigate further.

Because of a greater theoretical consistency, style-2 usually seeks knowledge, interesting facts, entrepreneurial groups, physical fitness activities, status, structured and functional environments, and leadership roles with upward movement and public recognition. Like style 1 they will desire to win their competitions and may see many people as opponents instead of allies. They will likely focus on learning more than style-1, systematizing, and owning their own work-space and ideas. They may focus on building self-confidence and fabricating certain relationships that they know will help advance their position in the world.

Style-3's main objective is to seek knowledge, practical applications, and authority equal to or greater than their responsibility as well. The learning preference takes a giant leap in comparison to styles 1 and 2. Style-3 will have an excessive need to uncover, discover, and recover the truth/facts about anything that has a perceived value. This type will likely have a very logical/analytical approach to problem-solving deeply rooted in rational thought as opposed to feelings and intuitions. Their capacity for useful insight and absorbing large amounts of information will be one of their greatest strengths.

The Achiever

The achiever style-1's desire framework represents some consistency in the power (not as consistent as the dominator) and greater consistency in the economic factor and regulating elements and lesser consistency in the aesthetic and altruistic elements. The greatest difference between the achiever and the dominator is the economic element is much higher than the power element. In the dominating style, power is more consistent than the economic impulse.

Their main objective is to seek practical means of achieving status, success, and control over their own life and destiny. Their goal is primarily associated with personal gains and real-world outcomes that bring security and benefits to the self. Their basic desire is to use their practical experiences as boosters while leveraging their ability to control and direct the most advantageous outcomes for themselves. They desire reliable systems that have proven their worth in the past.

Their basic learning preference means they can strongly influence using the ideas and rules they know little about. Rather than studying to know, they may simply cram to pass. They don't like spending inordinate amounts of time in the part of their brain that gets bogged down with unimportant or unnecessary details or that solves complex problems.

Motivational Direction and Consistency Graph
The Achiever

Trait	0	10	20	30	40	50	60	70	80	90	100
ORIGINALITY					30						
EFFICIENCY								70-80			
INDIVIDUALITY						50					
POWER							60				
SACRIFICE		10	20								
COMPLIANCE					40						
CURIOSITY						50					

They will likely seek entrepreneurial groups, mastermind groups, and relationships that better their public standing in the world. They may like physical activities, status, structured environments, and leadership roles defined by who you know and that come with upward movement and promise. They usually focus on personal gains, systematizing, and owning their own space and ideas. They focus on building self-confidence and developing relationships that will advance their position within the world. They focus on innovative and intuitive processes for making progressive upward associations that promise clout and solidarity with important people.

Potential blockers are created when they seek to direct and control or agree or disagree with others rather than understand their plight much like the dominator. They tend towards self-interest and may meet their own needs first and then the needs of others if they qualify. This is due to the limited sacrificial piece. They are usually unwilling to sacrifice of their own for others unless there's a benefit to doing it. They can be suspicious of others and will keep an emotional distance from those who may desire to be close to them.

Their strength lies in their unshakable confidence, ability to advance their ideas, own their own work-space, direct and control their own destiny, and manage difficult situations. They can be a strong leader who takes personal pride and initiative in an effort to climb the ladder within their work and personal life. They are likely able to present well due to their individualism and will be direct, practical, and more innovative than the dominator tends to be.

Inner and outer conflicts associated with the achieving style include overindulgence in practical matters without respect for any creative intuition in other people. Potential conflict responses include disregarding other people's creative opinions, seeing others as intruders, and overemphasizing their personal needs. Boundaries may be drawn but may contain more wiggle room than allowed by the dominating style.

Much like style-1, the achieving style-2's main objective is to seek practical means of achieving status, success, and control over their own life and destiny. their goal is primarily associated with personal gains and real-world outcomes that bring security and benefits to the self. Style-2's basic desire is to use their practical experiences as boosters while leveraging their ability to control and direct the most advantageous outcomes for themselves and their future.

Their basic learning preference means they can strongly enforce the ideas and rules they know only something about—not everything. Rather than studying to know everything, they will learn just enough to get over the hump. They don't like spending inordinate amounts of time in the part of their brain that gets bogged down with unimportant or unnecessary trivia or details.

Style-3's main objective is the same in that it is to seek practical means of achieving status, success, and control over their own life and destiny. The difference lies in their learning preference. Their basic learning preference means they can strongly enforce the ideas and rules they know *everything* about. Rather than studying to know something, they will learn everything there is to know about a subject. They appreciate spending inordinate amounts of time in the rational part of their brain that solves complex problems and discovers new things and ideas about things.

The Instructor

The main objective of the instructor style-1 is to create a distinct difference between them and the rest of the world while expressing their intuitive and innovative ideas among their peers or within a public forum. Greater consistency in individualism, and aestheticism and lesser consistency in regulation and theoretical thinking will account for this desire framework. Greater consistency in individualism always accounts for better influencing and presenting dexterities. Power and economic influences are held at bay or nominal in these cases. The theoretical component is lesser and as a result will expose the innovative side to their thinking.

Their basic desire is to prove their freedom, resourcefulness, autonomy, and independence to the world while schooling and promoting to their peers their innovative, imaginative, and often astonishing ideas. They desire the freedom and permission to march to the beat of their own drum without having to wear a conventional strait-jacket. Their basic learning preference means they can strongly promote and enforce the ideas and rules they know little about.

Rather than studying to know, like all lesser theoretical types, they may simply cram to pass. They don't like spending inordinate amounts of time in the part of your brain that gets bogged down with unimportant or unnecessary details. Unlike the achiever and dominator, the instructor types will rely more heavily on their keen *intuition* and past *experiences* for decision-making.

These styles will seek continued education, entrepreneurial groups, mastermind groups, and relationships that allow them to be center stage—presenting to groups and sharing their "out-of-the-box" ideas energize them. Their brain can accept and enjoy the spotlight much more than dominating types. They will usually focus on personal gains, being the maverick, subversive and spontaneous creative expression, and using your own methodology for making personal gains within the world. They tend to focus on being distinctive and unique while also maintaining influence and affiliation with others.

Motivational Direction and Consistency Graph
The Instructor

	0	10	20	30	40	50	60	70	80	90	100
ORIGINALITY					40	50					
EFFICIENCY						50					
INDIVIDUALITY						50	60				
POWER						50	60				
SACRIFICE					40	50					
COMPLIANCE					40	50					
CURIOSITY						50	60	70			

Potential blockers are created when they only direct and control or agree or disagree with others rather than understand their plight. This is due to the fact that although their economic and power drives are not super consistent, they're average or above average, nonetheless. They tend towards self-interest and independence because their sacrificial system is not in play. Their unorthodox stratagems may lead to a subversive mentality that can cause them to be different for difference sake rather than their differences being of any real value.

Their strength lies within their innovative and creative ability, unshakable confidence, ability to advance your ideas, own their own space, direct and control their own destiny, and manage difficult situations in unconventional ways. They can potentially be strong leaders who take personal initiative in an effort to climb the ladder within their work and living spaces. They can be direct, expressive, atypical and innovative.

Inner and outer conflicts associated with this style include indulgences related to meeting personal needs and an excessive need to be independent of others and their ideas or the star of the show. Inner conflict responses include excessive autonomy needs with a heavy reliance on what they think other people know to be true.

Style-2's main objective is the same; to create a distinct difference between them and the rest of the world while expressing their intuitive and innovative ideas among their peers or within a public forum. The learning preference is a bit different as it denotes strongly promoting ideas and rules they have only recently learned about. Rather than studying to know everything, like the others, they will know just enough to get over the hump.

Style-3's learning preference means they can strongly promote and enforce the ideas and rules you have learned through excessive study. Rather than studying to know something, they will want to know everything. They can appreciate spending time in the part of their brain that wants to know why. They will rely on their keen intuition and past experiences combined with a deep neural knowledge-bank.

The Pragmatist

The pragmatist style-1's main objective is to develop efficient, functional, and practical, methods of achieving moderate management over their own life and destiny as well as the lives of others who will allow it. This style is more economically driven and regulated with less creative modalities. They desire to establish structured systems and reliable routines for life and work. They desire to achieve a balanced and cooperative relationship with the world and those people who will have a direct effect upon it in an effort to manage its outcomes by establishing order, routine, and reliable systems for living.

Motivational Direction and Consistency Graph
The Pragmatist

	0	10	20	30	40	50	60	70	80	90	100
ORIGINALITY	0	10	20	30	40	50	60	70	80	90	100
EFFICIENCY	0	10	20	30	40	50	60	70	80	90	100
INDIVIDUALITY	0	10	20	30	40	50	60	70	80	90	100
POWER	0	10	20	30	40	50	60	70	80	90	100
SACRIFICE	0	10	20	30	40	50	60	70	80	90	100
COMPLIANCE	0	10	20	30	40	50	60	70	80	90	100
CURIOSITY	0	10	20	30	40	50	60	70	80	90	100

Their basic learning preference means they can strongly push the ideas and rules they may know little about. Rather than studying to know, like the other style-1's, they may simply know just enough to pass. They don't like spending inordinate amounts of time in the part of their brain that gets bogged down with complex, unimportant or unnecessary details. They will rely on practical horse sense, past experiences, and real-world thinking.

They will want to seek some control, structure, and dependable means to achieve real-world results, which may include leading, management opportunities, cooperative environments where their views can be levied on others, and entrepreneurial exploits. They will likely focus on leading others through life's maze through levelheaded team efforts, structured reasoning, and street-smart routines that have worked in the past. They rely heavily on past experiences, common sense, and current knowledge.

Potential blockers are created when their somewhat static (rigid) mindset disables them from thinking too far outside the box or appreciating the diversity of ideas offered by others. Rather than seeking out and digging deep for new insights, they tend to rely on what they already know. Their over-reliance on what they "think" is right may block them from knowing what to do or doing the right thing.

Their strength lies in their ability to manage and work with others who think along the same lines as them without overly vacillating. They are structured in their thinking and can easily rely upon proven and already established methods for accomplishing tasks. Inner and outer conflicts associated with this style include a moderate decreased passion for controlling their own space with a high need for structured environments and outcomes. Inner conflict responses may include excessive black and white or either/or thinking even when all the facts may allow wiggle room. They may also be tempted to strictly enforce their own ideas on others and hold them to certain standards for living.

The pragmatist style-2 is the same as the others with a basic learning preference as situational. Rather than studying to know everything about a matter, they may only focus on what they need to know. Style-3 will have an excessive need to uncover, discover, and recover the truth/facts about anything. They will have a practical/analytical approach to problem-solving deeply rooted in rational complex thought. Their capacity for useful insight and absorbing large amounts of information will be one of their greatest strengths.

The Maintainer

The maintainers style-1's main objective is to maintain and even-keeled view of the world while not overstepping bounds or delving into any extremes that may cause you to stand out among others or to veer from the acceptable social norms most people expect. This style primarily has all their elements falling along the averages. Their basic desire is to achieve a balanced and cooperative relationship with the world system and those people who will have a direct effect on them in an effort to manage outcomes carefully without leaning too heavily towards any extremes or excessive ideas.

Their basic learning preference means they can gently push the ideas and rules they know little about. Rather than studying to know, they will learn enough to get by. they will likely rely on their balanced intuition and past reliable experiences. They will likely seek the status-quo within the areas of life and work and will seek simple and serene activities that won't overstretch their values or appear immoderate to others, thus keeping them in line with 68 percent of the population.

Motivational Direction and Consistency Graph
The Maintainer

	0	10	20	30	40	50	60	70	80	90	100
ORIGINALITY	0	10	20	30	40	50	60	70	80	90	100
EFFICIENCY	0	10	20	30	40	50	60	70	80	90	100
INDIVIDUALITY	0	10	20	30	40	50	60	70	80	90	100
POWER	0	10	20	30	40	50	60	70	80	90	100
SACRIFICE	0	10	20	30	40	50	60	70	80	90	100
COMPLIANCE	0	10	20	30	40	50	60	70	80	90	100
CURIOSITY	0	10	20	30	40	50	60	70	80	90	100

Their primary focus is developing simple predictable strategies that allow them to blend with the culture including but not limited to avoiding over-thinking, imagining new things, or over-controlling their environment. Potential blockers are created when their lack of passion impedes with their ability to make quick, risky or bold gains in their space. Their lack of attention to cognitive reason and complex thinking may disable them from quickly achieving the results they may desire.

Their strength lies in their ability to maintain middle ground and avoid extremes and excesses that may create unwanted exposure to unnecessary challenges or inconvenient controversies. Their indifference to individualism can help them achieve the trust of others, equilibrium, and non-threatening appearance.

Inner and outer conflicts associated with this style include a moderate or decreased passion for self-mastery and the unquestionable truth as others see it. Inner conflict responses may include not digging into important matters deep enough when necessary and a nonchalant approach to problems, challenges, and opportunities.

Like the rest, pragmatist style-2 learning preferences means they can gently push the ideas and rules they understand. Rather than studying to know everything, they will learn enough to get them to the next step. Pragmatist style-3's have an excessive need to unearth the truth/facts about most anything of interest. They will have a creative/analytical approach to problem-solving deeply rooted in unconventional/rational thought. Their capacity for useful insight and absorbing large amounts of information will be one of their greatest strengths.

The Freedom Seeker

The freedom seeker style-1's main objective is to seek and establish freedom, autonomy, independence, uniqueness, and control of their own space and time while seeking "out-of-the-box" approaches to problems, challenges, and opportunities. This style encompasses excessive individualism and lesser economic driving and regulated thinking. Their basic desire is to find alternative "out-of-the-box" approaches to creating the life they want as well as opportunities to present their self-directed ideas to the world. They will see their maverick approaches to tasks as worthy and acceptable regardless of other opinions to the contrary. Their basic learning preference means they can gently push the ideas and rules they know little about. Rather than studying to know, like the others they will learn enough to get by. They will seek the spotlight through presenting, teaching, innovating, or within groups where they play a larger role in developing and expressing their own ideas.

Motivational Direction and Consistency Graph
The Freedom-Seeker

	0	10	20	30	40	50	60	70	80	90	100
ORIGINALITY	0	10	20	30	40	50	60	70	80	90	100
EFFICIENCY	0	10	20	30	40	50	60	70	80	90	100
INDIVIDUALITY	0	10	20	30	40	50	60	70	80	90	100
POWER	0	10	20	30	40	50	60	70	80	90	100
SACRIFICE	0	10	20	30	40	50	60	70	80	90	100
COMPLIANCE	0	10	20	30	40	50	60	70	80	90	100
CURIOSITY	0	10	20	30	40	50	60	70	80	90	100

They will focus on intuitive presentations, teachings, and creative expressions that involve unorthodox, boundary-pushing innovations while drawing unconventional, subversive, and maverick differences between others and themselves. Potential blockers are created when they take an unconventional or controversial approach to problems, challenges, and opportunities in an effort to explore differences and separate themselves from the status-quo. If they're a low compliant thinker, they may guess rather than take the time to explore all aspects of a situation before making an important decision.

Their strength lies in their ability to think outside the box, push the boundaries, move the goalpost, and develop unconventional ideas. They're creative problem solvers who take the time to "experience" the world around them while showing others how to take more chances. They believe there's more than one way to skin a cat and may innovate their way to the top.

Inner and outer conflicts associated with this style include a high need to stand out from others within the world while not gaining the necessary knowledge and confidence to support their rebel spirit. They may also run the risk of dreaming more and doing less. At times they might feel like a unicorn or creative dreamer.

Style 2's basic learning preference means they can gently push the ideas and rules they have recently learned. Rather than studying to know everything, they will learn enough to get over the hump. Style-3 will spend a lot of time researching and accumulating facts to support their intuitive, complex, and interesting ideas. Their excessive need to know will drive them deeper into the learning experience.

Freedom seeking style 3's strengths lies in their ability to think innovatively, push the envelope, and expand their ideas well beyond the norm. They are creative problem solvers who take the time to seek and find the necessary truths around issues while teaching others and learning how to leverage their calculated risks.

Inner and outer conflicts associated with style 3 include a high need to stand out among others within the world with little reliance on their excessive knowledge, which would accompany them in avoiding the pitfalls that attend their rebel spirit. They may also run the risk of thinking or imagining more than they may be willing to do.

The Forfeiter

The forfeiter style-1's main objective is to seek creative, cooperative, and traditional avenues of assisting others with their life goals while sidestepping challenging people, difficult circumstances, and strong ideas. This is due to greater consistency in sacrifice and lesser consistency in power, individualism, and efficiency.

Motivational Direction and Consistency Graph
The Forfeiter

ORIGINALITY	0	10	20	30	40	50	60	70	80	90	100
EFFICIENCY	0	10	20	30	40	50	60	70	80	90	100
INDIVIDUALITY	0	10	20	30	40	50	60	70	80	90	100
POWER	0	10	20	30	40	50	60	70	80	90	100
SACRIFICE	0	10	20	30	40	50	60	70	80	90	100
COMPLIANCE	0	10	20	30	40	50	60	70	80	90	100
CURIOSITY	0	10	20	30	40	50	60	70	80	90	100

Their basic desire is to cooperate with others through creative expression without abandoning traditional and predictable methods that have worked in the past. Meeting the needs of others while forfeiting their own needs will make them feel accomplished and trustworthy within the world. These attributes stem from lesser consistency in efficiency and power with greater consistency in sacrificial bents and regulation.

Like the other styles, type-1's will not be interested in over-investing or over-indulging their rational mind through excessive study or investigation. This is known as intuitive or fractured learning. They learn more through intuition, past experience, and instinct rather than exploring arduous learning paths involving textbooks, excessive seek and find, or classroom settings.

They will usually seek quiet and creative outlets, creative expression, the outdoors, hobbies, imaginative expression, the arts, and alternative solutions to solving other people's problems. They usually focus on assisting others and their needs while effectively neglecting their own. Finding creative and alternative solutions that produce a sense of purpose or support a meaningful cause is commonplace for this type.

Potential blockers are created when they settle for what they can get as opposed to fighting for what they want. You may see mundane work as a necessary evil and therefore may put more energy into dreaming rather than doing what you love. Their strength is two-fold and lies in their ability to think unconventionally and go with their gut feelings. They're a creative person who is likely excessively benevolent, cooperative, and usually principled. They think in a strict, boxed manner and may walk a straight line for fear of being a bad person.

Inner and outer conflicts associated with this style can include surrendering to the circumstances and a desiring to set a standard blueprint for others to follow. If it's right for them it's right for everyone. Holding others to strict standards of living in the world may block them from experiencing stronger relationships that include differences. They may at times be overly hard on themselves.

Like the other styles afore mentioned, learning preferences will differ based on theoretical consistencies. I won't bother repeating how this works any further as you probably have gotten the idea how this works by now. All I will point out is the greatest theoretical differences will include spending too much time looking for answers they already have and a fear of looking dumb.

The Storyteller

The storyteller style-1's main objective is to seek autonomy as well as creative, cooperative, and traditional avenues of assisting others with their life goals while sidestepping challenging people and ideas. They will have an original/unconventional approach to problems, challenges, and opportunities and may find it hard to be understood by others. When faced with established rules, systems, or protocols, they may display a standalone Gypsy-Spirit that defies conventional thought.

Motivational Direction and Consistency Graph
The Storyteller

ORIGINALITY	0	10	20	30	40	50	60	70	80	90	100
EFFICIENCY	0	10	20	30	40	50	60	70	80	90	100
INDIVIDUALITY	0	10	20	30	40	50	60	70	80	90	100
POWER	0	10	20	30	40	50	60	70	80	90	100
SACRIFICE	0	10	20	30	40	50	60	70	80	90	100
COMPLIANCE	0	10	20	30	40	50	60	70	80	90	100
CURIOSITY	0	10	20	30	40	50	60	70	80	90	100

This is due to greater consistencies in personal sacrifice, aesthetic and individualistic elements, and lesser consistencies in regulatory, economic, and power elements. Basic learning preference include strongly enforce the ideas and rules they may know little about. Rather than studying to know, they will cram to pass. They don't like spending inordinate amounts of time in the part of their brain that solves math problems. They are better at relying on their intuition, past experiences, and instincts.

This style will likely seek creative and innovative outlets, creative expression, the outdoors, imaginative expression, the arts, and alternative and sometimes-unconventional solutions to solving personal as well as other people's problems. They will focus on creative expression and assisting others and their needs while oftentimes neglecting their own. Finding creative and alternative solutions that produce a sense of purpose in the world is commonplace for this type.

Potential blockers are created when they settle for what they can get as opposed to fighting for what they want. This style may see mundane work as a necessary evil and therefore may put more energy into dreaming rather than doing what they love. They will be interested in gaining enough practical knowledge to solve immediate problems but will not likely pursue knowledge for knowledge's sake.

Their strengths are three-fold and lies in their ability to think outside the box, present ideas well, and express with intuition. They are creative problem solvers who are likely benevolent, cooperative, and usually unconventional. Inner and outer conflicts associated with this style include a high need to innovate without accessing the knowledge to support it. Certain causes and missions may sidetrack them and take president over achieving what they really want in life.

Theoretical differences in style-2 and style-3 can create inner and outer conflicts associated with a greater need to innovate while feeling restricted by a need to seek the truth by uncovering many more facts before deciding what to do. Excessive investigation with little conclusions can haunt a style-3 creating frustration for those who are more conventional and efficiency-minded.

The Nonconformist

The nonconformist Style-1's main objective is resigning to enjoying the life they have while experiencing the world around them in creative and meaningful ways. They are typically interested in environmental cause and effect strategies useful to the enhancement of the earth and its inhabitance as well as unconventional approaches to life and work.

This stems from higher aesthetic, theoretical, and individualistic elements (on the scale) with lesser regulation elements. The basic desire is to find creative ways to express inner creativity and experience world surroundings. They will seek personal fulfillment through unconventional and creative expression, inspirational activities, and "out of the box" thinking.

Learning preference include disinterest in using the rational mind through excessive study to solve problems and not pursuing knowledge for knowledge's sake. They learn more through intuition, past experience, and original instinct rather than taking the arduous path involving textbooks, tedious lessons, or lackluster classroom settings.

Motivational Direction and Consistency Graph
The Nonconformist

	0	10	20	30	40	50	60	70	80	90	100
ORIGINALITY											
EFFICIENCY											
INDIVIDUALITY											
POWER											
SACRIFICE											
COMPLIANCE											
CURIOSITY											

This style usually seeks a mission or cause greater than the self to invest their time, intuition, and talent, where returns can be both rewarding and helpful to their personal psyche without unnecessary conflicts or confrontations. They usually focus on attractive presentations, teachings, and creative experiences that involve nature or their "own tribe" for the purpose of making an unconventional difference in the world. They may be active in volunteering their time, resources, and talent to worthy or environmental causes.

Potential blockers are created when they take a back seat and don't drive their agenda to a conclusion. Oftentimes appreciating the spotlight, they inadvertently focus too much attention on their own issues. They can be somewhat insecure and will only project an illusion of self-confidence that may falter if someone calls their bluff.

Strengths lay in their ability to think "outside the box" and work tirelessly for a cause or mission larger than themselves. they're intuitive and imaginative thinkers who take the time to "experience" the world around them as opposed to just passing through it without a sense of meaning or real impact.

Inner and outer conflicts associated with this style include a predisposition to sacrificial thinking or yielding their position when things get tough. At times they may find themselves settling for what they can get instead of fighting for what they want. Greater theoretical consistencies generate styles 2 and 3 and will result in more investigative researching and a greater need to know why.

The Starving artist

The main objective for the starving artist style-1 is to seek freedom and autonomy as well as creative, cooperative, and unconventional avenues of self-expression. Their gypsy spirit mindset will cause them to seek self-expressive venues and opportunities where they can harmonize with their surroundings. This is due to excessively consistent drives in aesthetics and individualism with excessively less consistencies in ambition and efficiency.

The starving artist will have an original/unconventional approach to problems, challenges, and opportunities and may find it hard to be understood by others. When faced with established rules, systems, or protocols, they may display a standalone wondering spirit. This stems from lesser consistency in regulated thinking.

Their basic learning preference includes strongly embrace ideas and rules they may know little about. Rather than studying to know, they cram to pass. They don't like spending inordinate amounts of time in the part of their brain that solves math problems. They fair much better at relying on intuition and animal instincts.

This style will seek creative and innovative outlets, creative expression, the outdoors, imaginative expression, the arts, harmonious environments, and alternative and sometimes-unconventional solutions to world problems. They will focus on imaginative expression and finding innovative and alternative solutions that produce a sense of purpose in the world. Seeking inspiring opportunities for their artistic expression is commonplace for this type.

Motivational Direction and Consistency Graph
The Starving artist

Category	0	10	20	30	40	50	60	70	80	90	100
ORIGINALITY											
EFFICIENCY											
INDIVIDUALITY											
POWER											
SACRIFICE											
COMPLIANCE											
CURIOSITY											

Potential blockers are created when they settle for what they can get as opposed to fighting for what they want. You may put a lot of energy into dreaming bigger than you may be able to do. You may feel misunderstood and might struggle with figuring out your next move. Their strength is three-fold and lies in their ability to think outside the box, tap into their inner self, and express with their intuition. They are very creative thinkers who can be keen, environmentally friendly, and resourceful.

Inner and outer conflicts associated with this inspirational style include a high need to innovate without accessing the knowledge to support it. Certain causes and missions may easily sidetrack them and take precedence over achieving what they really want in life.

Greater theoretical advantages create a more scientific and experimental approach to life. Rather than needing to know why, this type will need to *experience* the unusual. This might show up through the use of psychedelics, alternative lifestyles, and indulgences way outside of the mainstream.

The Yearner

The yearner Style-1's main objective is to seek and establish freedom, autonomy, independence, and control of their own space and time, while at the same time, regulating and establishing important boundaries. This stems from greater consistency in regulation, aesthetics, individualism, and power, and lesser consistency in economic drive.

This style will *yearn* for alternative approaches to creating the life they want as well as opportunities to present their self-directed ideas to the world. Although they may think like an individualist, they may end up doing what is traditionally expected in the end. Learning preference include gently pushing the ideas and rules they know little about. Rather than studying to know, they may only learn enough to get by. They tend to rely on their creative intuition and past successes when gathering information for moving ahead.

They may yearn for the spotlight through presenting, teaching, innovating, or within traditional groups where they play a larger role in developing and expressing their own ideas but may lack the courage to make it happen. They will focus on systematic, traditional presentations and learnings salted with some creative expression that involve "how I believe things ought to be."

They may at times desire to push boundaries but in the end might second guess themselves. Potential blockers are created when they prefer a conventional or traditional approach to problems and opportunities when what they really want is to be separated from the status-quo. They may experience a strong desire to be independent but may experience trepidation when it comes to pushing the envelope.

Motivational Direction and Consistency Graph
The Yearner

	0	10	20	30	40	50	60	70	80	90	100
ORIGINALITY	0	10	20	30	40	50	60	70	80	90	100
EFFICIENCY	0	10	20	30	40	50	60	70	80	90	100
INDIVIDUALITY	0	10	20	30	40	50	60	70	80	90	100
POWER	0	10	20	30	40	50	60	70	80	90	100
SACRIFICE	0	10	20	30	40	50	60	70	80	90	100
COMPLIANCE	0	10	20	30	40	50	60	70	80	90	100
CURIOSITY	0	10	20	30	40	50	60	70	80	90	100

Strength lay in their ability to think outside the box and develop unconventional ideas. They're creative problem solvers who take the time to "experience" the world around them while showing others "how to live within a *reliable* and *safe* system." Inner and outer conflicts associated with this style include a high need to stand out from others in the world while not gaining the necessary knowledge and confidence to support their imaginative spirit.

They may also run the risk of dreaming more than they are willing to do. At times they might feel like breaking out of their established rules prison. Greater consistency in the theoretical dimension will engender greater effort in understanding why and may lead towards more experimentation. When boundaries are crossed, this style will tend to justify their reasons as opposed to verifying their subversion.

The Enforcer

The enforcer Style-1's objective is to seek practical applications, authority equal to or greater than their responsibility, position power, and control over their own space as well as those who may find themselves within their space. This is due to very consistent (high on the values-scale) regulation, power, and efficiency.

This style's basic desire is to structure, direct, and to willingly take and maintain control of their space and future destiny. They are strongly self-interested and self-directed (not to be confused with selfish) and will work long and hard to gain what they believe belongs to them. They desire to own their personal work, space, and life.

Learning preferences include very strongly enforcing ideas and rules they know little about on others. Rather than studying to know, they may quickly cram to pass. They may not like spending time in the part of their brain that methodically and painstakingly sifts through the unnecessary details or that solves difficult math problems.

This style will usually seek entrepreneurial groups, physical fitness activities that prove their winning side, status, structured environments, and leadership roles with upward movement. They desire to win their competitions and will see others as opponents instead of allies. They will likely focus on practical applications, structuring, systematizing, owning their own ideas, building self-confidence, and fabricating relationships that will assist in advancing their position within the world. Structuring their surroundings by drawing hard no-nonsense lines and functioning within them is commonplace with this type.

Potential blockers are created when their only desire is to direct and control or agree or disagree with others rather than understand their plight. They tend towards self-interest and may meet their own needs first and then the needs of others after their own needs are met or others qualify for their costly attention.

Strengths lay in their unshakable confidence, their ability to own their own space, the need to direct and control their own destiny, and to manage difficult and complex situations. These styles can be strong leaders who takes personal initiative in an effort to climb the ladder within their work and life. They tend to only work within real-world systems that function well.

Motivational Direction and Consistency Graph
The Enforcer

ORIGINALITY	0	10	20	30	40	50	60	70	80	90	100
EFFICIENCY	0	10	20	30	40	50	60	70	80	90	100
INDIVIDUALITY	0	10	20	30	40	50	60	70	80	90	100
POWER	0	10	20	30	40	50	60	70	80	90	100
SACRIFICE	0	10	20	30	40	50	60	70	80	90	100
COMPLIANCE	0	10	20	30	40	50	60	70	80	90	100
CURIOSITY	0	10	20	30	40	50	60	70	80	90	100

Inner and outer conflicts associated with this style include overindulgence in practical matters without respect for others' creative imagination and intuition. Conflict responses include disregarding people's creative opinions and ideas, drawing strict boundaries that carry harsh consequences when crossed, seeing others as intruders rather than partners, and overemphasizing personal needs over others. Greater consistencies within the theoretical element always leads to a "know-it-all" type behavior. Knowledge is used as a controlling agent.

The Experimenter

The experimenter style-1 is the same as the starving artist but with greater theoretical drive. Your main objective is to seek unconventional, complex, and outlying avenues of self-expression through experimentation or very creative means. Your gypsy-spirit mindset will cause you to seek self-expressive venues and opportunities where you can experiment with new and exciting experiences.

These styles will have an original/unconventional approach to problems, challenges, and opportunities and may find it hard to be understood by others. When faced with established rules, systems, or protocols, they may display a standalone wondering spirit that defies conventional thought.

Their basic learning preference includes putting a lot of energy into interesting and complex investigations. They will experiment with different experiences as a way to learn new things and may be out of the mainstream among their peers.

Motivational Direction and Consistency Graph
The Experimenter

	0	10	20	30	40	50	60	70	80	90	100
ORIGINALITY											
EFFICIENCY											
INDIVIDUALITY											
POWER											
SACRIFICE											
COMPLIANCE											
CURIOSITY											

They will likely seek creative and innovative outlets, creative expression, the outdoors, imaginative expression, the arts, harmonious environments, and alternative and sometimes-unconventional experiences. These types will likely focus on imaginative expression and finding innovative and alternative solutions that produce a sense of purpose in the world. Seeking inspiring opportunities for their complex expression is commonplace for this type.

Like the starving artist, potential blockers are created when they settle for what they can get as opposed to fighting for what they want. They put a lot of energy into dreaming bigger than they may be able to do. You may feel misunderstood much like a unicorn among a world of horses. This style's strength is three-fold and lies in their ability to think outside the box, tap into their inner self, and express with their intuition. They are creative thinkers who are likely keen, innovative, and unrelenting in their pursuit of truth.

Inner and outer conflicts associated with their complex style include a high need to achieve a type of nirvana. Certain experimental missions may sidetrack them and take precedence over achieving what they really want in life. There are no other theoretical consistency levels associated with this type other than a greater consistency.

13
BEING THE BEST VERSION OF YOUR BEST SELF

Human motivation is inside all of us. The four primary emotions are alive and kicking in all of us. We all have a particular worldview and a self-view. Every human being in the world has a trajectory that began in the womb and has lasted until now. Our thoughts and choices are a result of prior causes largely unconscious to all of us. All of our goals, plans, and alleged willpower are causal states of the brain, leading to emotional triggers, which lead to certain behavioral outcomes that affect the world and people around us.[107]

Our specific wants, needs, and desires are always dependent on our emotional framework for greater or lesser flow. Emotions and behaviors outmaneuver our desires. In other words, what I want will not always align with what I ultimately end up doing. For example; I desire a raise, but I struggle to ask for it. I'm outlining the fundamentals of being human. Understanding and embracing our humanness is axiomatic to enjoying our life and fulfilling our purpose.

Laying the groundwork for you to be the best version of yourself is important. Houses don't exist apart from foundations; at least not good houses. Great houses take time to build. Your purpose, like a great house will take time to be discovered. It doesn't come easy; it has to be cultivated in order to grow like a well-watered garden. Your purpose is a part of yourself—it's organic.

Dreaming

Part of beginning your journey to your best self begins with simple daydreams—dreaming about what it would be like to do what you love or care about. To be free from the decisions and

---

[107] Sam Harris, *Free Will*, Pg. 34

distractions of others not designed for your best interest and free to do what you already are, lays the groundwork for being the best version of you possible. You can dream on the clock if you're working as long as it doesn't negatively impact your performance, but it's probably better to dream at lunch or with a cat on your lap or by a pond.

You should first dream about having coffee by the sea or being able to shop in the middle of the day for that hard to find birthday card. When I became free from working for someone else's dream I spent every morning having coffee by the beach for six months. You can dream about what you would like to do—you don't have to use my dreams; you can have your own because your dreams belong to you.

Dreaming begins with a wish. What do you wish for? What are your future hopes? You have to think about where you are as it compares to where you want to be and then fill in the gap. How wide is the gap between where you are right now and where you want to be? If what you're doing right now is not your personal plan, then you need to plan what you are going to do.

If you are working for someone else give it all you've got until you can change it. When I worked for others in the past, I worked as though it all belonged to me. This will ensure a promising future. Don't ever use your current position as a stepping-stone. Give it all you've got until someone gives you more or opportunity knocks, and you open a different door.

Are you happy where you are or are you wishing for something quite different from your current reality? Maybe you're wishing for freedom from people in general or more specifically that obtuse person who makes it their mission to discourage you. How about excessive noise, mean bosses, intermittent uproars, and unpredictable weirdness?

You may begin by saying something like; "I wish it were quieter," or "I wish I were at the beach right now." Or maybe you might say, "I wish I were spending time with my grandson today." Maybe you wish you had some real peace and solitude. Either way, you must wish for it before it can be visualized.

You have to want it and believe it's within your ability to have it. Dreams are plans that stem from our wishes and hopes. We must have dreams before we can have goals. Goals are dreams with deadlines. Once you put a date on a dream and create a deadline you set yourself up for either a goal or a failure. This is why I don't recommend goals when dreaming—not yet anyway.

Dreaming is like painting a moving picture within your mind of what this or that could look like. You may picture yourself with a nice home office or you might picture yourself renting space at your favorite location or having an online business or working from a laptop at Starbucks. I made ten thousand dollars sitting in Panera Bread once.

The process of dreaming your mental images really needs to take hold because this is what you're going to build upon when your dream eventually comes to pass. I dreamed of an awesome home office up to the point of getting the money together to build it. Then I set a goal of completion when I hired a contractor friend to build it. Dreams create hope and hope bridges the gap between your faith and your limiting beliefs.

If you don't have faith in *you*, nobody else can have faith *for* you. Hope is both a birthplace and a bridge to believing. Faith is an action that moves you out of a limiting belief in self and into a sense of ability through the process of hoping. Hope is like a handle you can grab onto in order to pull yourself forward.

Help Yourself

Here it is on the chin; no one wants to help you. People care about themselves just like you, so don't be too shocked. If you're going to make your dreams come true, then you alone are responsible to make it happen. Not helping you isn't a character deficiency in others; it's a time deficiency—most people just don't have the time or resources to help you. If you don't want to help yourself and you think everyone else should help you, reading further will be of no benefit to you. Otherwise, keep reading and find out how to locate yourself and develop it into something productive. It's going to take time, chance, and some risks on your part.

You're going to have to be self-motivated or this will never work. Thomas Edison failed 6,000 times before the light bulb and Mike Schmidt of the Philadelphia Phillies for twenty years straight failed at bat 2 out of 3 times yet was inducted into the baseball hall of fame. Apparently, failure only happens when you stop trying.

I wanted to learn how to build websites, so I started investigating how to do it on the Internet and bought a few cheap books on the subject. I talked to a few people who knew how to build them. I went to a studio and watched a guy build one in front of my own two eyes and then I went home and tried it myself.

This went on for about three years. I hired my brother to build me a website in 2004 and talked to him about it as he built it. I did all this in my spare time. Fifteen years later I'm pretty good at it and I don't do it for a living. I've been paid $5,000.00 several times to build websites that took a few days' time. I build all my own websites and when I can't figure something out, I find someone who can. I learned how to use WordPress over the last 9 or 10 years in my spare time and have saved thousands by doing my own site building.

I'm a very consistent theoretical. I love to learn. Like me, you need to capitalize of your already built in assets. Maybe your best asset is leading; it would be a good idea to find something to lead even if it's just a small group you put together that meets on Friday mornings. Your greatest asset might be individualism; find a place to present your innovative ideas. I understand that not everyone is self-motivated. Some folks experience a lower dose of emotional energy—so what. You can still dream or align yourself with someone who thinks like you and piggy-back on their efforts.

The point I'm making is that we all can do *something*—don't do be one of those people who does absolutely nothing. There are many things we can do that aren't dependent on any specific integrated motivational orientation or a certain behavioral and emotional consistency. Here are a few things you can do in an effort to stand out regardless of your brain type or motivational orientation.

Brand Yourself, Nobody Else Will

Part of establishing yourself in the world and laying the groundwork for being your best self is being known for something. I'm known as a *thought leader* because that's what people call me. The odds are good that you're known for something as well. I didn't come up with that, everyone else did. When I first heard it in 2014, I didn't even know what it was.

To common every-day people I'm known as a resource, a marriage counselor, an artist, and a behavioral consultant. All these expressions come out of *who I am* not what I do. These are known as identifiers. Your personal ID is a result of bringing value in these areas. In the business world I'm a personality consultant, a motivational consultant, executive consultant, thought leader, and a behavioral profiler.

I'm valuable as a human being and as a particular resource to people and businesses. When you're seen as a person of value you become worth more rather than worth less. We call someone "worthless" when they bring no value to bear on any given situation. If you're considered "valuable," it means you are value-able or able to bring value in a particular instance. If your value ability solves problems and increases awareness that result in solved problems, people will pay you for it. Your value stems from your skills, emotional intelligence, behavioral orientations, character base, and integrated motivational orientations. You are already packaged for sale.

If you have a lot of value, brand it. Register it on the Internet. I created "stevesisler.org" many years ago. If you Google, my name it's accessible. The Internet is a giant landscape where you can leave breadcrumb trails. People will follow the breadcrumbs and then find you lightning fast. When someone finds you online and you have something they need, they might want it. They might even buy it.

Be Different

Don't just be different—be different with value. Be wicked different. When people remember you, it creates public awareness. I was speaking with someone once and they said, "*I heard of you.*" A relative had someone approach them during a conversation, the person asked them if they knew me. When they replied "yes," the person went on and on about how great they thought I was.

The individual doing the listening told a relative of mine later, "*You would have thought Steven was Jesus Christ to listen to them.*" We all laughed ourselves silly, but isn't it interesting the impression I apparently left? What kind of impressions are you leaving people with? Do they think you're like Jesus or a devil? Are the differences between you and everyone else substantial or substandard? I ask this because if you're going to answer to yourself, you'd better be worth being with all day. If you don't like yourself, you'll never work for yourself.

This is why you have to be different with value. This is all about laying the groundwork for being your best self. A niche is when you carve an area out of an existing area that doesn't have many spectacular things in it. You make your area spectacular and then eliminate any competition around you. If you're selling cookies, then you had better make a spectacular cookie or it'll get lost in boring land.

When your cookie is spectacular, rename it. Call it a "snookie" and wrap it in amazing packaging. Create an awe-inspiring website around your snookie and say, *"if it isn't the best snookie you ever had it's free."* Now you have my attention and everyone else's. This is different with value.

The Panache Test

You need panache because most people go unnoticed. You need to standout without looking nuts. I'm a corporate consultant and I wear jeans, cowboy boots and spurs. I capitalize on being casual and a bit different. It doesn't really matter because I deliver results.

Dashing style
Spurs
A helmet plume
Bold
Élan

These things get you noticed. Well, maybe the helmet plume is a bit much. The point is this; you have to pass the panache test. You pass this test when someone mentions something about your ethos or your appearance because it got their attention. I was asked to come back for another speaking engagement and the client said, "You're bringing your spurs, right?" When what you say, what you do, and what you wear is dazzling, people take notice. I had a person tell me they were going to tape my conversations with them. Have dashing answers that come out of left field.

I was in a conversation once and based upon the discussion I told them they were talking about "zoo phenomenon." "What's that," they asked. It's when you spend a boatload of money to go to the zoo and all the cool animals either end up missing or they're so-called sleeping in some undisclosed location. They never forgot it. Always aim for the bull's eye. If you wear a button-down shirt, starch and press it. If you have a good physique, capitalize on it and don't hide it. Sit up and don't slouch. All these little things set you apart as different. Smile and whiten your teeth.

Position is Everything

Can I find you on the Internet? When I Google you do you come up on the first page? Do you come up at all? It doesn't matter how good you are any more, it matters whether or not you are accessible or if people can find you by accident. How many things do you buy because you saw it by accident?

You have to position yourself correctly. Many years ago, when I was a house painter, I painted a huge house and charged less than it was worth because it was on the main street through town. I secured ten more houses by positioning myself on that main street. In 2007 I didn't have my own blog, so I posted comments on other people's blogs who have thousands of followers.

When you make a post, your name can be linked to your website. If your post is unique and dazzling, someone might click it. One person clicked my name on a popular blog, and it led to $48,000.00. It's 2019 and I'm still working with a client that was gained by that post. Why wait to get eighty-five thousand followers when somebody else already has them?

Strategic Relationships

Develop strategic relationships with people you aspire to help. This is all part of setting yourself up and positioning yourself to be in demand. This doesn't mean you ignore everyone else. When I started my consulting firm, I created a FRANK list for starters. FRANK is an acrostic for *friends, relatives, associates, neighbors,* and *kids*. I consulted for free with these five groups for about five months. After six months I had a non-paid sales team of about 40 people. All my paid work came from the sales generated by these relationships.

They were so impressed with the results that they immediately told someone. In 2005 my first client paid me $8,000.00 for 4 hours of work and then $280.00 per hour after that to talk to me. I'm still working with them 14 years later. This was because some one person in the FRANK list said; *"You have to hire this guy. He can help you."*

Here's the bottom line; you may need to get your act together. You might need a wind-blown look in your hair and a good salt spray in your face. Throw your shoulders back, sport a great attitude, and find a place to make horse-sense out of nonsense. It doesn't really matter what kind of motivational orientation you have to begin believing you have something to offer this world. So maybe you should wrap it up with a smile and give it to someone.

Practice Makes Expert

If you do something enough times, you'll become not only good at it, but you'll likely become an expert. In his book *Outliers: The Story of Success*, Malcolm Gladwell makes a really good case for this. Gladwell states, *"Practice isn't the thing you do once you're good. It's the thing that makes you good."* Gladwell sites illustration after illustration proving that the people, we call experts today have spent at least 10,000 hours becoming good at whatever it is they do well.

Whether it's Mozart, Bill Gates, or Edison, everyone has this common (or uncommon) thread of persistence and years of doing something over and over again. When I read this book a few years ago I began to apply its message to my own life in this wise; "what have I done for prolonged periods of time over the years and has it contributed to my success?"

I realized that I have studied and read the Bible for more than sixteen thousand hours in the last 35 years. I may not be able to quote chapter and verse like I used to (I used to memorize entire chapters in the 80's), but I am so familiar with the basic patterns and principles outlined in these scriptures that they are nearly automatic in life and mind.

This alone has helped me help others in dramatic ways and with unconventional clarity. This kind of wisdom familiarity has enabled me to teach, speak, motivate, and learn some of the greatest principles off all time. Whether it's ancient king Solomon, king David, the Moses figure, Agur, St. Paul, St. Jude, Epaphroditus, or Elihu, I've been infused with these stories and how they thought, acted, and solved problems in their own day.

Over the past 15 years I have also spent at least 10,000 hours researching and studying human behavior, the brain, human and workplace motivation, temperament, body language, and human nature. The ten-thousand-hour rule is by far the reason why you are perceived as an expert at anything. If you were born with a gift or endowed with supernatural powers, the ten-thousand-hour rule may not apply to you in the same way. Although Mozart was very gifted at birth, he also got a late start and didn't compose his greatest works until twenty years after he was discovered.

According to Gladwell it also takes about ten years of continued chess playing to become a grandmaster chess player although Bobby Fischer did it in nine, which is considered by many to be an anomaly. It also takes ten to twelve years to master a martial art. My brother sports a first-degree black belt and he told me that the black belt is only the first base in the martial arts ball game. Apparently if you haven't reached black belt status you're still in the dugout.

The fact is this, if you want to be an expert, you're going to have to do something for a long time. Many today want to be a shining star early in life. They want to avoid the time it takes to become really good at something. They want to get it quick and then reap untold fortunes from doing something without work. King Solomon said those who want to get rich quick "come to ruin." Becoming excellent is typically a slow and steady paced process for most people. This doesn't mean you can't excel at something early or find a niche in your twenties, it simply means most of us take time to grow into ourselves.

Non-Expert Shooting Stars

For some, fame and fortune can happen in a rather cataclysmic fashion. This is what is known as a shooting star. Shooting stars can rise quickly only to often burn out almost just as quickly as they were discovered. If you have ever seen a shooting star in the night sky you know what I mean by this. 99% of child actors are shooting stars. Not all shooting stars have this behavior, but most of them do. This usually happens when the brain isn't able to stand up to the pressures brought on by having excessive riches before you have all the wisdom to know what to do with them.

"What'choo talkin' bout Willis?" This was the famous line spoken into everybody's living room by Gary Coleman between 1978 and 1986. Regardless of Gary's funny line and expression, it wasn't enough to keep him on top any more than Jimmy Walker's famed *"Dyn-o-mite"* expression kept him on top. Whether success is a product of time and chance, your alien ingenuity, or unexpected inheritance, you still have to have the scruples maintain it. For many, success is like a hot chick; once you land her you spend the rest of your days trying to keep her.

Some people win millions of dollars playing the state lottery, but how many actually keep their winnings for prolonged periods of time? Not many. Brad duke, who won a $220 million-dollar jackpot in 2005, immediately took a $63,000 trip to Tahiti with seventeen friends. Duke also spent a whopping $65,000 on several new motorcycles. After winning $220 million and initially spending it like an out of control madman, Duke started both low and high risk investing when he had only $85 million left. This low-risk investment of forty-five million combined with a high-risk investment portfolio of thirty-five million saved his skin. He probably got the dope slap from a close friend who observed his idiotic spending trends.

David Edwards on the other hand won a $41 million Powerball and took home $27 million in August of 2001 after taxes. Six years later, the money was all gone. Edwards was later evicted from his $1.2 million home in Palm Beach Garden, Fla. for not paying his association dues. Shortly thereafter, Edwards was evicted from a storage shed he was apparently living in. The items in storage were auctioned to pay Edwards' storage fees—what a shame.

Duke was ultimately a shining star while Edwards was a shooting star because of the decisions they each made. Some people receive money, but not only kept it, they create more with it. These examples of quick or undeserved wealth prove that not everyone who falls into increase or is rushed into fame can keep it.

To spend your time thinking, "If only I had a million dollars" will not help you move forward into your best-self position. It will actually delay it. You don't have a million dollars, so now what? Why don't you check your ten-thousand-hour list for starters and see where it can help you help someone else.

The Ability to Spot Stupid

The decision to be a shining star never lies within our fortunes, but rather within our brain and our ability to spot stupid quickly. Knowing where to spend your time and talent takes brains. Spotting stupid is an art that is developed over time. It begins with realistic approaches to life as well as a balanced view of self and your ability.

An unbalanced view of self is usually your first step towards idiot land. We have to view ourselves with sober judgment. This means having yourself in proper view in terms of what you are actually able to do and what you may not be skilled at. Spotting stupid is far more intuitive than logical. Although logic is seen as logical only *after* logical solutions to problems are applied, intuition can spot a problem *before* it actually becomes one if you're paying attention. I have outlined several simple steps to spotting stupid that may help you avoid danger before it rips your throat out:

1. If you are in a situation that causes you to take pause for even just a moment, this could be a sign of stupid. If this happens you should stop, drop, and think.
2. If you are in a position to make a choice that might cost you a decent amount of time, money, reputation, or friends, make it a rule to ask three smart friends what they think.
3. If something doesn't "feel" right, there's probably a pretty good chance it's wrong. Take some time to find out more about your decision and the consequences it could bring to bear.
4. If you're making a large purchase, make sure you do your homework. Don't be too hasty. Remember the words of king Solomon, *"Calmness lays great errors to rest."*
5. Huge decisions that have lasting affects should be thought through with several smart people. Taking this on all by yourself is not a good idea at best.

Decisions; we all have to make them. But some of us make better decisions than other people do. Making good decisions will ensure a shining star path as opposed to a shooting star path. Bringing smarter people than yourself into your equation will mitigate unnecessary outcomes and increase your chances of a best self. I used to be hastier than I am now, but I've learned to involve smarter people in major decisions. This has been super helpful.

Good decision-making is great when you have ten thousand decisions to make in ten years. We will never be expert decision-makers, but we can certainly become better decision makers. In order to ensure this, you have to humble yourself and admit you're an infallible being who is capable of making poor decisions.

Knowing Who You Are Not

What are you spending your time doing over the long haul? What have you invested thousands of hours into? Is this something you can capitalize on? It's a powerful thing when you are quick, accurate and concise with something. This is part of knowing the difference between who you are and who you are not.

Knowing who you *are not* saves a lot of time and energy. Some people believe they're good at something when they actually terrible at it. Find out what you're great at and don't waste time with things that come very hard—focus on what comes easy. This brings us back to realistic ideas about our ability and ourselves.

Being Excellent

Being excellent is what set's you above those who are only good. Matter of fact, you'd be surprised at how little education you may actually need if you are already excellent at something. Education is more or less overrated these days. If the things you're excellent can be done well despite your lack of "official" training or "formal" education, you might not need any. Because you deliver the results far and away better than expected, official training is reduced to the "pointless" category.

I recommend putting your eggs in the basket that works. So many people do what they don't like and relegate what they do like to hobby status. If you're excellent at something because you've accumulated over ten thousand hours doing it, this should be part of your best-self strategy. To many are making a living instead of living off of what they make.

This chapter has been about things anyone can do regardless of their IMO status. Think about your own IMO; what comes natural to you? Start thinking of ways to capitalize on who you are versus what you do. If they're one and the same, then good for you! If not, entertain the possibility of aligning the two.

About the Author

Steve has consulted on "personality difference" with over one hundred .com companies in 18 countries including the US Military, UNC's Cadet Program, Beechnut Nutritional Corp, Signature Brands, LLC, Mastermind Talks of Toronto, The COO Alliance, and Book-in-a-box.com, to name just a few. Steven has spoken over 3,000 times over the last 34 years.

He has lectured at the EO's Entrepreneurial Master's Program at M.I.T. for the last 6 years, and has spoken in Athens, Perth, Brisbane, Sydney, Adelaide, Canada, Spain, New Zealand, Newfoundland, and has shared the stage with world-class entrepreneurs such as David Asbrey, founder of Bullet Proof Coffee, Cameron Herald, former COO of 1-800-Got-Junk?.

For more than 34 years, Steven Sisler has been an innovator in the areas of human relationships, people intelligence, personality consultation, family dynamics, emotional intelligence, and motivational speaking. As a behavioral analyst, axiologist, and personality expert in both behavior and values analysis, Steve is a frequent guest on world-class podcasts such as The Art of Charm, Satori Prime, The Unmistakable Creative, The Competitive Edge, and Ben Greenfield's world-class fitness podcast. Totaling over 2 million downloads, Steve is making a difference around the world.

Steve is currently working with his partner, *Zeke Lopez* on a multi-year project, creating improved behavioral, axiological, and motivational assessment tools based upon the Aristos Personality model which will integrate both behavior, axiological, and motivational factors into one cohesive framework.

Steve has authored several books including: *The Four People Types and What Drives Them, The Angry Brain: A Contemporary View of the Anger Emotion and How it Relates to Human behavior, Character, and temperament* and *There's More to Management Than a Big Desk.*

Steven Sisler can be reached at behavioralresourcegroup.com, theimoreport.com, and stevesisler.org. or by calling 781.585.3105 during business hours 8:30-4:00 CST.

Printed in Poland
by Amazon Fulfillment
Poland Sp. z o.o., Wrocław

31045169R00171